Invitational Counseling

A Self-Concept Approach to Professional Practice

Invitational
Counseling

A Self-Concept Approach to Professional Practice

William W. Purkey
The University of North Carolina at Greensboro

John J. Schmidt
East Carolina University

Brooks/Cole Publishing Company

I(T)P ™ An International Thomson Publishing Company

Pacific Grove • Albany • Bonn • Boston • Cincinnati • Detroit • London • Madrid • Melbourne
Mexico City • New York • Paris • San Francisco • Singapore • Tokyo • Toronto • Washington

A CLAIREMONT BOOK

Sponsoring Editor: *Claire Verduin*
Editorial Assistant: *Patsy Vienneau*
Production Editor: *Tessa A. McGlasson*
Manuscript Editor: *Catherine Cambron*
Permissions Editor: *Catherine Gingras*
Art Editor: *Kathy Joneson*
Typesetting: *Kachina Typesetting, Inc.*

Cover Design: *Sharon L. Kinghan*
Interior Design: *Vernon T. Boes*
Marketing Team: *Nancy Kernal, Romy Fineroff*
Printing and Binding: *Malloy Lithographing, Inc.*

For more information, contact:

BROOKS/COLE PUBLISHING COMPANY
511 Forest Lodge Road
Pacific Grove, CA 93950
USA

International Thomson Editores
Campos Eliseos 385, Piso 7
Col. Polanco
11560 México D. F. México

International Thomson Publishing—Europe
Berkshire House 168-173
High Holborn
London WC1V 7AA
England

International Thomson Publishing GmbH
Königwinterer Strasse 418
53227 Bonn
Germany

Thomas Nelson Australia
102 Dodds Street
South Melbourne, 3205
Victoria, Australia

International Thomson Publishing—Asia
221 Henderson Road #05-10
Henderson Building
Singapore 0315

Nelson Canada
1120 Birchmount Road
Scarborough, Ontario
Canada M1K 5G4

International Thomson Publishing—Japan
Hirakawacho-cho Kyowa Building, 3F
2-2-1 Hirakawacho-cho
Chiyoda-ku, Tokyo 102
Japan

Printed in the United States of America

10 9 8 7 6 5 4 3 2 1

Library of Congress Cataloging-in-Publication Data
Purkey, William Watson.
    Invitational counseling : a self-concept approach to professional
practice / William W. Purkey, John J. Schmidt.
        p.   cm.
    Includes bibliographical references and index.
    ISBN 0-534-33902-6
    1. Counseling. I. Schmidt, John J., [date]. II. Title.
BF637.C6P86 1995
158'.3—dc20

95-8766
CIP

In memory of Sidney Jourard,
who first recognized the profound significance
of an invitational approach to professional practice.

CONTENTS

CHAPTER ONE

Introduction to Invitational Counseling

1

What Is Invitational Counseling?   2
An Overview   6
Why Invitational Counseling?   19
Summary   20
Opportunities for Further Reading   21

CHAPTER TWO

Foundations of Invitational Counseling

23

The Perceptual Tradition   24
Self-Concept Theory   30
Summary   41
Opportunities for Further Reading   41

vii

CHAPTER THREE

Ingredients of Invitational Counseling

43

Beliefs about Self, Others, and
Professional Helping   44
Intentionality   51
Responsibility   58
Levels of Professional Functioning   59
Summary   68
Opportunities for Further Reading   68

CHAPTER FOUR

Characteristics of Successful Counselors

70

Being Personally Inviting with Oneself   71
Being Personally Inviting with Others   74
Being Professionally Inviting with Oneself   76
Being Professionally Inviting with Others   79
Summary   81
Opportunities for Further Reading   82

CHAPTER FIVE

Dimensions of Invitational Counseling

83

Stages 84
Choices 92
Factors 97
Limitations 109
Summary 110
Opportunities for Further Reading 111

CHAPTER SIX

Development of Proficiency
113

Skill Development 114
Brief Therapy 129
Conflict Management 131
In Search of Proficiency 139
Summary 144
Opportunities for Further Reading 145

CHAPTER SEVEN

Integrating Approaches to Counseling
147

Professional Counseling 148
Counseling as a Process 151
An Eclectic Approach 155
Elements of Compatibility 160
Summary 162
Opportunities for Further Reading 162

CHAPTER EIGHT

An Expanded Perspective for Professional Counseling

164

Contemporary Counseling   165
Settings and Services   171
The Future of Counseling   173
A Place for Invitational Counseling   177
Summary   178
Opportunities for Further Reading   179

APPENDIX A

Development of Invitational Counseling   181
Historical Events   182
Major Publications   183

APPENDIX B

Inviting Oneself Personally   185
Inviting Others Personally   187
Inviting Oneself Professionally   189
Inviting Others Professionally   190

REFERENCES   195
NAME INDEX   209
SUBJECT INDEX   213

FOREWORD

It is refreshing to read a book on counseling that is not simply a compendium of techniques, strategies, and prescriptions of what to do and when. Most current texts are implicitly, if not explicitly, based on the specific treatments paradigm, which attempts to identify specific treatments for specific problems. In the nearly 25 years since Paul stated this paradigm in 1967, very little research has supported it.

The present book is based on a different, earlier paradigm that dates back to work of Snygg and Combs first published in 1949. This is the perceptual psychology paradigm, sometimes called phenomenology. With a philosophical as well as a theoretical basis, the paradigm is basically common sense, but with empirical research support. Simply stated, the perceptual psychology paradigm holds that all behavior is determined by the perceptual field of the behaver at the moment of behaving. It follows from this premise that if behavior is to change, the person's perceptual field must change. Counseling, then, is a method of facilitating such change.

Most textbooks mystify the counseling process. The counselor must choose a diagnosis from scores of possibilities and label the client's problem. Then the counselor selects a specific technique from scores of possible techniques, and intervenes to direct or lead the client to a solution decided upon by the counselor. The counselor is the expert, assuming responsibility for the total process.

In contrast, invitational counseling demystifies the process. It presents counseling as a human relationship. The counselor invites the client to join in a relationship in which both embark on an exploration of the client's life. The client has the major responsibility for the journey. The counselor provides the conditions for the client's self-exploration, by caring for and respecting the client and creating a safe environment.

For counseling to be effective, the client must invite the counselor into his or her world. The counselor is then able to see things as the client sees them—a necessary condition for a productive relationship, since each client is unique.

Invitational counseling recognizes the importance of the context in which counseling occurs—people, places, programs, policies, and processes. This institutional environment of counseling is an important but often neglected context in most texts on counseling.

This book is in the humanistic tradition of Rogers, Maslow, and Jourard. The important element in counseling is not the counselor's techniques and skills but his or her beliefs and attitudes about people, which manifest themselves in a relationship of respect, understanding, and genuineness in which the client is enabled to become his or her best self.

C. H. Patterson

PREFACE

ɜ‍ɐ

. . . a beautiful occupation.
And since it is beautiful it is truly useful.
Antoine de Saint-Exupéry
The Little Prince
1943, p. 48

ɜ‍ɐ

Counseling is a relatively young profession, but it is beginning to mature. With this maturity, a theme that continues to appear in the counseling literature is the search for new paradigms of professional functioning that will assist counselors to be a beneficial presence in clients' lives and that professional counselors can accept regardless of their theoretical orientation or the setting in which they practice. We believe the model presented in this book offers a fresh approach to professional helping.

This book is written for counselors in training, practicing counselors, and counselor educators as well as those related professional helpers who work with clients in a variety of counseling, consulting, and allied human service roles. We have written *Invitational Counseling: A Self-Concept Approach to Professional Practice* for counselors who accept a perceptual orientation to understand and explain the complex processes that contribute to human development and learning.

This book has a threefold application. It can be a supplementary text for courses in counseling that emphasize self-concept theory and a perceptual approach to professional helping. The book can also be used as a text in courses that benefit from a specific theoretical orientation. Finally, the book can serve as a guide for practitioners who are seeking an integrated model for professional counseling, particularly one that spans treatment, prevention, and developmental services.

An expanded and enriched version of an earlier work, *The Inviting Relationship* (1987), this new book offers a fresh approach for today's counselors who are seeking ways to integrate what they know, who they are, what they do, where they work, and what they accomplish into a viable and practical model of professional functioning. We refer to this approach as invitational counseling, which is founded on the perceptual tradition, self-concept theory, and an emerging view of human development and learning called invitational theory (Novak, 1992; Purkey & Novak, 1984; Purkey & Stanley, 1991). Invitational counseling uses a developmental perspective to tie together seemingly unrelated aspects of professional counseling, aligning them so they make a new kind of sense. These aspects include the characteristics and beliefs of counselors, the skills and processes they employ, the relationships they create, the environments they inhabit, and the outcomes they achieve.

In this book, *counseling* is defined in broad terms. It is more than individual, one-to-one helping relationships, more than psychological education, and more than information giving. As such, invitational counseling is a combination of counseling and consulting processes that value an ecological approach to the work of addressing human dilemmas, creating optimal learning environments, and enriching life experiences.

Invitational Counseling consists of eight chapters. The first four chapters define invitational counseling, introduce its major assumptions and theoretical foundations, and present elements of its structure. These chapters set the stage for understanding the integrative nature of invitational counseling and offer empirical support for its rationale.

Chapters 5 and 6 explain the process of invitational counseling, which includes identifiable stages, explicit choices, and definable steps. In addition, proficient communication, group leadership, and evaluation skills common to conventional forms of professional counseling are highlighted. When adopting invitational counseling, counselors work their way through hierarchical levels of learning to reach proficiency, as they would with other counseling approaches.

The final two chapters examine the counseling profession today and tomorrow and explain how invitational counseling makes sense as an integrative approach. Chapter 7 emphasizes the integrated orientation of invitational counseling, and Chapter 8 focuses on the expanded roles and varied settings that will likely be available for professional counselors of the future. Trends indicate that counselors will require broad-based models of professional practice like invitational counseling.

An annotated reading list is included at the end of each chapter to encourage the reader to explore concepts related to invitational counseling. In addition, two appendixes provide a collection of inviting activities and a historical account of the development of invitational counseling.

Invitational Counseling will benefit counselors in many professional settings, including schools, mental health services, marriage and family clinics, religious institutions, colleges, universities, and businesses. We believe that readers will find this book personally and professionally rewarding.

As is true for most accomplishments, the writing of this book was greatly facilitated by the encouragement and critiques of colleagues and students. In particular, we want to thank William Stafford, C. H. Patterson, David Sherrill, Daniel Shaw, and Paula Stanley for their valuable comments and suggestions. We also appreciate Claire Verduin, publisher, for her support, and the excellent reviewers who helped us fine-tune an earlier draft of this work: Steve Backels, Penn State University-Harrisburg; David Botwin, University of Pittsburgh; Ronald Collins, Montana State University-Billings; Peter Emerson, Southeastern Louisiana University; Stephen S. Feit, Idaho State University; Brenda Freeman, University of Wyoming; Joan Hartzke-McIlroy, Lewis and Clark College; Diane McDermott, University of Kansas; Katina Mendis, Eastern Montana College; Robert Nielsen, North Dakota State University; and Paula Stanley, Radford University. Lastly, we are greatly honored to have this book introduced by C. H. Patterson, a pioneer in the perceptual tradition and renowned theorist of professional counseling.

William W. Purkey
John J. Schmidt

CHAPTER ONE

Introduction to Invitational Counseling

ख

Here, you see, is the greatest, the most inglorious default, namely, to encounter the nothingness represented by one's lack of essence and to interpret this lack as a kind of deformity to be corrected or made up for by others. It is precisely the opposite of a deformity! The lack is an *invitation to be—an invitation* to be something worth being, an invitation to fill up the nothingness with an essence that is worthy of existing and undeserving of being lost.

Van Cleave Morris

Existentialism in Education: What It Means

1966, p. 28

ख

Professional counseling is an emerging and dynamic profession that includes services offered by counselors and related specialists in educational, industrial, medical, residential, recreational, correctional, pastoral, and countless other work settings. As the profession has developed throughout the 20th century, counselors have searched for viable theories and effective practices that would allow them to be a beneficial presence in the lives of those they serve. Furthermore, they have searched for theories and practices that they could integrate into comprehensive human service programs. In this search, counselors, psychotherapists, and other professional helpers have proposed many models and approaches to counseling.

As used in this book, the term *professional counseling* refers to a wide range of developmental, preventive, and remedial services that include individual helping relationships, group work, and consulting practices. There now exists a need in the counseling profession for a dependable structure that counselors can use in selecting, organizing,

1

and employing various approaches to professional helping. The model offered in this book is designed to provide this structure.

This book provides a framework for professional practice called *invitational counseling*. This framework has three goals: (1) to provide a perspective for understanding and organizing the wealth of scientific knowledge being generated in the burgeoning field of counseling, (2) to serve as an encompassing structure for compatible counseling theories and techniques, and (3) to present a practical guide for counselors and allied professionals in many human service settings. This entire book is an invitation to celebrate human ability, value, and individual responsibility.

What Is Invitational Counseling?

Invitational counseling is a model of professional helping, based on self-concept, that incorporates compatible theories, systems, and practices into an overarching framework for human service. This framework is based on four basic assumptions that give invitational counseling identity, direction, and purpose:

1. People are able, valuable, and capable of self-direction, and they should be treated accordingly.
2. Helping is a cooperative, collaborative alliance in which process is as important as product.
3. People possess relatively untapped potential in all areas of human development.
4. This potential can best be realized by places, policies, and programs that are intentionally designed to invite development, and by people who consistently seek to realize this potential in themselves and others, personally and professionally.

These four assumptions stand at the core of professional helping and, therefore, at the center of invitational counseling.

The early origins of invitational counseling may be found in the writings of Sidney Jourard. In *Disclosing Man to Himself* (1968), he wrote, "I now believe there is no biological, geographical, social, economic, or psychological determiner of man's condition that he cannot transcend if he is suitably invited or challenged to do so" (p. 59). From this beginning point, Purkey (1978), Purkey and Novak (1984), Purkey and Schmidt (1987), Purkey and Stanley (1991, 1994), and others have expanded Jourard's seminal thoughts into a theory of professional practice. Appendix A details the historical developments and significant publications related to invitational theory.

Invitational theory is anchored in the belief that intentional choice, coupled with action, has the potential to improve both the immediate human condition and people's long-term growth and health. The theory addresses human experiences that contain essential elements, occur at identifiable levels, include understandable spheres of behaving, require a hierarchy of choices, and pertain to styles of human interaction.

The essence of invitational counseling is that counselors should be intentionally optimistic, respectful, and trusting toward themselves and others, personally and professionally. Invitational counseling is as much a particular "stance"—a therapeutic attitude or disposition—as it is a methodology. As Parsons and Wicks (1994) noted, "A genuine counseling relationship does not arise out of the use of certain techniques, but can only develop when the counselor is willing to invest oneself in the process as a whole person" (p. 185). Accordingly, invitational counseling can be applied to interactions in a wide variety of *places* involving many different *people, policies, processes,* and *programs.* These five *P*s are central to invitational counseling and will be referred to repeatedly throughout this book.

Invitational counseling employs helping skills that assist people with immediate concerns. At the same time, it seeks to go beyond remediation to help people recognize their opportunities for achieving lives of rich significance and to mobilize higher levels of functioning. This going beyond immediate concerns to seek improved and enriched levels of functioning is a hallmark of invitational counseling. In this way, it provides an integrated model for professional practice.

An Integrated Model

Invitational counseling offers a model for professional helping within which counselors can incorporate compatible approaches for establishing helping relationships. This model enables counselors to assess the compatibility of various approaches to counseling and to select those that provide the most caring and appropriate professional service. For example, invitational counseling recognizes the importance of the "core" conditions—genuineness, empathic understanding, positive regard, and concreteness—as outlined and researched by client-centered therapists (Carkhuff, 1969a, 1969b; Patterson, 1959, 1984, 1985a, 1985b; Rogers, 1957, 1959). It uses the insights and assumptions of perceptual psychology (Combs, Richards, & Richards, 1976; Combs & Gonzalez, 1994; Combs & Snygg, 1959) and the observations of self-concept theory (Purkey, 1970; Purkey & Novak, 1984; Purkey & Schmidt, 1987). Invitational counseling also accepts the assumptions of Alfred Adler's individual psychology regarding the "creative self," goal-directed behavior, social interest, and behavior as a function of subjective perception (Ansbacher & Ansbacher, 1956; Dinkmeyer, Dinkmeyer, & Sperry, 1987). The field theory of Kurt Lewin (1951) and the personal construct theory of George Kelly (1955, 1963) are among those that have influenced the development of invitational counseling.

By providing an integrated model for professional helping, invitational counseling offers a systematic way of addressing personal existence and human potential. Other counseling approaches limit themselves to a particular theoretical framework or to a specific remedial type of relationship. By contrast, invitational counseling takes a broad approach to helping people realize their relatively boundless potential in all areas of worthwhile human endeavor.

While respecting the contributions of various theories and models, invitational counseling also confronts the philosophic and theoretical differences in these approaches. Some practices used in counseling and education are *not* congruent or compatible with invitational counseling. Any approach that employs fear, coercion, aggression, duplicity, seduction, embarrassment, ridicule, subversion, or physical punishment—regardless of good intentions or successful outcomes— cannot be viewed as invitational counseling.

Invitational counseling as an integrated approach is presented in greater detail in Chapter 7. In particular, elements of compatibility are explored in the form of questions counselors can ask themselves to assess whether a particular approach to counseling is congruous with invitational counseling. By identifying coherent approaches, counselors are able to be consistent in their professional practice.

A Professional Practice

As a professional practice, invitational counseling identifies ways that counselors and allied professionals employ their approaches and skills in arenas far beyond the remediation of immediate problems. Counselors who accept invitational counseling seek to assist people in recognizing their potential to develop optimally: to become more self-reliant, more emotionally and physically healthy, more innovative and creative, more able to set realistic goals, and more capable of achieving those goals. All of this takes place within the context of a larger invitation to the counselor and client to discover meaning and direction in one's personal and professional life. Most models of counseling adhere to these goals, but many of these are models limited in terms of scope. They tend to focus on one particular practice, system, or method. By comparison, invitational counseling offers a rationale for using few or many approaches and techniques, depending on the nature of the counseling situation.

Professional helpers who practice invitational counseling work to maintain a particular stance based on the belief that professional counseling is a cooperative, collaborative process—a therapeutic partnership. This spirit of shared responsibility manifests itself in relationships that involve "doing with" rather than "doing to" processes. The "doing with" stance is at the heart of invitational counseling. This stance provides an expanded perspective in which compatible approaches can be woven into an integrative framework of professional helping. This perspective embraces a philosophy about the perceptual tradition and self-concept theory that accepts a holistic view of human development.

A Holistic View

Invitational counseling considers a range of elements, levels of functioning, and factors in providing appropriate services for people who seek assistance. These elements and conditions emphasize a wide-angle view of both human development and the counseling relationship. Invitational counseling resists the temptation to compartmentalize people into separate behavioral, emotional, intellectual, educational, physical, or other artificial categories. Instead, the goal is to identify pertinent issues and investigate them from all angles to help clients select appropriate pathways in realizing their potential. The same philosophy guides thinking about ways that organizations can best enhance people's lives, improve relationships, encourage learning, stimulate career development, and enrich environments.

The notion that people cannot be reduced to distinguishable parts or fragmented by causal or scientific explanations is not a new concept in counseling. Alfred Adler was among the theorists of the early 20th century who took this stance. His theory of individual psychology, which continues to have a strong influence on the practice of professional counseling, embraces the premise of "the irreducible wholeness of the individual. The person is seen as a dynamic, unified organism moving through life in definite patterns toward a goal" (Dinkmeyer, Dinkmeyer, & Sperry, 1987, p. 11). Accordingly, counselors who adopt invitational counseling focus on the unity of the human personality.

This holistic view is encompassed in self-concept theory, which views the self as a dynamic whole consisting of limitless perceptions about the self and the world. When people seek assistance with educational, career, personal, and professional issues, counselors should consider all aspects of people's development. A holistic orientation has become popular not only in professional counseling but in health services in general. People want not just strategies for treating their illnesses, but ways of becoming and staying healthy throughout the life span. George and Cristiani (1990) summarized this philosophy: "By working with the whole person and teaching responsibility for both oneself and one's health, the holistic counselor works to help clients function more fully. Thus the approach relates to one's total life-style to enable one to become healthier and happier" (p. 77). Similarly, invitational counseling not only looks for ways to correct undesirable situations, but equally focuses on preventing problems and creating healthy, fulfilling lives.

Invitational counseling is congruent with numerous approaches to professional helping that find common ground in their view of human existence. The integrated nature of invitational counseling and its expanded view of professional practice make it attractive to counseling in various settings. With this brief definition, it is appropriate to summarize the essential components of invitational counseling.

An Overview

Philosophically, invitational counseling is based on the belief that each individual has a relatively untapped potential for intellectual, psychological, and physical development, and that this potential is best realized in a humane environment of people, places, policies, programs, and processes that intentionally invite the realization of this potential. Invitational counseling includes characteristics that define elements of a professional stance, levels of functioning, choices within the helping relationship, and styles of interacting. In addition, the process of inviting consists of three stages of helping and assumes the use of appropriate and proficient skill. These characteristics, processes, and skills are presented throughout this book. By way of introduction, this overview presents some definitive characteristics of invitational counseling. These include the elements of a professional stance, levels of functioning, spheres of behaving, and choices and styles of interacting.

Elements

Invitational counseling begins with a particular stance that the counselor assumes regarding self and others, personally and professionally. This stance is based on four elements—optimism, respect, trust, and intentionality—that provide substance, structure, and direction in the counseling relationship. As Corey, Corey, and Callanan (1993) pointed out, "Practicing counseling without an explicit theoretical rationale is somewhat like flying a plane without a map and without instruments" (p. 216).

The dynamic ways in which the four elements of optimism, respect, trust, and intentionality flow together and interact result in the counselor's being a beneficial presence in his or her own life and the lives of others. The first element that contributes to this flow is optimism.

Optimism. Optimism, as Seligman (1991) demonstrated, is essential for a good and successful life. Optimists do better in school, succeed more at life tasks, and even age better and live longer. By being optimistic about themselves, they also are more optimistic about others.

Invitational counseling encourages an optimistic vision of human existence: that individuals are valuable, able, responsible, and capable of self-direction, and are to be treated accordingly. Invitational counseling assumes that one of the deepest urges of human nature is to be intimately involved in mutually beneficial and caring relationships, and that what people desire most is to be affirmed in their present worth while being summoned cordially to realize their potential. Goethe described the process with these words: "If we take people as they are, we make them worse. If we treat them as if they were what they ought to be, we help them to become what they are capable of becoming" (Frankl, 1968, p. 8). When people exhibit behaviors that appear to contradict these assumptions, it is believed to be because little has been expected of them, or they have met with repeated negative experiences and have therefore lost respect for themselves, trust in their abilities, and faith in their potential.

A counselor's optimism is reflected in other characteristics as well. Confidence is one of these characteristics. Counselors who project an aura of confidence convey to their clients the belief that by working together, establishing goals, and staying the course, they will make significant progress. In contrast, the counselor who begins with doubtful comments and critical observations sets an uncertain tone for the relationship.

Another characteristic of optimism is perseverance. People are often faced with seemingly immovable barriers. As a result, frustration often feeds discontent to the point where some give up—counselors as well as clients. Invitational counseling requires that professional helpers not give up easily, even when clients give up on themselves. When counselors persevere, they reflect the optimism that is essential to invitational counseling. Often, such perseverance goes unrewarded for a long time after the counselor and client have ended their relationship. For example, one high school counselor who insisted that a student stay in school and graduate wrote, "It was several years later that the student sent me a note saying, 'I am finishing college this month and wanted to say thank you for not giving up on me.' "

A corollary to optimism and its related characteristics is that no person, place, policy, program, or process can be absolutely neutral. In invitational counseling, *everything counts*. Whatever happens, and whatever way it happens, adds to or takes from present existence and future potential. Every inviting or disinviting force, no matter how small or in what area, has limitless potential to influence the course of human events.

Respect. Nothing is more important in invitational counseling than respect for people. Central to this attitude is an appreciation for the rich complexity of each human being and the unique value of each culture. Being different is not a detriment; often diversity is a benefit to the entire group. Respect is manifested in such behaviors as civility, politeness, courtesy, and caring.

Respect is also reflected in appropriateness: knowing *when* to invite and when *not* to invite; *when* to accept and when *not* to accept. Appropriateness is an important ingredient of respect and will be considered later.

Responsibility is a second ingredient of respect. From an invitational perspective, each individual is the world's greatest authority on his or her own existence, and each is ultimately responsible for him- or herself, for his or her own actions, and for acting on his or her own behalf. According to Bugental (1989), the counselor is always in some measure external to the ongoing affairs of the client's life. No matter how much a client may want the counselor to take over, and no matter how much the therapist tries to guide the client's decisions, the reality is that the client is solely responsible for his or her own life. At the same time, the counselor has responsibility for encouraging the client's development of autonomy and respecting that autonomy.

In addition to appropriateness and responsibility, a respectful relationship is imbued with acceptance. The counselor accepts the client unconditionally, and assumes mutual responsibility with the client for what transpires in the helping relationship. Consequently, invitational counseling fosters equality, collaboration, and shared commitment. These are also conditions that contribute to a third element of invitational counseling: trust.

Trust. Trust is based on the recognition of the interdependence of human beings. This interdependence is most likely to be enhanced when people give a high priority to human welfare, when they view places, policies, programs, and processes as contributing to or subtracting from this welfare, and when they have freedom and willingness to trust their feelings. As Carl Rogers explained, counseling based on withholding oneself as a person and dealing with others as objects does not have a high probability of success. From the viewpoint of invitational counseling, helping is a cooperative, collaborative activity based on mutual trust.

Unfortunately, it sometimes happens that people who are most likely to benefit from invitational counseling are least likely to trust the process, for two reasons. On the one hand, their mistrustful self-perceptions permit few new perceptions to filter into their self-systems. On the other hand, their mistrust leads others into thinking that these people do not want to be involved in invitational counseling.

The element of trust is established in an inviting pattern of action, as opposed to a single inviting act. Establishing this pattern (which we refer to as a *stance*) takes time, and so patience is a vital commodity in invitational counseling. The world was not built in a day, and neither is trust. By demonstrating patience, the counselor's behavior serves as a valuable model for the client. Meier and Davis (1993) pointed out that a good way to develop trust in the initial stages of the counseling relationship is to encourage the client to take the lead in the counseling process. This allows the client to set the initial tone and style of making personal contact with the counselor.

Trust is established and maintained through sources identified by Arceneaux (1994). These sources include *reliability* (consistency, dependability, and predictability), *genuineness* (authenticity and congruence), *truthfulness* (honesty, correctness of opinion, and validity of assertion), *intent* (good character, ethical stance, and integrity), and *competence* (intelligent behavior, expertness, and knowledge). Trust is the product of these interlocking human qualities.

There are at least two actions that can damage trust in helping relationships: blaming others and making excuses. When counseling relationships dwell on blaming others, they become unproductive. In such situations, whether the client perseverates in blaming others or the counselor focuses on who's to blame, the client's development of responsibility is hindered. In the same way, making excuses threatens the establishment of trusting relationships because it capitalizes on irresponsible behaviors and advocates helplessness on the part of the client. Neither blaming nor excuse-making is appropriate to invitational counseling, as both jeopardize trust.

Sometimes, as Bennis and Nanus (1985) noted, one must withhold trust in order to defend oneself. However, if defending oneself means putting on a psychological suit of armor—being always suspicious, always on one's guard, always defensive—the price is too high. Being overly trusting involves the risk of being deceived or disappointed, but it is still the wiser course. Spending one's life believing that others are insincere, unreliable, or incompetent is, at heart, being disinviting with oneself. Without trust, as Stafford (1992) noted, "it is unlikely that anything of significance will occur in the counseling relationship" (p. 201).

In many ways, trust parallels respect. Trust is established in part by how respectful individuals are toward one another. This notion may seem too simple. Many people think that all one needs to do is ask to be trusted, and others will oblige. But gaining another's trust is not so easy. An individual's trust is often difficult to win, particularly when that person has been neglected, harmed, or damaged in other relationships.

While consistent patterns of actions are obviously important, even the smallest inviting act can have far-reaching consequences. As mentioned previously, a basic premise of invitational counseling is that everything counts. Sometimes the invitation can be as simple as a smile, a touch, or a single word. Human potential, though not always apparent, is always there, waiting to be discovered and invited forth.

Intentionality. By definition, an invitation is a purposeful act intended to offer something beneficial for consideration. Invitational counseling stresses that an intentional pattern of behavior based on publicly affirmed ideals is the foundation for any therapeutic relationship. From this viewpoint, human potential can best be realized by places, policies, programs, and processes that are specifically designed to affirm human worth and encourage its development, and by people who are intentionally inviting with themselves and others, personally and professionally.

Because the purposeful nature of invitational counseling encourages consistency in direction, the more intentional a counselor is, the more accurate his or her judgments will be. Clients rely on counselors to demonstrate consistency in their behaviors both in and out of the professional helping relationship. A counselor who maintains a high level of intentionality is more likely to create a credible image in the eyes of people who seek assistance.

The four elements of invitational counseling—optimism, respect, trust, and intentionality—when blended together provide professional counselors with a dependable stance that can be used to benefit themselves and others. These elements also influence the counselor's level of functioning.

Levels

There are four levels of functioning in invitational counseling, which include both harmful and helpful behaviors. Everyone functions at each level from time to time, but one's typical level of functioning eventually determines one's degree of success or failure in personal and professional life. In practice, counselors can use these levels to assess their own professional conduct as well as to assist clients in understanding their actions. The four levels of functioning introduced here are explained further in Chapter 3.

Level I: Intentionally disinviting. The most toxic and lethal level of functioning involves those actions, places, policies, programs, or processes that are deliberately designed to discourage, demean, or destroy. Examples of Level I functioning might be a counselor who is deliberately insulting to a client, a hospital policy that is intentionally discriminatory, a prison program that is willfully designed to demean inmates, or a school environment made purposefully unpleasant to "keep students in line."

Unfortunately, some individuals resemble Elmira Gulch in the 1939 film version of L. F. Baum's *Wizard of Oz*. Like Elmira, they take pleasure in hurting people or seeing them upset. Such individuals, whose stance is based primarily on pessimism, contempt, suspicion, and evil intent, and whose level of functioning is intentionally disinviting, could benefit from professional counseling. Their deliberate signals to themselves and others that they are unworthy, incapable, and irresponsible may be understandable—and even forgivable—but never justifiable. Disinviting people, places, policies, programs, and processes cannot be justified regardless of effectiveness or efficiency. From the viewpoint of invitational counseling there is no justification to remain at this bottom level. Counselors need to consider this principle when accepting invitational counseling as their guide to professional practice.

Level II: Unintentionally disinviting. When people create places, policies, programs, and processes that are unintentionally disinviting, they repeatedly puzzle over questions such as these: "Why are we having so many personnel problems?" "Why are people avoiding this place?" "Why are they not following our policies?" "Why are our programs not working?" "Why are we losing so many clients?" Professionals who typically function at Level II are usually well-meaning people, but the behaviors they exhibit, the places they create, and the policies, programs, and processes they design and maintain are often uncaring, chauvinistic, condescending, patronizing, sexist, racist, dictatorial, or just plain thoughtless. Examples appear again and again in individual accounts of being disinvited: "I feel insulted when the director always asks a female to take minutes," reported one counselor. Another commented that she found her supervisor's habit of calling her "sweetie" demeaning. An older adult complained that her pastoral counselor always shouted in her presence as though she were hard of hearing. Although unintended, such behaviors can be viewed by others as very disinviting.

Unintentionally disinviting processes can also be directed at oneself, as in cases where people consistently refer to themselves in negative terms. Some individuals speak of themselves in terms so demeaning that if anyone else spoke to them in such ways they would be highly insulted ("I'm so stupid," "I'm such a klutz," "I can't write," "I'm just a counselor"). They are unaware that they are being unintentionally disinviting with themselves.

Level III: Unintentionally inviting. This third level of functioning may be pictured as the domain of the natural-born professional. Counselors who function at this level are generally well liked and reasonably effective. The behaviors they exhibit and the places, policies, programs, and processes they create and maintain are often congruent with the spirit of invitational counseling. However, because they have little or no understanding of the principles involved, they are unaware of the reasons for their success. There is a certain sophisticated ignorance associated with these counselors. They know *what* they are doing, but they do not know *why*. They can identify the skills and tactics they apply in their helping relationships, but are uncertain about the reasons why they have chosen these specific strategies. When they encounter problems, or when things stop working, they sometimes have a difficult time figuring out what went wrong or how to start things up again. Even worse, they sometimes lack consistency in direction. When faced with threatening situations or challenges, they may drop to Level II or even Level I functioning. They may be unreliable in their responsibilities and uncertain in their decisions. A requirement of those who practice invitational counseling is to create and maintain an intentionally inviting stance, even in the most difficult circumstances.

Level IV: Intentionally inviting.   In invitational counseling, everybody and everything add to, or subtract from, human existence and potential. Ideally, the five factors of people, places, policies, programs, and processes should be so intentionally inviting as to create a world where each person is cordially summoned to develop intellectually, physically, and psychologically. From this standpoint, Level IV is the wellspring of invitational counseling. The more intentional an act, the more it lends itself to understanding, consistency, and direction.

Accepting the responsibility to be intentionally inviting can be a tremendous asset for counselors. Those who view their role to be intentionally inviting not only strive to reach Level IV, but once there, they continue to master the other important elements of invitational counseling.

Many people believe that they already know what they need to know about inviting, but in fact it is an extremely complex matrix of interacting forces. These forces will be detailed later, but it will be helpful here to introduce the four spheres, choices, and styles of behavior involved in invitational counseling.

Spheres

In addition to identifying the core elements of optimism, respect, trust, and intentionality and identifying levels of functioning, invitational counseling embodies four spheres of behaving. These spheres, pictured in Figure 1-1, will be introduced here and examined further in Chapter 4 as characteristics of inviting counselors.

Being personally inviting with oneself.   Being a professional counselor involves special pressures. Counselors can experience considerable stress as a result of continuous interaction with clients who are troubled, unsure of themselves, and seeking to improve their lives. It is essential that counselors be personally inviting with themselves—conserve their own energy levels and nurture themselves physically, emotionally, intellectually, and spiritually. Some examples of being personally inviting with oneself include taking pleasure in stillness, keeping in shape physically, reserving time for oneself, and finding satisfaction from sources completely removed from one's professional life. It is vital for counselors to have their personal lives in reasonably good order when endeavoring to be of service to others.

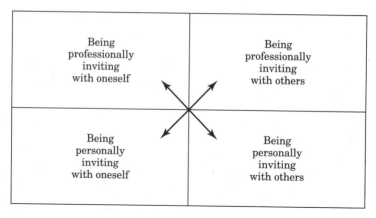

FIGURE 1-1 Spheres of Behaving

Being personally inviting with others. The second sphere addressed by invitational counseling is the importance of relating with others at a deeply personal level. Counselors are first human, and only after that professional. Betty Siegel, a friend of the authors, expressed it well: "All the professional success in the universe will not make up for lack of success with those you love and who love you." Professionals who employ invitational counseling work to nurture their "life support systems"—family, friends, mentors, students, colleagues, and lovers who make living, learning, and helping worthwhile.

Being professionally inviting with oneself. Counselors who consistently invite themselves to grow professionally are in a favorable position to be a beneficial presence in the lives of clients. By contrast, counselors who allow themselves to stagnate become professionally obsolete. Invitational counseling requires that professionals be actively and continuously committed to upgrading their skills, knowledge, and mastery of their profession.

In practical terms, being professionally inviting with oneself means participating in professional programs, seeking additional certification and licensure, spending time reading journals, joining and contributing to professional associations, and researching and writing for professional publication. Those who neglect to invite themselves professionally will become outdated. The sad part is that they may be unaware of their growing obsolescence.

Being professionally inviting with others. Being professionally inviting with others is best accomplished by building on the strengths of the previous three spheres. The first three spheres are necessary but not sufficient for functioning optimally in the fourth sphere of behaving. Once the first three spheres are functioning smoothly they serve as a launching pad for the fourth. Much of the remainder of this book concerns being professionally inviting with others.

The four spheres of invitational counseling make explicit what is implicit or often overlooked in professional practice: becoming a professional counselor requires optimal development in all four spheres. When the four spheres are fully functioning, counselors may reach the point beautifully described by Anne Morrow Lindbergh in her book, *Gift from the Sea:*

> I want first of all—in fact, as an end to these other desires—to be at peace with myself. I want a singleness of eye, a purity of intention, a central core to my life that will enable me to carry out these obligations and activities as well as I can. I want, in fact—to borrow from the language of the saints—to live in grace as much of the time as possible. I am not using this term in a strictly theological sense. By grace I mean an inner harmony. (1955, p. 23)

To live a harmonious life, personally and professionally, requires success in making caring and appropriate choices, which is another part of invitational counseling.

Choices

The interaction of elements, levels, and spheres of invitational counseling leads to four choices: (1) sending, (2) not sending, (3) accepting, and (4) not accepting. Every human relationship is influenced by these choices. The first two choices are in the domain of the person who chooses to send or not to send.

Sending. A behavior is not an invitation until it is a purposeful action. Thinking about doing good things is not sufficient. To respect is to act respectfully, to trust is to act trustingly, to care is to act caringly, and to love is to act lovingly. Invitational counseling requires that good intentions are acted upon.

Not sending. Sometimes, well-meaning counselors do not accomplish their intended goals because of lack of planning or poor timing. On some occasions, it is best *not* to take action. Timing is central to invitational counseling. Knowing when to remain silent is as important as anything spoken: not saying or doing anything can be the most inviting thing a counselor can do.

A graduate student in counseling at the University of North Carolina at Greensboro provided an example of the value of not sending with the following story: "This past weekend my wife was talking to my son and me about something she wanted done. I was in a hurry to get outside to finish raking leaves and went out of the room without my wife knowing I had left, and she continued to talk. Steven, our five-year-old son, finally said, 'Mommy, stop talking. Nobody is listening.'" Counselors who employ invitational counseling work to avoid inviting when "nobody is listening."

Accepting. The remaining two choices of accepting or not accepting are made by the receiver of invitations. In accepting, the receiver agrees to a relationship. Taking the risk to reach out and accept a cordial summons from another human being to begin a relationship can be the most courageous thing a person can do. By accepting an invitation, a person is saying, "I trust that you will use this acceptance for my welfare and not my detriment." Symbolically, the person is placing oneself in the hand of the inviter. A betrayal of this trust can be devastating. When a counselor invites a client to engage in a dialogue, and the client accepts, it is vital that the counselor treat this acceptance with the greatest sensitivity and respect. Acceptance indicates to the sender that the receiver is willing to begin a dialogue.

What is viewed by one person as acceptable may be seen as unacceptable by another. These differences in perception will be explored in Chapter 2.

Not accepting. The acceptability or unacceptability of an invitation is in the eye of the beholder. When the receiver sees an invitation as inappropriate or uncaring, views the sender as untrustworthy, or does not feel able or willing to accept the invitation, it is unlikely to be accepted.

When invitations are not accepted, it is helpful for the sender to consider the components of invitational counseling to see how more acceptable invitations might be created. For example, dialogue may present more acceptable options. Exploring options through dialogue is particularly important for counselors who find their clients resistant to change. It is helpful to remember that not accepting is different from rejecting. Clients need time to assimilate new understanding and support before committing themselves to a plan of action.

Each of the four choices requires equal attention in invitational counseling. Sometimes the most inviting thing a counselor can do is not to invite or not to accept. The same is true of clients, who can learn that sometimes saying no is a way of saying yes to themselves. Accepting responsibility for making choices is fundamental to invitational counseling.

Styles

Of all the elements of invitational counseling, the four styles of functioning may be the most useful for professional counselors. The four styles are as follows: (1) invisibly inappropriate, (2) visibly inappropriate, (3) visibly appropriate, and (4) invisibly appropriate. Invitational counseling identifies these four styles and highlights their impact on professional helping relationships.

Invisibly inappropriate. What is the difference between a gaze and a stare; a touch and a feel; a smile and a smirk? Although such differences are hard to describe, experienced counselors are keenly aware of them. They may sense that something about the counseling relationship is not right, although they would have difficulty explaining what that something is. Rogers (1951, 1959) addressed the importance of the counselor's listening to the inner self and trusting intuition. Clients, too, report that at times they feel uncomfortable in relationships, although the reasons escape them. These reasons may be revealed by considering the components of invitational counseling, beginning with optimism, respect, trust, and intentionality. From the beginning of the counseling relationship, something may be missing. Everything on the surface may seem appropriate, but feelings of inconsistency, unreliability, and uncertainty are present. When counselors and clients become aware that something is out of kilter, it is helpful to face these feelings as directly as possible. By doing so, invisibly inappropriate forces become visible, making them much easier to confront and resolve.

Visibly inappropriate. Everyone has encountered actions, places, policies, and programs that were visibly inappropriate in some way or another. These disinviting forces are so obvious that they call attention to themselves. Depending on the perceptions of the people involved, these forces are easier to change than invisibly inappropriate ones. Examples of visibly inappropriate forces are a counselor who delights in telling sexist or racist jokes; outpatient clinic signs that read, "Take a number and be seated!" "No food or drink allowed!" or "Do not touch this TV!"; a written school policy that supports corporal punishment; an area supervisor who consistently refers to male subordinates as "hunks" or females as "broads"; a personnel officer whose behaviors are blatantly discriminatory. All of these represent visibly inappropriate styles of functioning. Recognizing and challenging these styles for what they are often sets the stage for a more appropriate and caring style of functioning.

Visibly appropriate. This third style of functioning is the most common throughout the human service professions. The counselor who employs this style is technically proficient. His or her strategies and objectives are precise. Paraphrasing is done with skill, wait-time is used with perfection, and body language is centered, balanced, and encouraging. Clients, too, often behave in a visibly appropriate style, responding in cooperative ways, disclosing information in an appropriate manner, expressing their feelings fluently, and working toward identified goals. In situations where a counselor and client communicate in visibly appropriate ways, most observers would agree that they have established a therapeutic relationship. However, as good as this style is, invitational counseling proposes a more advanced style of functioning, the invisibly appropriate style.

Invisibly appropriate. When a counselor functions consistently and expertly in a visibly appropriate style, the effort and the skill involved gradually become less obvious. The performance of these skills becomes part of the counselor so that his or her behaviors do not call attention to themselves. With time and effort, the counselor reaches the invisibly appropriate style of functioning. Only another highly skilled and experienced counselor can recognize and appreciate the talents of this masterful professional helper.

George Burns, the great comedian, expressed the process of functioning in an invisibly appropriate style this way: "I improved so much I finally got so good that nobody knew I was there" (Burns, 1976, p. 58). This would seem to be a goal for counselors: to help with such grace and style that the counseling process itself becomes invisible. The client leaves each counseling session with a growing sense of self-control, self-confidence, and self-responsibility.

Functioning in an invisibly appropriate style is analogous to learning to drive a standard-shift automobile. The beginning driver is clumsily shifting and grinding gears while the car jerks and stalls. After considerable driving experience, and with intentional effort, that same driver shifts gears with such skill that the vehicle accelerates from low to high speed with barely a whisper. The better the performance, the more invisible the effort. This seems to be true in almost any line of human endeavor, but it is particularly true of invitational counseling.

Why Invitational Counseling?

Most practicing counselors seek a logical rationale when choosing theories and models for professional functioning. The following seven-point rationale is offered for invitational counseling.

First, invitational counseling has potential for broad application. It cuts across traditional boundaries, counselor roles, therapeutic classifications, and professional practices. In addition, it focuses not only on people but also on places, policies, processes, and programs that influence people's lives. This wide-angle approach is generally not true of other counseling theories and approaches. Thus, invitational counseling has the potential for application in a great variety of situations.

Second, it is complementary. Invitational counseling incorporates various approaches to the professional helping relationship that fit its theoretical tenets. It provides a partial bridge between seemingly dissimilar viewpoints—for instance, between supposedly directive and nondirective approaches. At the same time, invitational counseling is based on theoretical and philosophical assumptions, and approaches to professional helping that violate these assumptions are ruled out.

A third quality of invitational counseling is that it is relatively easy to conceptualize and understand. The fundamental ideas and concepts of inviting relationships can be explained in terms that relate to people's everyday experience and developmental levels. The practical qualities of invitational counseling allow the process to be entered into by people of almost any age.

Fourth, invitational counseling is therapeutic in the highest ethical sense and is congruent with all major assumptions regarding the nature of healthy human development. It respects the autonomy and self-directing powers of the individual and advocates personal responsibility. Further, it strives for mutual cooperation, respect, and trust. Each participant in invitational counseling is expected to establish rules under which his or her actions are governed. At the same time, each participant accepts the belief that others have the right and responsibility to establish their rules as well.

A fifth feature is that invitational counseling lends itself to both process and outcome research. Invitational counseling consists of stated theoretical foundations and systematic processes. These foundations and processes are observable, measurable, and subject to empirical research and evaluation. Invitational counseling helps counselors to generate questions about their work. These questions can in turn be used to develop strategies for attaining and furthering the goals of counseling.

Sixth, invitational counseling represents a democratic approach to the professional helping relationship. Democracy, as Stuhr (1993), Novak (1994), Lappe and DuBois (1994), and others explain, is more than a political system. It is also an ethical ideal that involves a deep commitment to the concept that those who are affected by decisions should have a say in their formulation, implementation, and evaluation. Implied here is the Jeffersonian faith that people are able to act intelligently upon issues that impact their lives.

Seventh and perhaps most important in establishing a rationale for invitational counseling is that it is optimistic. Because invitational counseling maintains that people are valuable, capable, and self-directing, it focuses on the positive and uplifting aspects of human existence and development.

Embedded in the seven-point rationale for invitational counseling is the notion that the counselor is only one part of the client's life. No matter how much or in how many ways clients seek to have their counselors take charge, invitational counseling assumes that the client is the only one who is responsible for his or her own life. Positive regard, respect, and optimism concerning the client's right to self-determination are at the center of invitational counseling.

Summary

In this chapter professional counseling is introduced as an inviting process. This process, called invitational counseling, is anchored on four assumptions: (1) people are able, valuable, and capable of self-direction, and should be treated accordingly; (2) counseling should be a cooperative process where process is as important as product; (3) people possess relatively untapped potential in all areas of human development; and (4) this potential can best be realized by places, policies, processes, and programs that are intentionally designed to invite development and by people who consistently seek to realize this potential in themselves and others, personally and professionally.

Invitational counseling is based on invitational theory, which has contributed to the development of several conceptual models of professional functioning. This theory stresses the importance of creating and maintaining a stance of optimism, respect, trust, and intentionality. To accomplish this goal, levels, spheres, choices, and styles of interpersonal relationships are identified. Each of these elements will be analyzed in future chapters.

Counselors who embrace invitational counseling seek to incorporate compatible counseling theories and techniques into an expanded perspective of professional counseling. By combining the remediation of existing concerns with an optimistic, action-oriented vision of human potential, these counselors assist clients in realizing their value, abilities, and self-directing powers.

Opportunities for Further Reading

No theory or model comes to fruition without the aid of everyone and everything that precede it. Invitational counseling is no exception. The annotated list of books that follows this and all other chapters salutes the many scholars who have profoundly influenced the authors of this book. To these authors we express our heartfelt thanks.

BLOOM, B. S. (1976). *Human characteristics and school learning*. New York: McGraw-Hill. Bloom presented some startling evidence of the endless perfectibility of the human being when given an optimally inviting environment.

DEWEY, J. (1933). *How we think*. Lexington, MA: Heath. This classic text deals with the problems people have and how they face them. Dewey pointed out that everything the professional helper does, as well as the manner in which he or she does it, invites others to respond in one way or another.

FREEMAN, A., & DEWOLF, R. (1989). *Woulda, coulda, shoulda: Overcoming regrets, mistakes, and missed opportunities*. New York: Silver Arrow Books. This popularized explanation of cognitive theory presents a clear view of how to recognize thoughts that are exaggerated, unfair, or simply wrong.

HUNT, J. McV. (1961). *Intelligence and experience*. New York: Ronald Press. Hunt maintained, on the basis of detailed research, that intelligence is not fixed and that development is not predetermined. This book offers both rigor and enthusiasm to support the notion that human potential, though not always apparent, is always there, waiting to be discovered and invited forth.

JOURARD, S. M. (1971). *The transparent self: Self-disclosure and well-being*. Princeton, NJ: Van Nostrand. Jourard proposed in this deeply perceptive book that there are no barriers to human potential that cannot be transcended when people are properly invited to realize this potential.

MEIER, S. T., & DAVIS, S. R. (1993). *The elements of counseling* (2nd ed.). Pacific Grove, CA: Brooks/Cole. This succinct 100-page book provides brief, practical, and ready-to-use skills for the beginning counselor. It also provides information on practical concerns, such as record-keeping and keeping up with research.

NOVAK, J. M. (Ed.). (1992). *Advancing invitational thinking*. San Francisco: Caddo Gap Press. This volume of edited works presents a range of perspectives and practices relating to invitational theory. In particular, an article by William Stafford addresses the relationship between counseling and invitational theory.

PETERS, T. J., & WATERMAN, R. H. (1982). *In search of excellence: Lessons from America's best-run companies*. New York: Harper & Row. Peters and Waterman focused on eight characteristics that distinguish highly successful companies. These characteristics involve a number of elements found in invitational counseling, including optimism, trust, respect, and intentionality.

ROGERS, C. R. (1980). *A way of being*. Boston: Houghton Mifflin. This collection of writings and speeches by Carl Rogers provides an insight into Rogers's own professional development and his vision for the future of professional helping.

CHAPTER TWO

Foundations of Invitational Counseling

૨ઢ

It seems clear that relationships which are helpful have different characteristics from relationships which are unhelpful. These differential characteristics have to do primarily with the attitudes of the helping person on the one hand and with the perception of the relationship by the "helpee" on the other.
Carl R. Rogers
On Becoming a Person
1961, p. 49

૨ઢ

Counseling theories, organizational systems, and communication models categorize only some of the many philosophical, psychological, theological, and sociological contributions that function as building blocks for the practice of professional counseling. Practicing counselors choose approaches based on various theories and models. Most approaches to professional counseling are based on assumptions about what humans are like and how they develop physically, socially, psychologically, and spiritually. The same is true for invitational counseling.

Invitational counseling springs from the mainstreams of three theoretical perspectives: the perceptual tradition, self-concept theory, and invitational theory. Invitational theory was introduced in Chapter 1. In this chapter, two deeper foundations of invitational counseling are presented. Figure 2-1 illustrates the pyramid formed by these three perspectives as they serve as successive platforms in the development of invitational counseling. Whereas invitational theory is an emerging view, the perceptual tradition and self-concept theory have long contributed to the educational, psychological, and sociological

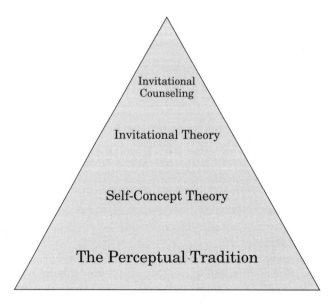

Invitational
Counseling

Invitational Theory

Self-Concept Theory

The Perceptual Tradition

FIGURE 2-1 Foundations of Invitational Counseling

basis for counseling in a variety of professional settings. For this reason, counselors who embrace invitational counseling should be versed in both the perceptual tradition and self-concept theory, including the research that has advanced both perspectives.

The Perceptual Tradition

Human behavior is always a product of how people see themselves and the situations in which they are involved. Although this fact seems obvious, the failure of people everywhere to comprehend it is responsible for much of human misunderstanding, maladjustment, conflict, and loneliness. Our perceptions of ourselves and the world are so real to us that we seldom pause to doubt them. Since persons behave in terms of their personal perceptions, effective helping must start with the helper's understanding of the nature and dynamics of perceiving.

A. W. Combs, D. L. Avila,
and W. W. Purkey
Helping Relationships
(2nd ed.), 1978, p. 15

❧

The perceptual tradition includes all systems of professional thought in which humans are viewed as they normally see themselves. The term *perceptual* refers not only to the senses but also to meanings—the personal significance of an event for the person experiencing it. These meanings extend far beyond sensory receptors to include such personal experiences as feelings, desires, aspirations, and the ways people view themselves, others, and the world.

The starting point of the perceptual tradition is that each person is a conscious agent in the process of his or her own development. The individual experiences, interprets, constructs, decides, acts, and is ultimately responsible for those actions. Behavior is seen as a product of the way people see themselves and the situations in which they find themselves. The best indicators of the choices people make throughout their lives are the beliefs they hold (Bandura, 1986; Rokeach, 1968). This view is in contrast to other approaches that depict behavior as basically a complex bundle of stimuli and responses or the product of a host of unconscious urges. In the perceptual tradition, primary importance is given to each person's perceived world, rather than to "objective" reality or "unconscious" forces.

Origins of the Perceptual Tradition

The perceptual tradition, which looks at the world as it is experienced by the perceiving person, could probably be traced back to the dawn of history. It is likely that our human ancestors, huddled around a fire in some forgotten cave, pulled their animal skins close around their shoulders and shared thoughts about their fears, desires, and the ways they felt about themselves, others, and the world around them. Thousands of years later, with the advent of written history, people began to give disciplined thought to their own perceptual worlds. Writers would describe this awareness in terms of "spirit," "psyche," "persona," "ego," "consciousness," "soul," or "self"—all acknowledging that there is an inner consciousness and spirit of personal existence.

A turning point in people's thinking about their nonphysical existence came in 1644, when René Descartes published *Principles of Philosophy*. In this masterpiece, Descartes proposed that doubt was a principal tool of disciplined inquiry—yet he could not doubt that he doubted. He reasoned that if he doubted, he was thinking, and there-fore he must exist. Other philosophers of the period, among them Benedict Spinoza and Gottfried Leibniz, added their thoughts about the mysteries of perceived experience.

At the turn of the present century, when North American psychology began to take its place among the other academic disciplines, there arose a great deal of interest in perception. During this time, two major American schools of psychology, *structuralism* and *functionalism*, explored and explained how people perceive themselves, others, and the world. These early schools of psychology were laid low in the early 1920s by the behavioral revolution headed by John B. Watson and his colleagues. The behaviorists argued that people's internal worlds were too subjective for scientific study; only external events and conditions were important.

Although behaviorism dominated North American psychology throughout the present century, a number of scholars from various disciplines persisted in the belief that each person consciously experiences events, interprets those experiences, gives them personal meaning, and acts accordingly. This view did not deny the influence of external factors or unconscious processes, but it placed them within the context of human experience. At this time, modern philosophy and science saw the development of phenomenology, the study, classification, and description of phenomena. Edmund Husserl (1859–1938) is often credited with the development of this philosophical field of study (Husserl, 1952, 1977). A mathematician, scientist, and astronomer, Husserl applied transcendental phenomenology to understand what must be assumed about human perception and conception in order to fully appreciate the human experience. Following the teachings of Franz Bretano, Husserl reintroduced the abstraction of *intentionality*, which, as we have noted, is an essential concept of invitational counseling. The existentialists who followed this period did not all agree on every aspect of Husserl's philosophy, but they were influenced by his work. Together, these scholars helped to keep the perceptual tradition alive.

Among the perceptually oriented psychologists of this era were George Kelly, with the concept of personal constructs (1955, 1963); Gordon Allport, with his theory of personality development (1937, 1943, 1955, 1961); Sidney Jourard, with self-disclosure (1964, 1968, 1971b); Kurt Lewin, with field theory (1951); Abraham Maslow, with his hierarchy of motivational needs (1968); Carl Rogers, with client-centered therapy (1951, 1961); and Kurt Goldstein, with his self-actualization work (1939, 1963). Additional support for the perceptual approach came from Germany, where Gestalt psychologists provided data from carefully controlled studies that indicated the active, selective nature of the perception process. As Diggory (1966) noted, the ability of these psychologists and allied professionals to argue substantive matters of learning theory and motivation with the behaviorists helped to give perceptually oriented scholars credibility in the eyes of hostile critics.

Although many of the early researchers and writers on perception were psychologists, psychotherapists, and counselors, contributions to the perceptual tradition were made by theologians, educators, philosophers, anthropologists, sociologists, and other scholars. The philosophical theologians Paul Tillich and Martin Heidegger added greatly to conceptions of individuality and personal responsibility. Anthropologists Ivan Malinowski, Ruth Benedict, Margaret Mead, and others forwarded the concepts of human resiliency, adaptability, and potentiality. Well-known sociologists, such as Talcott Parsons and Wilbur Brookover, also contributed to the framework of the perceptual tradition by demonstrating the importance of the social environment on individual perception.

One of the most influential contributors to the perceptual tradition was George Herbert Mead. His classic work *Mind, Self, and Society* (1934) described the development of a person's perceptual world and explained how it becomes differentiated through interactions with significant others. Mead argued that personality, rather than being anchored in biological variables, environmental pressures, or unconscious forces, is highly active, constantly aware, and heavily influenced by social-psychological factors. Mead and countless other researchers and writers made major contributions to the perceptual tradition.

In recent years, many writers and researchers who shared an interest in perception banded together and developed their own unique theories and approaches to understanding human experience. These theories and approaches became identified by such names as phenomenology, existentialism, personology, humanism, holism, perceptualism, and transactionalism. Although differing in name, these various theories sought to understand human existence by focusing on the perceiving person and the ways that person experiences self, others, and the world.

The focus of this book does not permit a proper recognition of the scholars from many disciplines who have contributed to the perceptual tradition. However, among the many worthy contributors there is one man whose ideas can be singled out as representative of the perceptual approach to understanding people and their behavior. This person is Arthur W. Combs, and his contribution has come to be called perceptual psychology.

Perceptual Psychology

I believe the humanist movement in psychology is but a single expression in that discipline of the same deep stirrings in human thought going on everywhere else. Each humanist is attempting to bring some aspect of the basic concept into clearer figure, to give it organization and direction, to discover with greater clarity and sharpness its meaning for the science of behavior. We have called ourselves by different names: Personalists, Transactionalists, Phenomenologists, Self Psychologists and Perceptualists, to name but a few. Like the blind man approaching the elephant, we have acquired a multitude of part answers. There is a need now for a unifying system which will provide: (A) a frame of reference capable of encompassing and giving meaning to these diverse contributions, and (B) a theoretical structure for research and innovation. The theme of this paper is to suggest that perceptual psychology can provide a start toward that end.

Arthur W. Combs
"Why the Humanistic Movement Needs a Perceptual Psychology"
Journal of the Association for the Study of Perception
1974, p. 2

ٶ

One of the most eloquent voices in objecting to the passivity of behaviorism and the unconscious forces of Freudianism was that of Arthur W. Combs. The continued insistence of Combs and his colleagues (David Aspy, Donald Avila, Walt Busby, Sidney Jourard, Earl Kelley, Hal Lewis, Ann Richards, Fred Richards, Betty Siegel, Donald Snygg, Daniel Soper, Richard Usher, and Hannalore Wass, among many others) on stressing how people see themselves, others, and the world was a significant contribution to psychology, counseling, and education. The work of Combs and his colleagues served as a rallying point for many splinter theories.

According to Rollo May (1961), the book *Individual Behavior: A Perceptual Approach to Behavior,* by Snygg and Combs (1949; Combs & Snygg, 1959), was the first to state the position of the American school of phenomenology (the study of human consciousness). In this book and others that followed, Combs and his associates (1962, 1965, 1969, 1974, 1976, 1978, 1984, 1989, 1994) proposed that perception is the primary component in human behavior. They maintained that the basic drive of each individual is the maintenance, protection, and enhancement of the perceived self: one's own personal existence as viewed by oneself.

As explained by Combs, Avila, and Purkey (1978), the perceptual tradition seeks to understand human behavior through the eye of the beholder—from the perspective of the person's personal and unique experience. All behavior is dependent upon the individual's own frame of reference and is a function of the perceptions that exist for the person at the moment of behaving. While the counselor may not be able to change what a client is encountering in his or her life, the counselor can assist the client in perceiving these encounters in a more positive and realistic way, aiding the client to better respond to life situations. The assistance the counselor offers begins with an understanding of basic assumptions regarding the role of human perception.

Basic Assumptions

Some primary features of the perceptual tradition are reflected in the following 16 assumptions:

1. There may be a preexistent reality, but an individual can only know the part that comprises his or her perceptual world, the world of awareness.
2. Perceptions at any given moment exist at countless levels of awareness, from the vaguest to the sharpest.
3. Because people are limited in what they can perceive, they are highly selective in what they *choose* to perceive.
4. All experiences are phenomenal in character. The fact that two individuals share the same physical environment does not mean that each will have the same experiences.
5. What individuals choose to perceive is determined by past experiences as mediated by present purposes, perceptions, and expectations.
6. Individuals tend to perceive only what is relevant to their purposes and make their choices accordingly.
7. Choices are determined by perceptions, not facts. How a person behaves is a function of his or her perceptual field at the moment of acting.
8. No perception can ever be fully shared or totally communicated because it is embedded in the life of the individual.
9. Phenomenal absolutism means that people tend to assume that other observers perceive as they do. If others perceive differently, it is often thought to be because others are mistaken or they lie.
10. The perceptual field, including the perceived self, is internally organized and personally meaningful. When this organization and meaning are threatened, emotional problems are likely to result.
11. Communication depends on the process of acquiring greater mutual understanding of one another's perceptual field.
12. People not only perceive the world of the present, they also reflect on past experiences and imagine future ones to guide their behavior.
13. Perceptions create their own reality. People respond not to reality, but to their perceptions of reality.

14. Reality can exist for an individual only when he or she is conscious of it and has some relationship with it.
15. A person may perceive the "facts" involved in a situation, but may grossly distort the meaning of these facts.
16. Client distress may be more a process of perception of a situation than the situation itself.

As reflected in the 16 assumptions, the perceptual tradition proposes that all behavior is a function of the individual's perceptual field. A person's behavior may make little sense when observed from the external views of other people, but this same behavior makes great sense when understood from the vantage point of the internal view of the experiencing person. As Zimmerman, Bandura, and Martinez-Pons (1992) demonstrated in their research regarding self-efficacy, a determinant of aspiration is a belief in self-efficacy. For example, students who possess a high sense of academic efficacy are far more likely to persevere in school and thus meet with academic success. Similar findings were reported by Schunk (1984, 1989, 1990) in studies of self-efficacy, self-regulated learning, and academic success.

Thanks to the contributions of perceptually oriented scholars—such as Aspy's (1972) perceptual characteristics of effective helpers, Chamberlin's (1981) "preflections" of the future, Bandura's (1982) self-efficacy model, Meichenbaum's (1974, 1977) cognitive behavior modification, Seligman's (1991) learned optimism, and Powers's (1973) integration of perception with systems theory, among many others—perception continues to play a major role in understanding human behavior. Perception is also the foundation to self-concept theory.

Self-Concept Theory

Your habitual way of explaining bad events, your explanatory style, is more than just the words you mouth when you fail. It is a habit of thought, learned in childhood and adolescence. Your explanatory style stems directly from your view of your place in the world—whether you think you are valuable and deserving, or worthless and hopeless.

Martin E. P. Seligman
Learned Optimism
1991, p. 44

✿

Of all the perceptions we experience in the course of living, none has more profound significance than the perceptions we hold regarding our own personal existence—our view of who we are and how we fit into the world. "The world has many centers," wrote Thomas Mann, "one for each created being." This center of the created being has come to be known as the *self-concept*.

Every person seems to have a special recording studio that records each perceived inviting or disinviting message that arrives over countless sensory pathways. These recordings are filed in such a way that they can be taken out by the experiencing person and played back again and again. As long as the perceived recordings affirm one's personal value, ability, and responsibility and contain elements of hope, respect, and trust, the individual is likely to behave accordingly. When the recordings are of messages that announce personal worthlessness, inability, and irresponsibility and contain pessimism, contempt, and suspicion, the person loses faith in his or her self and abilities. Few people, if any, can withstand the continued disesteem and contempt of fellow human beings.

Definitive statements about the characteristics and origins of self-concept remain in the realm of theory. However, an analysis of the various explanations of self and a review of related research provide valuable insights into how people see themselves. Extensive reviews of research on self-concept are available (Hamachek, 1991; Hattie, 1992; Purkey, 1970; Walz & Bleuer, 1992; Wylie, 1979), and so an extended review here is unnecessary. The following summary of self-concept theory expands upon previous work by Combs, Avila, and Purkey (1978), Harper and Purkey (1993), Purkey (1970), and Purkey and Novak (1984).

Qualities of the Self

Self-concept may be defined as the totality of a complex and dynamic system of learned beliefs that an individual holds to be true about his or her personal existence and that gives consistency to his or her personality. Embedded in this definition are five important qualities of the self. The self-concept is (1) organized, (2) dynamic, (3) consistent, (4) modifiable, and (5) learned. These qualities can be illustrated by a simple drawing. There are obvious weaknesses in using a drawing to represent the multifaceted, multilayered, highly abstract, and hierarchical constellation of active ideas called self-concept, yet drawings are helpful in expressing complex ideas. Figure 2-2 illustrates the organization of self-concept.

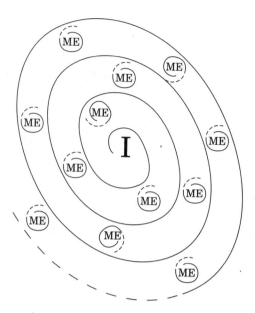

FIGURE 2-2 Self-Concept Analogy

Self-concept is organized. Most self-concept theorists, such as Combs (1982, 1989), Combs, Richards, and Richards (1976, 1988), Hattie (1992), Jourard (1964, 1971b), Purkey (1970), Rogers (1947, 1961, 1967), and Wylie (1979), agree that the self has a generally stable quality that is characterized by orderliness and harmony. To picture this internal symmetry, consider Figure 2-2, and imagine that the large spiral represents the organized unity of the self, the "global self." The global self is orchestrated and balanced within itself, but it also contains smaller units. These can be thought of as subselves and are pictured as small "me" spirals. These subselves represent the self-as-object, the various "me's" that are the objects of self-perception. For example, "me as a counselor" would represent the self-perceptions a particular counselor holds about being a professional helper. Each of the "me" spirals within the global system is organized and balanced within itself, yet each is influenced by and in turn influences the global self.

The numerous "me" spirals also represent specific beliefs that a person holds to be true about his or her personal existence. These beliefs can be divided into *attributes* (such as strong, tall, loyal, short, fat, bright, young, friendly, trustworthy, sexy) and *categories* (such as student, husband, mother, Christian, Moslem, Jew, atheist, tennis player, American, African, homosexual, veteran, lover). These perceived attributes and categories usually are linked together (for example, "good student," "loyal American," "sexy lover," "excellent counselor") and positioned in a hierarchical order within the global self. This order is critical, for it gives meaning and stability to the entire self-system.

Each person's self-concept maintains countless "me's," but all are not equally significant. Some are seen as highly important and are positioned close to the center of the global self. This center is marked with an "I" in Figure 2-2 to indicate immediate personal awareness. It is this "I" that Erich Fromm so beautifully referred to as "life being aware of itself" (1956, p. 8). Humans are aware of themselves as well as their perceived past and future. This self-awareness, this consciousness, gives consistency to the human personality.

Other "me's" are less central and therefore located toward the periphery of the global self. Subselves closest to the "I" have the most influence on daily functioning; the individual "hears" these subselves the loudest for they are closest to the center of the self. By the same token, those subselves farthest away from the "I" have the weakest voices and thus have diminished influence on behavior. For example, perceiving oneself as a devout Christian may have vastly greater impact on a person's behavior than perceiving oneself as a casual golfer.

The open areas between the lines of the global spiral in Figure 2-2 represent the space each person requires to evaluate him- or herself fairly and grow properly. Some people can become so crowded internally with often contradictory "me's" that they experience a sort of sensory overload, continuously adding "me's" without letting go of any. When this happens, a person may behave in confusing and inconsistent ways.

A graduate student of one of the authors suggested an imaginative way of understanding the difference between the central "I" and the "me's" that surround it. The "I" can be imagined as a source of light. Light travels in all directions through the universe, but it is only visible when it strikes something. By analogy, the "I" of personal existence becomes visible only when it reflects off the various "me's." The "I" cannot see itself directly, any more than the human eye can see itself. It is through the mirrored reflections of countless "me's" that the "I" defines itself.

As early as 1961, C. M. Lowe postulated that some parts of the self-system are peripheral and are therefore relatively unstable, while other parts are more central to the self (close to the "I") and are highly resistant to change. For example, consider the comment, "Oh, I couldn't do that; it's just not me." Anyone who has attempted to give up a cherished belief about oneself, or to accept one that does not seem to fit, can understand how difficult a task it is to change one's perceptions of personal existence.

In her classic studies of individuals in distress, Horney (1939) reported that individuals tend to cling to their beliefs as a drowning person clings to a straw. Closely held beliefs about oneself are difficult to change. They can persevere even against reason, experience, time, and education (Abelson, 1979; Pajares, 1992; Schommer, 1990). Fortunately, change is possible, and this fact has important implications for counseling.

A second organizational feature of the self is that each subself (represented by a small "me" spiral) has its own generally negative or positive value. For example, being a divorced person might be very close to the center of the self, but this could be valued negatively by the experiencing individual. He or she might think, "Being a divorced person is a most significant part of my life, and I am constantly aware of it. But I am not comfortable with this fact and tend to hide it from others." Thus, each subself carries its own plus or minus charge that contributes to the global self, positively or negatively.

A third organizational quality of the self is that perceived success and failure tend to generalize throughout the entire self-system. From his research, Diggory (1966) concluded that when one dimension of the perceived self is important and highly valued, a failure in that dimension lowers the individual's self-evaluation in other, seemingly unrelated abilities. Conversely, success in a highly valued activity tends to raise self-evaluations in other apparently unconnected abilities. This spread-of-effect phenomenon has been documented by Blailiffe (1978), Ludwig and Maehr (1967), and others.

To illustrate the spread-of-effect phenomenon, return to Figure 2-2 and imagine that each subself (small "me" spiral) is a tiny bell. When one bell rings, all others chime in, echoing to some degree the positive or negative note sounded. This process can be illustrated by the perceptions of a person who is a professional tennis player. If this professional considers himself to be an excellent athlete, and being an outstanding player is close to the "I," the center of the self, and highly valued, then consistent success on the tennis court raises self-regard in other, apparently unrelated areas, such as outside business ventures or public speaking. However, one caveat is necessary: A high achiever in any endeavor may become unhappy with success if the achievement is not perceived as valued in the eyes of significant others. Individuals require positive regard from others as well as from themselves. Only those with a clearly atypical personality could, over time, retain a positive self-concept in the face of consistently disinviting external forces.

One final organizational feature of self-concept is that each person's self is marvelously unique. Like fingerprints or dental charts, no two people hold identical sets of beliefs about themselves. This uniqueness makes for an infinite variety of human personalities. It also helps explain problems in communication. Because no two people ever perceive exactly the same way, it is often difficult for them to agree about what it is they experience. For example, a counselor will need great sensitivity to understand the perceptual world of the Western Apache, where questions display "an unnatural curiosity," handshaking "violates a person's territory," and talking about trouble "increases its chances of occurrence" (Basso, 1979). There may be sharp perceptual differences between counselors and those they seek to help. To the degree that a counselor can enter the perceptual world of the client, to that degree can he or she also understand, accept, and reflect the feelings of the client.

Self-concept is dynamic.   Combs and associates (1959, 1962, 1978, 1994) have postulated that the maintenance, protection, and enhancement of the perceived self (one's own personal existence as viewed by oneself) are the basic motivations behind all human behavior. For example, a corporate executive might be neglecting her official duties (the "executive me") that she does not see as a central part of herself, while spending many hours on the golf course improving her already superior skills and polishing her valued self-as-golfer image. People tend to behave in ways that are most central to the self and closest to the "I." In this way, the self-concept serves as a road map for living.

As explained by Spears and Deese (1973), self-concept is not the cause of a person's behavior. For example, in the case of student misbehavior, the self-concept does not *cause* the misconduct. A better explanation is that the disruptive person has learned to see himself or herself as a troublemaker and is behaving accordingly. In a similar explanation of self, Shavelson, Hubner, and Stanton (1976) referred to self-concept as a "moderator variable" that serves as the reference point, or anchoring perception, for behavior. More recently, Bandura (1982), Seligman (1991), and others have demonstrated that individuals who view themselves as inefficacious in coping with environmental demands and expectations tend to dwell on their perceived deficiencies and view potential challenges and difficulties as far more difficult than they really are.

To understand the dynamic nature of the self, picture the global spiral as a sort of personal gyrocompass: a continuously active system of subjective beliefs that dependably point to the "true north" of a person's perceived existence. This guidance system serves to direct actions and enables each individual to take a consistent stance in life. Rather than being viewed as the cause of behavior, self-concept is better understood as the gyrocompass of the human personality, providing consistency in personality and direction in behavior.

Early evidence regarding the dynamic nature of the self was

provided by Zimmerman and Allebrand (1965). They demonstrated that poor readers in school lack a sense of personal worth and adequacy to the point where they actively avoid achievement. For poor readers, to study hard and still fail provides unbearable proof of personal inadequacy. To avoid such proof and to suffer less pain, many students deliberately choose not to try. Their defense against failure is to accept themselves as failures. From their point of view, it is better not to try than to try and be embarrassed or humiliated. By not trying, they maintain control. Glock (1972) stated the situation succinctly: "A negative self-image is its own best defender" (p. 406). To understand why this is so, it is important to recognize that, from the person's perceptual vantage point, any amount of anxiety involved in a particular action, no matter how painful, seems preferable to other available avenues of behavior. Posner, Strike, Hewson, and Gertzog (1982) reported that for beliefs to change, a number of conditions must exist, including the individual's awareness that new information represents an anomaly with respect to existing beliefs, that this new information should be reconciled with existing beliefs, and that this reconciliation is impossible. This inclines the individual to reduce dissonance by creating a new or revised belief system. Counseling can be a tremendous help in such cases by assisting clients in reevaluating and reorganizing their perceptions.

Self-concept is consistent. A noteworthy feature of self-concept is that it requires internal consistency. To maintain this consistency of personality, people act in accordance with the ways they have learned to view themselves. From a lifetime of studying their own actions and those of others, people acquire expectations about what things fit and what behaviors are appropriate in their perceived world. All subselves that exist within the global self-system are expected by the perceiver to be consistent with all others, no matter how inconsistent they may be from an external viewpoint. When these expectations are not fulfilled, "cognitive dissonance" results, which is the uncomfortable state of incompatible perceptions. This discomfort is most apparent when one behaves in a way that is not in keeping with one's self-image.

If a new experience is consistent with experiences already incorporated into the self-system, the individual easily accepts and assimilates that new experience. However, if the new experience is in opposition to those already incorporated, the person will actively reject it, no matter how self-enhancing it might appear to the external observer. To summarize, people accept and incorporate that which is congenial to their established self-systems, but they reject and avoid experiences or meanings of their experiences that are disagreeable and incongruous. People seek support for their perceived self-identity, and avoid evidence that threatens it.

To understand the consistency of self, it is important to consider how things appear from a persons's *internal* point of view. Cases of anorexia illustrate this phenomenon. People who have anorexia see themselves as fat in spite of the fact that they are dangerously underweight. To reduce their "fatness" they avoid food, sometimes to the point of starvation. No matter how illogical, counterproductive, and self-defeating a particular behavior may appear to be from an *external* viewpoint, individual behavior has a certain internal logic. Counselors who can understand, accept (acceptance does not mean agreement), and reflect this logic to clients are in a good position to help clients reconsider their perception.

Sometimes the global self consists of contradictory subselves. Yet these various "me's" can coexist happily and may never encounter or challenge one another as long as the individual does not perceive the contradictions. For example, a father may neglect his own children while working actively with a youth group. It is only when a person faces some identity crisis, or becomes aware of the contradictions among self-perceptions, that resolution of the dissonance is likely to occur. If the perceived dissonance is not resolved, the individual is likely to suffer emotional distress.

Behaviors that are incompatible with one's self-concept are likely to result in psychological discomfort and anxiety. For example, at a human sexuality conference, a university infirmary physician noted the reluctance of some young adults to use contraceptives although they were having sexual relations. When questioned as to why they did not practice contraception, they reasoned that if they used contraception they would obviously be planning to engage in sexual activity, which they considered "bad" and could not accept. By not using contraceptive measures when they had sexual intercourse, they sustained the belief that they were swept off their feet in a moment of passion. Spontaneous sexual activity was far more acceptable to their self-image than a premeditated act would be. People behave according to their perceptions, even if the behavior seems to others to be odd, dangerous, or self-defeating. Everything a person experiences is filtered through, and mediated by, whatever self-concept is already present in the self-system. This screening and mediating process ensures internal consistency within the human personality.

The tendency toward consistency appears to be an essential feature of the human personality, for it provides the person with internal balance, a sense of direction, feelings of stability, and a certain dependability in behavior. If individuals altered new beliefs about themselves easily, or if their behaviors were unpredictable, the human personality would lack integrity. Under such conditions, human society would be difficult to imagine.

Counselors who understand the tendency toward self-consistency do not expect quick changes in themselves or others. People cannot be quickly shaped into something more suitable or desirable. It took a long time for individuals to get to where they are now, and it will take time for them to change. Whether a person's self-concept is healthy or unhealthy, productive or counterproductive, the person strives for consistency.

One additional example might be useful here. Doctors and nurses often find it difficult to get patients who are diagnosed as diabetic to care for themselves properly. Such patients find it difficult to accept their new "diabetic me" and the accompanying need to use insulin and follow dietary requirements. It takes time to assimilate this new "me" into the self-system. It is noteworthy that the English language allows a diabetic to reveal his or her self-concept by saying "I am diabetic." Certain conditions and diseases are not allowed this same freedom. One never hears, "I am cancerous." Instead, a forced distancing process takes place: "I *have* cancer." In general, people who have health concerns prefer to define themselves in terms other than their affliction: "I am a father, teacher, and poet, and I happen to be epileptic." Counselors who relate to clients primarily in terms of the clients' disabilities can be very disinviting.

One further insight relating to self-consistency is that being correct in one's assumptions about oneself has reward value, even if the assumption is negative. A student may take a certain pleasure in thinking, "See, just as I thought! I knew nobody in this damn school cares whether I live or die!" Being right—even about negative feelings toward oneself—can be self-satisfying.

Although self-concept tends toward consistency, significant changes in the self are possible. Each person is involved in an endless quest for positive self-regard and the favorable regard of significant others. Over time and under certain conditions, one's self-image can undergo significant alterations. The good news for counselors is that self-concept is modifiable.

Self-concept is modifiable. In each reasonably healthy person, new perceptions filter into the self-concept throughout life, while old ones fade away. This continuous flow creates flexibility in the human character and allows for infinite modifiability of the perceived self. A likely reason for the assimilation of new ideas and the expulsion of old ones is the quest to maintain, protect, and enhance the perceived self.

The basic assumption of the perceptual tradition—that each person is constantly seeking to maintain, protect, and enhance his or her psychological self—is a tremendous "given" for the counselor, for it means that the self is predisposed toward development. Rather than seeking ways to motivate clients, invitational counseling is based on the assumption that people are *always* motivated. People may not do what others wish them to do, but this does not mean that they are unmotivated. Counselors who accept this assumption can shift their energies away from a "doing to" process of trying to motivate people, and toward a "doing with" process of inviting people to explore their self-perceptions and choose the directions for this internal motivation.

From a perceptual point of view there is only one kind of human motivation—an internal and continuous incentive that every individual has at all times, in all places, during any activity. Understanding human motivation from this perspective is a tremendous advantage for counselors, for it assumes that motivation is a basic force that comes from within the human being. Counselors who accept this view can use their talents to encourage a cooperative spirit of mutual learning, which introduces another quality of the self: self-concept is learned.

Self-concept is learned. People change their self-perceptions, either for good or ill, in three general ways. The first way is through an extremely traumatic or ecstatic event. All of us have witnessed how the tragic loss of a loved one, or the joyous arrival of a baby, can have such impact that the very structure of a person's self-concept undergoes significant change (for example, "I am now a widow," "I am now a father," "I am now retired"). The impact of such momentous events, including religious conversion ("I am now saved"), abruptly interrupts the internal balance of the self-concept and points it in a new direction.

A second way that people change their self-perception is through a professional helping relationship, such as spiritual guidance, medical treatment, or professional counseling. An abundance of empirical research has demonstrated that counseling and related therapeutic approaches can be beneficial in altering both self-regard and regard of others. In addition, scientific and medical interventions continue to overcome challenges and help individuals live long and healthy lives. Various forms of professional service, both separately and in conjunction with one another, can have powerful effects on self-concept.

The third and greatest influence on self-concept takes place in everyday experiences and events. Repeated experiences, either inviting or disinviting, have a profound effect on the self. Children can be gradually but permanently crippled by abusive adults who themselves may have been psychologically crippled as children. In school, students who are repeatedly invited or disinvited gradually begin to see themselves as successes or failures. In business, workers who are consistently encouraged to participate in decision-making processes, or who are repeatedly excluded from such actions, will eventually see themselves as either valued participants or as mindless functionaries (Gitlow & Gitlow, 1987). Many people who seek professional help have lost the will to challenge the negative self-perceptions that dominate their lives. Asking a client to describe how significant people view him or her can reveal much about the client's self-perceptions.

One further characteristic of the self-concept is that developing it is a lifelong process. By exploring with clients the sources of negative self-perceptions and by encouraging them to consider their strengths, counselors can help clients to develop self-confidence and restore feelings of self-efficacy.

Unfortunately, it appears that there is a general decline in self-concept as children progress through school. Burnett (1993) reported a downward trend in self-concept as students moved from grades two to seven. Similar findings were reported by Harper and Purkey (1993) in their study of children in grades six through eight. This decline has significant implications for counselors in schools. What children believe about themselves is vital to their learning and overall development.

The Self-Concept as a Lifelong Process

As far as is known, no one is born with a self-concept. It emerges experience by experience, thought by thought, perception by perception. Gradually, the self is acquired and modified through the constantly accumulating experiences of the developing person. The construction of the self is a lifelong research project, developed through accumulated experiences and accompanied by the constant interpretation of events in ways congruent with what is already present in the self-system.

Of all contemporary theories and models of professional helping, none depends more on self-concept theory than invitational counseling. It gives major importance to the counselor's and client's selves and suggests ways to invite positive and realistic self-images in both parties. Because self-concept does not appear to be instinctive, but instead is learned through experience, it possesses infinite capacity for growth and actualization. This capacity offers great hope for the counselor and client.

In concluding this presentation of self-concept theory, it may be helpful to think of the self-concept as a lake. This lake is constantly fed by an experiential river that flows into the lake at one end and exits it at the other. The river can flow rapidly or slowly and can provide much or little freshness to the lake. In a healthy personality, the river constantly provides the lake with fresh concepts about the self, while outmoded ideas are flushed out of the lake and down the river. When this lifelong process of renewal and development is interrupted, and little is allowed to enter or leave the lake, the lake becomes stagnant. In invitational counseling, by analogy, individuals are invited to examine new ideas about their existence and to abandon outmoded concepts that are no longer beneficial.

Summary

This chapter has presented a review of the two pillars supporting invitational theory: the perceptual tradition and self-concept theory. These foundations have contributed significantly to the development of invitational counseling.

An understanding of the perceptual tradition is essential to the practice of invitational counseling. Therefore, a brief history of the perceptual tradition was presented along with some illustrations of the role of perception in everyday life.

Self-concept theory was also described in this chapter. The development of self-concept was outlined, along with its major organizational characteristics and the significant role it plays in human development. In particular, the significant impact of repeated inviting or disinviting events on the developing self was explained.

Finally, the overview of invitational theory presented in the first chapter gives a structure by which the perceptual tradition and self-concept theory can be applied in professional helping relationships. As such, invitational theory provides the roots for invitational counseling.

Opportunities for Further Reading

BUBER, M. (1958). *I and thou.* New York: Scribner's. The first English edition of this classic book appeared in 1937. In his poetic and somewhat mystical style of writing, Buber explored the phenomenon of human existence.

COOPERSMITH, S. (1981). *The antecedents of self-esteem* (2nd ed.). New York: Consulting Psychologist Press. In a series of carefully constructed studies, Coopersmith described the antecedents and consequences of self-esteem in children. He concluded that parental warmth, clearly defined limits, and respectful treatment are the primary forces in inviting positive self-regard in children.

COMBS, A. W. (1989). *A theory of therapy: Guidelines for counseling practice.* New York: Sage Publications. This small book provides a system for interpreting the role of professional helping in everyday life.

GOFFMAN, E. (1959). *The presentation of self in everyday life.* Garden City, NY: Doubleday. This widely quoted book presents a sociological perspective on the ways individuals present themselves to others and the ways they seek to guide and control the impressions others have of them.

HAMACHEK, D. E. (1991). *Encounters with the self* (4th ed.). New York: Holt, Rinehart & Winston. Hamachek focused on the private self-picture that each person carries inside, which defines who one is and what one can and cannot do. Hamachek explained how this picture is developed, changed, and expressed in everyday behavior.

HATTIE, J. (1992). *Self-Concept.* Hillsdale, NJ: Lawrence Erlbaum. Hattie provided an extensive review of research on self-concept and offered many insights based on research evidence.

MASLOW, A. H. (1968). *Toward a psychology of being* (2nd ed.). New York: Van Nostrand. This book is a continuation of Maslow's *Motivation and Personality,* first published in 1954. Maslow expands on his thesis that all science needs to do to help in positive fulfillment of the human condition is to enlarge and deepen the conception of its nature so that it includes the "inner view" of human existence.

MAY, R. (Ed.). (1966). *Existential psychology.* New York: Random House. The existential philosophers whose works appear in this book of readings agree that reality must be seen in terms of human experiences that transcend rational thinking. As May explained, "there is no such thing as truth or reality for a living human being except as he participates in it, is conscious of it, has some relationship to it" (p. 17).

ROGERS, C. R. (1969). *Freedom to learn.* Columbus, OH: Merrill. The theme of this book is that students can be trusted to learn and to enjoy learning when a facilitative person sets up environments that encourage responsible participation in selecting and reaching goals. Rogers revised this book in 1983 as *Freedom to learn in the eighties.*

SELIGMAN, M. E. P. (1991). *Learned optimism.* New York: Knopf. According to Seligman, optimism can be taught and learned, and can determine health and happiness. The book combines hard-edged science with practical advice on how to learn to be optimistic.

STEINEM, G. (1992). *Revolution from within: A book of self-esteem.* Boston: Little Brown. The importance of self-esteem in personal and professional functioning is documented again and again in this book. According to Steinem, one of the critical differences between the cruel despot and the creative leader is low versus high self-esteem.

WALZ, G., & BLEUER, J. (1992). *Student self-esteem: A vital element of school success.* Ann Arbor, MI: ERIC/CAPS. This book provides a comprehensive overview of self-esteem. Seventeen chapters offer 59 articles written by authorities on self-concept and self-esteem.

CHAPTER THREE

Ingredients of Invitational Counseling

ða

Of all the exciting developments that have taken place, there is none more basic than the realization that a counselor can gain the whole world and lose his or her own soul. . . . To me the most striking personal discovery of the past decade has been that people respond to my degree of caring more than to my degree of knowing.

C. Gilbert Wrenn
The World of the Contemporary Counselor
1973, pp. 248–249

ða

The opening chapters of this book introduced invitational counseling as a model of professional helping founded in the perceptual tradition and self-concept theory. This chapter presents the ingredients of invitational counseling and explores the four levels of professional functioning introduced in Chapter 1.

In building a house, designing a boat, or baking a cake, the first consideration after a blueprint, design, or recipe is chosen is the quality of the ingredients to be used. So it is with invitational counseling. Once the philosophy and theoretical foundations have been understood, the next step is to consider the ingredients.

This chapter analyzes four ingredients of invitational counseling. The first ingredient is the belief system a counselor maintains regarding self, others, and professional helping. The second ingredient consists of the four elements that make up the dispositional stance of a professional counselor. The third ingredient is the degree to which a counselor and client intentionally develop a therapeutic alliance. The final ingredient is responsibility, which is central to a counselor's respect and trust in the helping relationship. Each of these ingredients will be considered, followed by its integration into the four levels of professional functioning.

Beliefs about Self, Others, and Professional Helping

Indeed, people often do not behave optimally, even though they know full well what to do. This is because self-referent thought also mediates the relationship between knowledge and action.

Albert Bandura
"Self-Efficacy Mechanism in Human Agency"
American Psychologist
1982, p. 122

ಶ

For counselors to develop and maintain professionally inviting relationships, it is essential that they nurture their ability to take an internal frame of reference: to view people as they see themselves, others, and the world. Focusing on unresolved unconscious conflicts or on contingencies of reinforcement may remove problems, but from an invitational viewpoint, the counselor-client relationship has another goal: to realize one's relatively untapped potential in all areas of worthwhile human activity. To achieve this potential, counselors first pay close attention to their clients' perceptions.

Clients' Perceptions

Invitational counseling is based on the assumption that people choose their actions—the ways they elect to function—and that these choices are made on the basis of their perceptions. These perceptions make individual personalities possible. People's perceptions also explain individual differences in behavior that occur constantly in the course of daily interactions.

An example of individual differences in perception may be observed when a couple attends a movie. Upon leaving the theater, one praises the film, exclaiming, "It was the best I've ever seen!" The other person responds incredulously, "I thought it would never end!" Contrasting perceptions occurred even though they sat next to each other in the same theater for two hours, viewing the same film, even eating out of the same box of popcorn.

A similar indication of the relative uniqueness of perceptions is often witnessed by family counselors. The mother states that her rules are too lenient, while her teenage daughter complains, "Mom never lets me do anything!" Parents and children are sometimes at odds because of their individual perceptions of the same external events. They may agree on some aspects of what took place but differ dramatically in the meanings they attribute to them. Individual perceptions permit an endless variety of interpretations of the same event.

From birth, individuals assimilate countless perceived objects, situations, interactions, and relationships into their perceptual fields. Based on this assimilated content, they then choose actions that seem most appropriate at the moment of action. For example, a man who perceives himself as a capable company employee and good family provider may seek additional responsibilities at the office and at home. His consistently high performance results in his continued success at the office and at home. These achievements produce praise from both employer and family, who tell him what a capable employee and provider he is. These messages validate his self-enhancing actions. The cyclical process, as illustrated in Figure 3-1, continues to spiral in beneficial directions.

In contrast, Figure 3-2 illustrates this cyclical process in a negative, self-defeating manner. In this example, the student sees himself as being incapable of performing well in school. This perception leads to poor work and study habits, which result in inferior work and failing grades, criticism from significant others, and reaffirmation of the student's low self-concept.

Through countless and continuous interactions, people develop both negative and positive perceptions about themselves, others, and the world. While these perceptions undergo change over time, some fundamental beliefs remain relatively stable. It is these basic

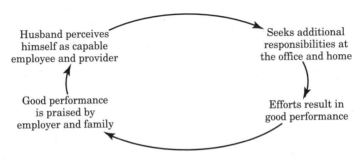

FIGURE 3-1   Cyclical Process of Self-Perceptions

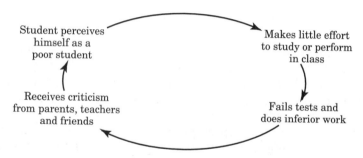

FIGURE 3-2 Cyclical Process of Self-Perceptions

perceptions that guide decisions and serve as a "frame of reference for judgment" (Combs, Richards, & Richards, 1976, p. 109). These core perceptions serve as psychological road maps for living and are the heart of one's self-concept.

Counselors' Perceptions

Countless variables have been related to counseling outcomes, including counselor traits (Felker, 1973; Vargas & Borkowski, 1983), counselor behaviors (Dell, 1973), environmental factors (Chaikin, Derlega, & Miller, 1976; Haase & DiMatta, 1976), and counseling skills (Ivey & Authier, 1978). Of these, a variable that appears repeatedly in the professional literature is the counselor's own perceptual world.

Early research by Combs and Soper (1963) related counselor perceptions to the effectiveness of counseling relationships. The now classic works of Carkhuff (1969a, b) stressed the importance of perceptual qualities of the therapist in successful helping relationships. This position supports the pioneering work of Carl Rogers, who as early as 1958 noted, "It seems clear that relationships which are helpful have different characteristics from relationships which are unhelpful. These different characteristics have to do primarily with the attitudes of the helping person on the one hand, and with the perception of the relationship by the 'helpee' on the other" (1958, p. 6). Additional research by Kegan (1982), Meichenbaum (1977), Patterson (1985b), Zarski, Sweeney, and Barcikowski (1977), and others continues to support the conclusions drawn by Rogers regarding the importance of counselor perceptions in the helping relationship.

A primary goal of counseling is to assist individuals in understanding themselves, others, and the world so that they may enhance their present existence and future development. Counselors who accept and reflect accurately their own feelings *within themselves* are in a favorable position to encourage such processes in others. Conversely, counselors who have difficulty with their own self-explorations, or who harbor feelings they are unable to accept and reflect within themselves, severely limit their value as helpers. A counselor's ability and willingness to self-examine, self-accept, and self-reflect are necessary for successful functioning, both personally and professionally.

Acceptance and Reflection of Perceptions

In invitational counseling, the counselor realizes that a client's perceptions are central to that person's total being. This realization permits the counselor to accept the perceptions that clients have even when these views contradict the counselor's own perceptions. The counselor who does not accept the client's perceptions, no matter how "wrong" these perceptions may be from an "external" viewpoint (in this case, the counselor's point of view), initiates an adversarial posture that is likely to weaken or destroy the helping relationship.

Accepting and accurately reflecting the client's perceptions creates a bond that allows the client and counselor to explore feelings and examine ways of experiencing the self, others, and the world. This pattern of accepting and reflecting is a different process from that of agreement. A counselor can accept and reflect a client's perception that she or he is a worthless person without *agreeing* to that perception. The time for confrontation regarding perceptions may come, but it should be preceded by the client's understanding that his or her feelings have been heard, accepted, and accurately reflected.

Counseling an alcoholic client provides an example of the hearing, accepting, and reflecting process. A counselor who refuses to hear, accept, and reflect the client's perception that she or he *is not* an alcoholic ("I'm just a social drinker"), but rather insists on forcing the alcoholic label on the client, is unlikely to promote a productive counselor-client alliance. On the other hand, if the counselor accepts and reflects the client's perception of him- or herself as a social drinker, involvement at this level can productively assess current drinking habits, behaviors, and any resulting problems perceived by the client. Again, acceptance does not mean agreement. The counselor may decide at some appropriate point to confront the client about the contradictions between what he or she perceives to be true about the use of alcohol and how he or she uses alcohol and behaves when drinking. When done appropriately, confrontation is a most caring and appropriate way to interact with a client (see Chapter 6).

The centerpiece for reflecting and understanding client

perceptions is *acceptance*. No matter what interviewing approach is used, whether it is the lifestyle questionnaire of Adlerian counseling (Dinkmeyer, Dinkmeyer, & Sperry, 1987), the script analysis of transactional analysis (Steiner, 1990), the paraphrasing and reflection of person-centered therapy (Rogers, 1961), or another therapeutic process, the essential element in invitational counseling is a genuine acceptance of the client's expressed feelings. In developing the ability to hear, accept, and reflect clients' perceptions, an essential ingredient is the counselor's ability to accept and reflect the counselor's own perceptions *within* him- or herself.

Three Existential Questions

Perceptual issues in human behavior are connected to three basic questions regarding personal existence. These questions heavily influence the counseling process, for the answers they generate largely determine the outcome of the helping relationship. At some point, people ask the following three questions as they move through the various stages of their lives.

The first question is, "What do I hold to be true about my own existence?" This is a fundamental self-concept question, for the answers may reveal the inner nature of a person's perceived being. The beliefs a person holds to be true about his or her personal existence serve as a guidance system in formulating the direction of his or her behavior. This perceptual guidance system indicates the true north, south, east, and west of a person's personality and the direction he or she should follow in life. Behaving in ways that are consistent with one's self-concept confers a certain reward value and a special satisfaction, whatever the final destination. People who hold realistic and positive beliefs about themselves and their abilities are more likely to encounter success, whereas those who harbor unrealistic and negative beliefs are more likely to meet failure.

The second question affecting the counseling relationship is, "What do I believe others think about me?" This is a question of acceptance as well as validation, for the answers it generates provide reasons for people to either justify their self-images or reexamine them. When people believe significant others see them as able, valuable, and responsible, they tend to behave in ways that support those beliefs. When people believe others see them as unable, worthless, and irresponsible, their behavior is likely to reflect this opinion as well. People tend to live up or down to the expectations of others, no matter in what direction these expectations may point.

The third question affecting the counseling relationship is, "How would I like others to see me?" Herein lies a fundamental conflict. Often, our own self-perceptions and the perceptions we think others have of us are contrary to how we would like to be seen by others. Countless opportunities for inner conflict and social discord exist among one's self-perceptions, one's perceptions of how others see oneself, and the ways one would like to be seen by others. Resolution of these conflicts, coupled with realization of the power one has to alter perceptions, is at the heart of invitational counseling.

These three questions are equally important for both client and counselor. Both internally process these questions, and an understanding of this process contributes to the success of the helping relationship. The counselor's efforts to be in tune with his or her own perceptions as well as those of the client increase sensitivity toward self and others. This sensitivity enables the counselor to maintain a professional stance in the counseling relationship.

A Professional Stance

Invitational counseling holds that four essential elements help define and give clarity to the role and function of a counselor. These were introduced in Chapter 1 and are reiterated here to emphasize their contribution to the counselor's professional stance. The first is optimism.

It makes sense that, in approaching their clients, successful counselors have a strong belief that they have the ability to help and that their clients have the ability to take control of their lives. This optimism is not an unbridled belief that anything is possible, but rather a clear assessment of the client and the situation. Many counseling relationships begin with an onslaught of negative reports and damaging data. Given this dismal opening, it is understandable that maintaining an optimistic stance is difficult. Nevertheless, invitational counseling asserts that there is no alternative to believing that the client is capable of making changes, improving skills, and accomplishing goals to achieve a better life.

Invitational counseling maintains that people possess untapped potential in all areas of human endeavor. The uniqueness of human beings is that no apparent limits to their potential have been discovered. Clearly, invitational counseling cannot be seriously embraced without optimism regarding human potential. When counselors view people as possessing untapped potential, they are able to use this optimism to establish beneficial places, programs, policies, and processes that reflect a genuine respect for themselves, their profession, and the people they seek to help.

Counselors who practice invitational counseling work to develop a positive and realistic respect for themselves, their profession, and their clients. This respect is translated into the expectation that the client is a responsible person and will progress in the helping relationship. Sometimes a counseling relationship can try one's patience because progress is not readily observed. In such a situation it is easy to become frustrated and use disrespectful behaviors to shock a client into improving. One example of disrespectful behavior would be the practice used by some schoolteachers and counselors in a program called "assertive discipline" (Canter & Canter, 1976). In this approach, teachers are encouraged to write the names of students on the blackboard as a public announcement of their offenses. Ridicule and embarrassment have no place in the invitational model and are contrary to invitational counseling. At no time is disrespect a responsible method of operation because it violates an essential condition for establishing trust.

Professional counseling requires a relationship in which clients are comfortable in disclosing themselves. This self-disclosure cannot be achieved without the element of trust. Clients are most likely to accept invitations to self-disclose when the counselor is seen as trustworthy.

Most approaches to counseling take the position that trust must be developed early in the relationship and that without trust a helping relationship is unlikely to be established. This position may have some truth, but in invitational counseling trust is seen as a result of a professional stance that evolves from an optimistic posture and maintains a high level of respect that incorporates responsible behaviors. The inviting process, described later in this book, illustrates the steps and actions counselors take to ensure trustful relationships with their clients. Trust is not expected to be established early in a helping relationship. Rather, it is constantly nurtured and strengthened by positive actions taken by counselors.

The first three elements of invitational counseling—optimism, respect, and trust—are intertwined in the professional stance. Combined, they reflect a fourth and most important element, one that gives a direction to the helping relationship and has been referred to as "counselor intentionality" (Ivey, 1994; Ivey & Simek-Downing, 1980; Purkey & Schmidt, 1987; Schmidt, 1984). Intentionality plays a paramount role in invitational counseling. It is the element that gives human activity purpose and meaning. Optimism, respect, and trust have direction and strength in accordance with the intentionality of the individual. Figure 3-3 illustrates the central role intentionality plays in invitational counseling. The figure is adapted from an idea of a colleague, Charlene Smith, who noted that intentionality is central

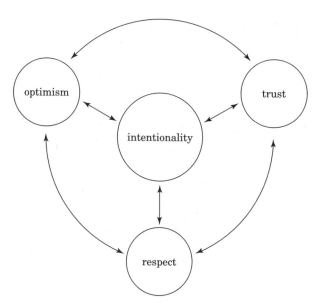

FIGURE 3-3 A Professional Stance

to the other three elements because it implies the choice or desire to be optimistic, respectful, and trustworthy. Because intentionality is so important in invitational counseling, it deserves detailed attention.

Intentionality

The introductory chapters of this book explained how important perception and self-determination are to invitational counseling. Both of these dimensions influence human intentionality. They are powerful factors in all counseling relationships. As Jourard (1964) explained, each individual's physical and psychological health is profoundly affected by the degree to which he or she has found meaning, direction, and purpose in his or her existence. Successful counseling relationships value the individual's perception of events and honor the right of self-determination. By the same token, intentionality is a barometer for successful living because, as Covey (1989) noted, "we are responsible for our own lives. Our behavior is a function of our decisions, not our conditions" (p. 71).

An intentional stance gives purpose and direction to helping relationships. It provides a guide for selecting the most beneficial goals for personal and professional success. Intentionality that respects and honors the individual while encouraging a purposeful direction is the heart of invitational counseling.

Defining Intentionality

The concept of intentionality in professional helping was introduced by Rollo May in 1969. He viewed intentionality as a major variable related to successful therapy. According to May, people's perceptions are always colored by intentions. Intentionality is the basis for these intentions, and provides the framework in which perceptions are organized and interpreted.

May (1969) described intentionality as "the structure which gives meaning to experience" (p. 223). He traced its philosophical and epistemological roots from the early writings of St. Thomas Aquinas, Immanuel Kant, and Franz Bretano, to the more recent works of Edmund Husserl and Martin Heidegger. May's analysis of intentionality as a derivative of the Latin words *intendere* and *tensum* emphasized the "stretching toward," "taking care of," and "purposeful" meanings the construct carries. He viewed intentionality as people's ability to link their inner consciousness and perceptions with their intentions and overt behaviors. By this definition, intentionality "is not to be identified with intentions, but it is the dimension which underlies them; it is man's capacity to have intentions" (p. 224).

Intentionality, as May defined it, has implications for the qualities of caring and empathy as well as for the qualities of direction and purpose. Intentionality allows counselors to form intentions based on their perceptions of counseling and enables them to use intentions to move the counseling relationship along on its journey toward a successful conclusion.

After a long period of neglect, the construct of intentionality has been rediscovered as a variable for counselors that may be vital to successful professional functioning (Ivey, 1994; Ivey & Simek-Downing, 1980; Purkey & Novak, 1984; Purkey & Schmidt, 1987; Schmidt, 1984). Ivey and Simek-Downing (1980) noted, "The broad construct of intentionality underlies several descriptions of theoretical goals of counseling," and relates to "counselors who are capable, can generate alternative helping behaviors in any given situation, have several alternative helping modes available to respond to the needs of the client at the moment, and the ability to utilize these responses to assist others to reach long-term goals" (p. 8). Intentionality enables counselors to create and maintain a caring purpose, a consistent direction, and a dependable posture for assisting their clients.

Ivey (1969, 1994) defined intentionality as "acting with a sense of capability and deciding from a range of alternative actions. The intentional individual has more than one action, thought, or behavior to choose from in responding to life situations" (1994, p. 11). Counselors who function with intentionality are able to respond to varying situations without becoming trapped in one response mode. By contrast, counselors who lack intentionality, according to Ivey (1994), consistently use "only one skill, one definition of the problem, and one theory of interviewing, even when the theory isn't working" (p. 12). Individuals who act with intentionality have a number of alternatives for their actions.

There are differences between May's (1969) and Ivey's (1994) definitions of intentionality. For example, Ivey referred to the counselor's lack of intentionality, implying that intentionality is a capability that is either present or absent. By contrast, May indicated that if a counselor does not see an appropriate alternative mode of counseling, it could be concluded that the counselor is trapped in an intentionality that makes it impossible for him or her to see any other alternatives. The notion of being trapped has more of a psychodynamic interpretation than a simple lack of capability.

A further difference between May's and Ivey's interpretations of intentionality is that Ivey placed more emphasis on conscious levels of awareness, whereas May maintained that the concept of intentionality "goes below levels of immediate awareness, and includes spontaneous, bodily elements and other dimensions which are usually called 'unconscious'" (1969, p. 234). Despite these differences in defining intentionality, both Ivey and May have presented this construct as an essential ingredient in the development of successful counselor-client relationships.

Invitational counseling embraces the concept of intentionality and offers an alternative definition to those proposed by both Ivey (1994) and May (1969). In writing about teacher-student interactions, Purkey and Novak (1984) described intentionality as a bipolar concept, with positive intentions at one pole and negative intentions at the other. Figure 3-4 shows this bipolar dimension of intentionality.

The Bipolar Potential

As presented in invitational counseling, intentionality can be a positive or negative concept, a constructive or destructive force. Counselors who understand and employ invitational counseling face a critical moral and ethical decision, for they are asked to embrace an intentionality that can be either a significant impetus for psychotherapy or a powerful force for psychopathology. Intentionality spans a wide

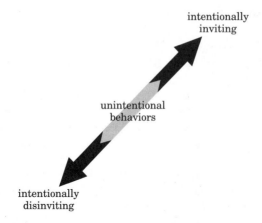

intentionally
inviting

unintentional
behaviors

intentionally
disinviting

FIGURE 3-4 Bipolar Characteristic of Intentionality

range of behaviors, and counselors can choose to be helpful or harmful. Counselors can be a beneficial presence or a lethal one in the lives of their clients.

The positive or negative potential of intentionality can be an awesome concept when applied to professional counseling. Counselors have the knowledge and skills to be a profound influence in the lives of fellow human beings. The abuse of such knowledge and skills can have devastating effects. This power gives counselors all the more reason to maintain a high level of ethical intentionality. However, even with the most careful attention to their own self-perceptions, purposes, and behaviors, at times, counselors will be unintentional in their behavior.

As noted earlier, Ivey (1994) referred to a person's inability to choose from a number of behavioral alternatives as a lack of intentionality. May (1969) viewed this inability as a person's being unconsciously trapped in an intentionality that prevents the exploration of other alternatives. By comparison, Purkey and Novak (1984) adopted the term *unintentional* to identify purposeless, accidental, or otherwise unintended behaviors. They conceptualized behavior as being on a bipolar axis, with levels of functioning running from intentionally disinviting through unintentionally disinviting, and unintentionally inviting to intentionally inviting. Figure 3-4 illustrates this continuum, as well as the uncertainty of unintentionality.

In Figure 3-4, the upper portion of the bidirectional arrow indicates actions, policies, programs, places, and processes designed to be inviting, while the lower portion illustrates those intended to be disinviting. The intentionality of each of the two ends of the axis is

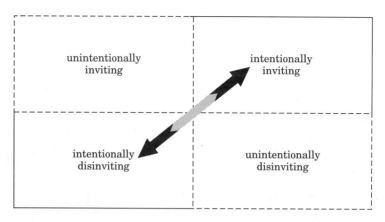

FIGURE 3-5   Four Quadrants of Intentionality

illustrated by the clarity and precision of the arrow at both poles. In contrast, the middle area, illustrating unintentionality, is vague and ill-defined. Actions, policies, programs, and environments that are intentional have purpose, whether positive or negative.

A more detailed analysis reveals that four areas of intentionality and unintentionality can be illustrated in terms of rectangular coordinates. These areas are pictured in Figure 3-5 as four quadrants. The solid lines forming the outer boundaries of the upper right and lower left quadrants illustrate the clarity and precision of those areas. By contrast, the outside broken lines of the other two quadrants illustrate their vagueness and uncertainty. Similarly, the internal broken lines among the four quadrants in Figure 3-5 also suggest the continuum of relationships among actions, places, policies, programs, and processes, and emphasize the unsettled boundaries that exist among these quadrants.

The exact ways in which unintentionality, defined by Purkey and Novak (1984) as being on a continuum, differs from Ivey's (1994) notion of a lack of intentionality, or from May's (1969) concept of being trapped in a particular intentionality, are still under investigation. What does seem clear at this point is that intentionality supports the process of caring.

So far, caring has not been emphasized as an essential element of invitational counseling. The reason is that caring and being intentionally inviting appear to be one and the same process. The root of *intention* is "to tend" toward something; in the same way, a parent "tends to" a child, and a teacher "tends to" students. In its most beneficial form, intentionality includes the essential condition counselors know as caring.

Caring: An Essential Condition

Of all the qualities that describe invitational counseling, none is more important than the counselor's ability to care genuinely about others. Gilbert Wrenn (1973) wrote that through his career as a counselor it was clear that what was most important in all of his helping relationships was not how much he *knew,* but rather how much he *cared* about those who sought his help. Knowledge and techniques are necessary for becoming an inviting counselor. Without sufficient knowledge and skill, caring can be counterproductive and create more problems than it solves. At the same time, knowledge and techniques are insufficient by themselves to enable one to become a professional helper, as Noddings (1984, 1992) and others have explained.

The research that defines effective helping relationships points to empathic listening, genuine regard, trustworthiness, respect for the individual, and related qualities of caring (Gladding, 1992; Vacc & Loesch, 1994). Caring—with its own ingredients such as warmth, empathy, and regard—is the quality that gives intentionality the power to be a beneficial presence in one's own life and those of others. These ingredients are essential in charting a course of personal and professional functioning.

Charting a Course

It is easy to recognize the significant roles that direction and purpose play in assisting people to lead successful lives. Who has not witnessed the influence that direction and purpose have on the outcome of events? Those parts of a person's life that are "tended to" the most are those that usually turn out as planned. Even the language used to describe events contains aspects of direction and purpose: "I knew it would!" "If only I had done what I wanted to do." "I should have followed through." "Just as I planned!" These comments illustrate intentional ties that contribute to, or detract from, successful living. As Abraham Maslow observed, "Each act of consciousness *tends toward* something, it is a turning of the person toward something, and has within it, no matter how latent, some push toward a direction for action" (1962, p. 230). This statement underscores the importance of direction, purpose, and goals.

Direction. People who seek the assistance of counselors are often in search of direction. They seek assistance because they need to choose a direction in life, or they are unsure of the course they have chosen. Sometimes they lack the skills to explore appropriate alternatives. Counselors who have direction in their own lives are in a good position to assist others.

David Campbell (1990) described the importance of direction in his book *If You Don't Know Where You're Going, You'll Probably End Up Somewhere Else.* Invitational counseling embraces this theme, and adds two corollaries: (1) if you don't know where you've been, you probably don't know where you are, and (2) if you don't know where you are, you probably don't know where you're going. Counselors who function at a high level of intentionality with positive direction are in a good position to help clients explore their perceptions and influence their futures.

Purpose. People sometimes appear to have direction in their lives but seem to lack an overall purpose. For example, a minister who directs his or her life toward pastoral leadership and church building may one day discover the need for more purpose in his or her life. While the minister's direction has produced desired results, it may have lacked an overall purpose. The person who only knows *what* to do is no match for the one who also knows *why* he or she is doing it. Knowing what to do reflects direction; knowing why reflects purpose.

Counselors who function with intentionality seek purpose by determining whether their relationships are successful or unsuccessful. Because they seek this understanding, they are able to describe both what they are doing and why they are doing it. Equally important, they are able to help their clients set goals for change.

Goals. An important part of professional counseling is to establish rational, reasonable, obtainable goals. Without these goals the counseling process can lose its meaning. Goal setting by the client and counselor establishes grounds for the client to make decisions, identify obtainable objectives, and lay out plans of action. Only when a client can articulate a plan of action can he or she begin to implement strategies for change.

Counseling relationships that fail to set goals are little more than conversations between the counselor and client. While these conversations may help to establish a relationship, they do little to move the client in a direction that enhances development, prevents difficulties, or resolves problems. Having clear direction, purpose, and goals are all part of invitational counseling. At the same time, there is a danger of establishing goals too quickly and precisely before clients have had the opportunity to express their feelings and to tell their stories. Counselors who apply this approach appreciate the responsibility they carry with regard to themselves, their clients, and the helping profession.

Responsibility

Invitational counseling is based on what Kurt Goldstein (1963) referred to as "the experience of real unity" with other human beings. This experience of unity is best developed through personal and professional responsibility. Responsibility involves acceptance of the personal control individuals have over the directions they take and the purposes they choose, coupled with a resistance to blaming or crediting others for one's own decisions. The role of the counselor is to assist clients in dealing with life's concerns and enrich their existence and potential. It is not the role of the counselor to correct problems, provide solutions, or take over a client's life. A counselor's responsibility can be analyzed under the categories of using appropriate skills, forming a beneficial alliance, and achieving and sustaining commitment.

Using Appropriate Skills

The demands placed on professional counselors are steadily increasing. The daily stress of surviving in today's world, handling career requirements fueled by economic uncertainties, keeping up with advancing technologies, and managing family responsibilities are a few of the issues counselors face. In addition, there are obligations resulting from escalating standards of counselor preparation and continuing education, coupled with growing demands for community service. In addition to this growing pressure, counselors are often expected to come up with "magic" answers, to "motivate" people, "modify" behaviors, "build" self-concept, "enhance" self-esteem. For example, a parent was overheard saying, "I'm *never* going back to that mental health counselor. I've taken my child to the clinic for two weeks, and she hasn't changed a bit!" In such circumstances it is tempting for counselors to work beyond their level of competence or to move faster than the client. Responsibility means using skills that are appropriate for the counselor and his or her training and appropriate for the client and his or her situation. Using appropriate skills requires that counselors evaluate the strategies and techniques they choose, monitor their own behaviors, and seek ways to form a beneficial alliance with their clients.

Forming a Beneficial Alliance

A second component of counselor responsibility is establishing a beneficial alliance that involves joint decision making. This alliance incorporates the element of mutual trust. The client places his or her faith in the counselor's professional skill, while the counselor maintains a realistic optimism about the client's ability to direct his or her own life. Counselors who operate from a "being with" stance recognize that they have equal responsibility with their clients for making the counseling relationship successful. They also understand that a productive relationship can be mutually beneficial. In its highest form, counseling is a growth experience for both client and counselor.

Achieving and Sustaining Commitment

Successful counseling relationships are measured in large part by the extent to which the counselor and client are committed to common goals. A challenge for the counselor in the initial stages of the relationship is to assess the client's willingness to make such a commitment. Simultaneously, clients assess their counselors' commitment to them. Sometimes a counselor's commitment is fragmented due to allegiance to institutions such as schools, hospitals, families, and others. When commitment is unclear or uncertain, responsibility becomes unsteady and the counseling relationship is weakened.

Invitational counseling encourages clear commitment to the client, but with an openness about the counselor's responsibilities to the institution and other groups. If the elements of optimism, trust, and respect are held at a high level, commitment will be achieved and sustained in the counseling relationship. Such actions are defined by the levels of functioning introduced in Chapter 1.

Levels of Professional Functioning

The four levels of functioning described in the invitational model are (1) intentionally disinviting, (2) unintentionally disinviting, (3) unintentionally inviting, and (4) intentionally inviting. These four levels are not absolute categories of human behavior; rather, they offer general descriptions of the messages people send to themselves and others. They serve as a guide to help counselors examine their own behaviors and assist clients in doing likewise.

As with all human interactions, no one level of functioning totally dominates behavior. People, like the places, policies, processes, and programs they create, flow from one level to another. Communication processes exist at each of the four levels, and all counselors function at various levels from time to time. However, it is the *typical* level of functioning a counselor exhibits that determines the sort of helper he or she becomes.

Because of the incredibly complex nature of communication, no one can ever be fully aware of what is being transmitted. In addition to what is communicated with verbal language and the language of behavior—the silent language—humans also communicate with the environments they create and maintain and the programs, policies, and processes they design and support. The most destructive of these communicative processes is to function at the intentionally disinviting level.

Intentionally Disinviting

Counselors who function at the intentionally disinviting level deliberately create and maintain actions, programs, policies, processes, and places that are designed to inform themselves and others that they are incapable, worthless, and irresponsible. Adding insult to injury, their intentionally disinviting behavior has direction, purpose, and goals. Perhaps they take a certain joy in functioning at the level of contempt, distrust, and pessimism, or perhaps they function from a defensive, protective, and suspicious stance. In any case, such counselors can themselves benefit from professional counseling. It may seem contradictory to say that a counselor, a helping professional, could willfully function at the intentionally disinviting level, yet some do— rarely perhaps, but it happens. This level of functioning may be thought of as *lethal functioning*.

Lethal functioning occurs in at least two ways. The first happens when even the most skilled professional helper becomes angry and frustrated and makes a decision based entirely on these feelings. One example is the psychotherapist who, in a moment of frustration, intentionally humiliates a client for missing an appointment. Another example is a school counselor who supports corporal punishment as "the only language some children understand." A third example is the process advocated by some professionals of locking juvenile offenders in prison with hardened criminals to "teach them a lesson." Intentionally disinviting methods such as these may be an indication of anger, frustration, fatigue, desperation, or lack of knowledge, but whatever the reason, such methods have no place in invitational counseling. Any behavior, policy, program, process, or environment that is designed to insult, hurt, humiliate, ridicule, embarrass, demean, or physically punish human beings is unacceptable, regardless of any intended benefits.

A second way that lethal functioning occurs is when counselors use their positions to behave unethically, immorally, or illegally. Examples of this type of lethal functioning are the family therapist with personal sexual problems who intentionally and consistently sides with a spouse of a particular sex in marital sessions; the prejudiced high school counselor who repeatedly discourages students of certain backgrounds from applying to college; or the counselor in private practice who entices clients to have sexual relations with him or her as part of the "therapy." Such lethal functioning is not only disinviting but also unethical.

Exactly why a few professional helpers elect to function at the intentionally disinviting level may never be known. But whatever the reasons—perceived personal inadequacies, embedded prejudices, over-riding jealousies, sexual dysfunction, negative self-images, or sadistic impulses—such people can themselves benefit from professional help. If counselors who employ toxic methods are unwilling or unable to change or seek help, then it is the responsibility of fellow professional helpers to carefully but firmly remove them from the profession. From the viewpoint of invitational counseling, no justification exists for intentionally disinviting actions, policies, programs, processes, or places. They may happen, and they may be understandable—even forgivable—but they are never justifiable.

Being human, counselors may slip into disinviting modes on occasion. They are, after all, human beings first, and professionals second. Most counselors who function at a disinviting level do so unintentionally.

Unintentionally Disinviting

Countless factors and variables influence the professional helper's daily activities. Interruptions from important work, pressures to complete tasks, demands from supervisors, physical ailments, noise level, disinviting clients and colleagues—even the temperature, weather, or time of day or month—can influence both the degree of intentionality and level of functioning. At times, these factors and variables can be such that counselors act or react in ways that are perceived by others as disinviting, even though this was not intended. Examples of un-intentionally disinviting behaviors include continuing to work at one's desk while someone stands there waiting to be recognized; drinking coffee during an interview without offering the client a cup; giving a finger-crunching handshake; telling off-color, sexist, or racist jokes; or arranging office furniture so that the counselor has a "throne." Some-times, such behaviors are caused by a simple lack of politeness and good manners. For this reason, civility and common courtesy are given high priority in invitational counseling. Other times, such behaviors are evidence that the counselor lacks the central characteristics re-quired by invitational counseling.

On some occasions, counselors send messages that in and of

themselves would be viewed by most fair-minded observers as inviting. However, because individual perceptions play such an important role, the person who receives these messages may view them as disinviting. When well-meaning counselors are viewed as disinviting, probably their functioning is careless or inappropriate.

Careless functioning. Sometimes, counselors appear to be blissfully unaware of what their clients would like in terms of direction and support. For example, many people who call or visit community college counseling centers to inquire about equivalency high school diplomas never follow up on their initial contact. One reason may be that they encountered a careless counselor: "Go over to the Registrar's Office in Building 403 and pick up forms 193-A and 7-B-4. Complete the forms and proceed to the Business Office in Building 306, Room B-3, for processing." For insecure and hesitant students, such directions are overwhelming. These directives appear to be living proof that the community college is no place for them. A more caring and appropriate approach would be for the counselor to have all the necessary forms on hand and assist the visitor in completing the application, including escorting the visitor to the next office and following up with a telephone call. Thoughtful acts that may be quickly forgotten by the counselor can have long-lasting positive effects on the client.

Experienced counselors understand that by spending time with people who are simply "looking for information," "seeing what's available," or "just stopping by" allows relationships to form in which deeper, more pressing interests are revealed. To pass up such opportunities by sending individuals to the "next window, please" is careless. It is also inappropriate.

Inappropriate functioning. The most well-meaning counselors can be caring, but through lack of experience or errors in judgment, they behave in ways that are inappropriate to the situation. Over-friendliness (smiling continuously), over-familiarity (patting, hugging), and even over-counseling ("What I hear you saying is . . .") are examples of inappropriate functioning.

Counselors should ask themselves: "Is this the most caring and appropriate thing to do at this moment?" Sitting on the hospital bed to hold the hand of a client who has just had surgery may be a very caring act, but the jarring pain it inflicts is most inappropriate. In the same vein, discussing a client's concerns with a colleague during a cocktail party may reflect caring, but it is entirely inappropriate.

An incident illustrating inappropriate functioning happened to one of the authors when he was asked to keynote a convention of counselors. Following the keynote address, all participants headed for small-group workshops. The keynoter approached the registration area to inquire where he might get a cup of coffee. The registrar interrupted his query with an abrupt question: "What group are you with?" The speaker explained that he was without a group, to which the registrar responded, "You will have to wait; coffee is served at 10:30." At that moment a janitor walked by and said to the speaker, "There is a coffee machine on the second floor. I'm going that way. I'll show you where it is." Clearly, the janitor was functioning in both a caring and appropriate manner.

Counselors who typically function in an unintentionally disinviting mode can benefit from additional training by learning or relearning counseling skills or by receiving counseling themselves. Perhaps such professionals are more object-oriented than people-oriented, do not engage in enough self-monitoring, or have difficulty focusing on the concerns of others. In any event, they should pursue avenues that will improve their professionalism—or seek other career opportunities.

On occasion, counselors who function at a disinviting level may see positive results from their efforts. This is not too surprising. People are helped by all manner of things and improve in all sorts of ways, sometimes in spite of the services rendered. As the fictional detective Charlie Chan noted: "Strange events permit themselves the luxury of occurring." However, when positive results occur regularly, it is a good indication that the counselor is functioning at an inviting level.

Unintentionally Inviting

Many counselors who function at the unintentionally inviting level have the personal qualities that contribute to successful counseling. These professionals are sometimes referred to as natural-born counselors. They are usually optimistic, respectful, and trusting. Yet the one element they lack is intentionality. They are helpful to clients and exhibit the concern and caring that clients require, but because they lack intentionality they are inconsistent in their work. This lack of consistency jeopardizes successful helping relationships. The result is that the counselor's credibility is vulnerable, for it depends too often on serendipitous counseling.

Serendipitous counseling. Because counselors who typically function at the unintentionally inviting level have personal qualities and professional training that are conducive to successful relationships, they are generally considered capable counselors. They know *what* they are doing, but they do not know *why*. This lack of understanding means that there is a barrier to their potential for further improvement. It also places clients at risk, since the counselor's approach is one of trial and error. The counseling relationship these counselors establish is not a product of intentionality, but rather a matter of serendipity or—to put it bluntly—luck.

An unintentionally inviting counselor may, for example, be intuitively able to establish excellent rapport with a client in the initial stages of the counseling process, but unable to move with the client through the exploration phase to the action phase of making decisions regarding future behaviors. The counselor is seen as empathic by the client, but after several sessions both the client and counselor appear to be spinning their wheels, covering old territory, and increasing their frustration over the lack of progress. In instances such as this, clients sometimes stop coming for counseling, not because they are upset or dislike the counselor, but because they are no longer receiving any benefit from the relationship. When this happens, a counselor who is unintentionally inviting may recognize the lack of success, but does not know the reason for it. He or she may even end up blaming the client for not following through with the commitment to counseling.

By analogy, counselors who function at the unintentionally inviting level are like amateurs who enjoy looking for Indian arrowheads. They know *what* to look for, but though they may discover a valuable artifact, their luck is no match for the professional archaeologist who knows *where, when, how,* and *why* to look for Indian relics. The professional archaeologist of counseling is the one who knows where, when, how, and why to be intentionally inviting with self and others, personally and professionally.

Counselors who owe their success to serendipity become far more effective when they recognize that they are responsible for using their talents to create and maintain a productive and purposeful direction in the counseling relationship. Such responsibility and direction enable counselors to be consistent in their actions and move them toward an intentionally inviting level of functioning.

Intentionally Inviting

A combination of direction, purpose, and skill allows counselors to achieve intentionality in their relationships. This in turn gives counselors the opportunity to reach the highest levels of professional helping. It is through intentionality that counselors are able to choose appropriate and caring strategies and to behave accordingly. In rough waters, the counselor who is functioning at the intentionally inviting level is consistent in direction and is able to stay on course. Intentionality also allows counselors to evaluate the direction of the counseling relationship, to monitor feedback, and to make changes as needed.

Orchestrating actions, places, policies, programs, and processes intentionally is the art of invitational counseling. Some counselors become so skilled that they are maestros of the profession. They practice their skills with such talented ease that the transitions between phases in their relationships with clients are indiscernible. Most counselors in training have watched tapes of the impresario counselor who performs a counseling demonstration while the audience is awed by the skills with which he or she develops and maintains the relationship and brings it to a close. It is admirable to have these skills, but the true test of an intentionally inviting counselor is the ability to make these skills a part of oneself. As noted earlier, counseling skills are not hung on the rack at the end of the day. The intentionally inviting counselor seeks to maintain a dependable stance in all relationships. This dependability is an expression of the counselor's self and goes beyond proficiency.

Beyond proficiency. A counselor's ability to maintain a consistent stance is important in personal and professional functioning. Consistency moves the counselor beyond the realm of technical proficiency toward a quality of character based as much on who the counselor is as what he or she knows. Helpers who have reached this point have a special style, which is reflected in their ability to distinguish between factors that are visibly appropriate and those that are invisibly so.

Visibly appropriate factors. Of all the behaviors exhibited by counselors in the inviting relationship, and of all the policies, programs, and places they create, the most noticeable are visible to the untrained eye. Organizing a peer helper program in a school, creating a cancer patient support program, being a "big brother" or "big sister" to some child, placing cheerful posters and living green plants in an outpatient waiting room, donating time to a retirement center, or creating a wellness program in a factory are all examples of visibly appropriate factors at work. Yet an even more powerful style in invitational counseling is to function in an *invisibly* appropriate fashion, with the counselor, in a sense, remaining invisible and able to keep the focus and attention on the client.

Invisibly appropriate factors. A distinctive feature of invitational counseling is its emphasis on invisibly appropriate actions, places, policies, programs, and processes. These are beneficial forces that do not call attention to themselves. Few people witness them, and only the trained eye of another professional can detect them. Still, they have a tremendous impact on the lives of human beings. A doctoral student at the University of North Carolina at Greensboro described the process as "artlessly" inviting—carried out with such skill and grace that the art itself is invisible to all but the trained observer.

Invitational counseling does not depend on an unbridled display of one's immediate emotions any more than skillful social behavior consists of rampant disclosure or unsparing authenticity. To maintain an inviting stance may at times require the curtailment of certain emotions and the display of feelings more appropriate to the immediate situation. In invitational counseling, authenticity is modified by the adjective *therapeutic*. The goal of invitational counseling is to be therapeutically authentic. The counselor's desire to be authentic should be monitored in relation to the client's welfare. To the degree that a counselor can hear, accept, and reflect clients' feelings—no matter how repugnant, abhorrent, unrealistic, or unacceptable these client disclosures may be from the counselor's point of view—to that degree the counselor is practicing invitational counseling.

A moving example of professionals functioning in an invisibly appropriate fashion was shared by a colleague, Nancy Dixon, at an invitational education conference:

> When I was in junior high school it was the dream of every young girl to become a member of the Dancing Boots, a precision team of 100 high school girls. I had even taken dance lessons so I would be sure to make the squad. But in the ninth grade I was in an accident that damaged my left knee. I could still dance and kick and do almost anything . . . except hop to the left. Whenever I hopped to the left I lost my balance and fell. Because of this, I decided not to try out for the Dancing Boots. But at the strong encouragement of my school counselor I changed my mind and tried out. To my great relief, not one time during the tryouts did anyone have to hop to the left. I made the squad and throughout high school we led every parade, performed at every half-time, and did every routine imaginable, but not one time did we hop to the left. After graduation and many years later, I returned to the high school for a class reunion. In talking with a former teacher, I commented on the miracle of never having to hop to the left. It was only then that I learned that the director of the Dancing Boots had been informed by the counselor that I could not hop to the left, so the director made sure that no one did.

Such invisibly appropriate functioning is the *créme de la créme* of professional helping.

Many beneficial things that people do often go unnoticed. While most people enjoy recognition for performing good deeds, it is the willingness to go unnoticed that distinguishes invitational counseling. Making a phone call or writing a letter on someone's behalf without their requesting it, speaking favorably of someone when the voices of criticism are strong, donating anonymously to a charity, or quietly cleaning up a mess made by some careless colleague are just a few examples of invisibly appropriate behaviors. While visibly appropriate forces are valuable in professional helping, invisibly appropriate factors are especially helpful because they focus on the individual or group for whom the action was intended. It is often these behind-the-scenes actions that make the greatest differences in people's lives.

At its best, invitational counseling becomes invisible. To borrow from the writing of Chuang-tse, an ancient Chinese philosopher, invitational counseling should "flow like water, reflect like a mirror, and respond like an echo." As in any art form, the process should not call attention to itself. In its purest form, therefore, invitational counseling remains unseen.

As an illustration of the invisibility of art, consider an audience observing the accomplished musician, the headline comedian, the world-class athlete, or the master teacher. What these artists do seems effortless. Only when we try to duplicate the artistry do we realize that true art requires painstaking effort, personal discipline, and intentionality. So it is with invitational counseling.

A beautiful example of the perfection of art is the behavior of W. C. Fields, the classic comic, who perfected the genius of the conscious error. By all accounts, W. C. Fields was one of the greatest jugglers who ever lived. Fields would deliberately drop an object apparently by accident in the middle of a difficult feat. Then he would catch it in a second, also apparently accidental move.

Another example of the perfection of art was given by Ginger Rogers, the beautiful Hollywood actress and dancer, in describing dancing with the incomparable Fred Astaire. "It's a lot of hard work, that I do know," said Rogers. "But it doesn't look it, Ginger," someone responded. Replied Rogers, "That's why it's magic." To paraphrase Alexander Pope, true ease in counseling comes from art, not chance, as those move easiest who have learned to dance.

The highest level of professional functioning has many names. World-class athletes call it finding the "zone." Fighter pilots refer to "rhythm." Comedians speak of finding the "center." Football teams call it "momentum." Those who employ invitational counseling can become so fluent—their carefully developed belief systems and techniques so honed—that the entire helping process is invisible to the untrained eye.

Summary

This chapter has described the major characteristics of invitational counseling, including an understanding of perception and self-concept; the ability to understand, accept, and reflect client perceptions; and the willingness to self-disclose appropriately and with care. Such understanding, acceptance, and skill, coupled with willingness, are embodied in the professional stance of invitational counseling.

The concept of counselor intentionality was defined and analyzed in this chapter. Its dimensions of direction and purpose were described and their interrelationships explored. Counselor responsibility and its components of appropriateness, respect, and mutual trust were also presented.

The qualities of successful counseling were related to four levels of professional functioning. Additional dimensions of invitational counseling include the ability to distinguish between visibly and invisibly appropriate behaviors and between unbridled and therapeutic authenticity, and recognition of the value of functioning in invisibly caring and appropriate ways.

Opportunities for Further Reading

ALLPORT, G. W. (1955). *Becoming: Basic considerations for a psychology of personality*. New Haven, CT: Yale University Press. In this often-quoted book, Gordon Allport articulated a new perceptual direction for psychology at a time when, for all practical purposes, only behaviorism and psychoanalysis existed. It is a prophetic work in humanistic thought.

CAMPBELL, D. (1990). *If you don't know where you're going, you'll probably end up somewhere else* (rev. ed.). Allen, TX: Tarbor Publications. This insightful book encourages the reader to establish a direction and purpose in life by planning one's future, assessing one's strengths, career interests and goals, and enjoying life to the fullest.

COMBS, A. W., SOPER, D. W., GOODING, C. T., BENTON, J. A., DICKMAN, J. F., & USHER, R. H. (1969). *Florida studies in the helping professions* (Social Sciences Monograph No. 37). Gainesville, FL.: University of Florida Press. This monograph brings together a series of research reports on the perceptual organization of effective helpers. The interpretation of these studies provided by Combs is that "good" and "bad" helpers can be distinguished by their perceptual characteristics.

GILLIGAN, C. (1982). *In a different voice*. Cambridge, MA: Harvard University Press. Carol Gilligan proposed in this influential book that women have culturally different standards of ethics than do men.

HALL, E. T. (1959). *The silent language*. New York: Doubleday. Hall's book was a pioneering study of nonverbal communication. By using his powers of observation as an anthropologist, Hall pointed out differences in cultures that make for inviting or disinviting behaviors.

JOHNSON, D. W. (1990). *Reaching out: Interpersonal effectiveness and self-actualization* (4th ed.). Englewood Cliffs, NJ: Prentice-Hall. This book combines theory and experience in explaining ways to develop effective interpersonal skills. In particular, Johnson focused on the skills needed to initiate and maintain friendships.

MAY, R. (1969). *Love and will.* New York: Norton. Rollo May explored numerous aspects of human interactions and therapeutic relationships. His chapter on intentionality presents an insightful discussion of the concept and its importance to both the client and counselor in professional helping. (Reprinted in 1989 by Doubleday, New York.)

PIETROFESA, J. J., LEONARD, G. E., & VAN HOOSE, W. (1978). *The authentic counselor* (2nd ed.). Chicago: Rand McNally. The authors of this book integrated a number of approaches in counseling into a synthesis of professional helping. Included in this text are descriptions of effective helpers and ways to achieve selected goals with specific clients.

ROGERS, C. R. (1961). *On becoming a person: A therapist's view of psychotherapy.* Boston: Houghton Mifflin. Rogers's purpose in this influential book was to share with the reader his personal experiences as a psychologist and counselor in his search for personal growth and professional creativity.

SCHMIDT, J. J. (1994). *Living intentionally and making life happen* (rev. ed.). Greenville, NC: Brookcliff Publishers. This is a readable self-development guide to intentionality and other essential ingredients for creating a successful life. It is an excellent resource for counselors who encourage clients to take control of their lives.

CHAPTER FOUR

Characteristics of Successful Counselors

ᜑ

One's own person becomes an instrument in the practice of the art, and must be kept fit, according to the specific functions it has to fulfill.

Erich Fromm
The Art of Loving
1956, p. 110

ᜑ

The basic elements, levels, and choices inherent in the inviting process cut across personal and professional interactions. This chapter elaborates on the four spheres of personal and professional functioning: (1) being personally inviting with oneself, (2) being personally inviting with others, (3) being professionally inviting with oneself, and (4) being professionally inviting with others. Each of these spheres is an essential characteristic of successful counselors, and is equally important to invitational counseling. Neglecting any one detracts from the other three. All the success in the world in one sphere will not make up for lack of success in the others. The optimal development of each characteristic contributes directly to the coalition of all four spheres.

All professional fields create obligations for practitioners, but professional counselors face distinctive pressures. These pressures include an accelerating trend toward higher standards of professionalism (Cecil & Comas, 1986; Schmidt, 1993; Vacc & Loesch, 1994), increasing demands for community service, and the intimate, fragile and often delicate human relationships involved in counseling. Because of these special obligations, it is vital that counselors consider all four spheres of personal and professional functioning.

70

Being Personally Inviting with Oneself

Just as I may be indifferent to myself, use myself as a thing, or be a stranger to myself, so I may care for myself by being responsive to my own needs to grow.

Milton Mayeroff

On Caring

1971, p. 47

ја

Counseling is a special sort of caring, and counselors are in a much better position to care for others when they care for themselves. The counseling relationship is seriously threatened or destroyed the moment a counselor interacts with a client in terms of the counselor's own desires. Specifically, counselors who adopt invitational counseling work to be personally inviting with themselves emotionally, intellectually, and physically and to satisfy their own desires outside the counseling relationship so they can better focus on the client's concerns when interacting professionally. Being personally inviting with oneself gives the counselor the strength to look beyond his or her own emotions to care for and about clients.

Inviting Oneself Emotionally

Inviting oneself emotionally means caring for one's mental health and learning to make appropriate choices in life. Counselors who know how to handle stress and reduce anxiety in their own lives, and who are able to function in psychologically healthy ways, are in a strategic position to help others in these same areas.

Being emotionally inviting with oneself requires attention to two areas of personal development: emotional control and emotional expression. Both of these processes relate to the concept of therapeutic authenticity introduced in Chapter 1.

Emotional Control. Effective counselors understand the need to have control of their emotions, particularly when assisting clients who face highly emotional issues. Counselors' ability to control their own emotions in the face of extreme adversity increases the likelihood that they will be able to understand, accept, and reflect—at a deeper than surface level—feelings strongly defended by others. Emotional control is established by the process of understanding perceptual worlds, appreciating emotional response patterns, recognizing the role of self-concept, and being sensitive to body language and other physical responses to emotional states.

Emotional control can exist in countless ways. Monitoring one's feelings, practicing positive and realistic self-talk, learning meditation and relaxation techniques, and using biofeedback are just a few of many ways to maintain emotional control. Counseling is an emotionally demanding profession, and so it is important that counselors establish emotional control within themselves. Emotional control, however, does not imply emotional denial. On the contrary, when appropriate and caring, effective counseling can include full and unabashed emotional expression.

Emotional expression. Psychologically healthy people allow themselves avenues for emotional release. Being personally inviting with oneself emotionally may mean whooping it up at a football game, cheering at a political rally, being silly at a party, crying at a sad moment, engaging in happy, childlike play, or encouraging "hoopla" at an annual convention. Not all emotional expressions need to be public, though. Simple, private means of emotional expression, such as a private laugh at one's own follies, feelings of anger at injustice, a silent prayer for a sick friend, or a full experience of the lump in one's throat when the national anthem is played, are equally essential.

It is a sad commentary on contemporary cultural values that emotions are often discouraged. For instance, one of the authors witnessed the "boys don't cry" syndrome while attending a movie with a group of adults and children. Upon leaving the theater a young boy asked, "Why were you all crying?" One man replied, "It was a joyous movie and so I cried." The boy said emphatically, "I didn't cry!" The man responded, "That's OK. We each express our joy in different ways." After a moment the boy confessed, "Well, I felt one tear . . . but I held it back." It is ironic that little boys are first taught not to cry, and then years later, in therapy, big men are taught to cry.

Counselors can be emotionally inviting with themselves by enjoying activities far removed from the stress of professional responsibilities. By taking up a new hobby, relaxing with a good novel, spending time alone, or experiencing spiritual renewal, a person can rejuvenate his or her energy level. Lists of ways to be inviting with oneself and others personally and professionally are provided in Appendix B.

One additional way that counselors can be personally inviting with themselves emotionally is by using counseling services. Counselors who are able to accept help are in a much better position to give it. Moreover, they can benefit from counseling by exploring emotional concerns and setting goals for continued development, including intellectual goals.

Inviting Oneself Intellectually

One of the most exhilarating discoveries of modern times is the concept that human capacity is vastly greater than anything ever imagined in previous generations. The mounting evidence that intelligence evolves according to inviting or disinviting environments is a concept of tremendous significance for counselors (Hunt, 1961, 1964, 1972). Rather than something the emerging human being is born with, intelligence is something one acquires through intellectual stimulation over a lifetime.

Being personally inviting with oneself intellectually requires participation in a wide variety of activities that increase knowledge, sharpen thought processes, and improve the overall power of the mind. Reading extensively on a variety of subjects that may be distant from one's professional interests; visiting zoos, museums, libraries, and science exhibits; and joining organizations such as nature clubs, discussion groups, and historical societies are examples of the many ways counselors can be intellectually inviting with themselves.

Counselors who are well read and intellectually alive are in a favorable position to create similar opportunities for their clients. A broad knowledge base coupled with diverse experience contributes to a counselor's ability to encourage the client's exploration of choices. Counselors who expand their intellectual horizons recognize the important relationship that exists between mind and body. Consequently, in addition to inviting themselves emotionally and intellectually, counselors invite themselves physically.

Inviting Oneself Physically

The ways counselors function are related to their physical health. When a counselor's physical self is neglected or in disrepair, it is unlikely that he or she will be able to maintain appropriate emotional wellness or expand intellectually. The importance of good health was underscored by Knowles (1977) who observed: "Most individuals do not worry about their health until they lose it. I believe the idea of a 'right' to health (guaranteed by government) should be replaced by the idea of individual moral obligation to preserve one's own health—a public duty if you will" (p. 59). This obligation is particularly appropriate for counselors.

Counseling is a profession that is as demanding physically as it is emotionally. It is important that counselors work to maintain proper physical health to cope with these demands. Counselors who expect their clients to eat moderately, exercise regularly, and drink reasonably will be a more credible model if they practice these behaviors themselves. Commitment to physical wellness includes restricting high-cholesterol foods and moderating consumption of sugar, salt, alcohol, and other substances that impede healthy living. The commitment to health also includes exercising regularly, eliminating smoking or other drugs that contribute to physical problems, and drinking water in preference to other liquids. Of course, many superb counselors are physically challenged in various ways. The point made here is that one should work at good health within the constraints of one's own special condition. Although specific ideas are too numerous to mention here, ways to be personally inviting with oneself intellectually, emotionally, and physically are provided in Appendix B.

Being personally inviting with oneself, while necessary, is not sufficient. People are social beings and require the company of others. Counselors who practice invitational counseling involve themselves deeply with those they love and who love them.

Being Personally Inviting with Others

> Love has really been ignored by the scientists. It's amazing. My students and I did a study. We went through books in psychology. We went through books in sociology. We went through books in anthropology, and we were hard-pressed to find even a reference to the word "love." This is shocking because it is something we all know we need, something we're all continually looking for, and yet there's no class in it. It's just assumed that it comes to us by and through some mysterious life force.
>
> Leo Buscaglia
> *Love*
> 1972, pp. 16–17

ঽ

To develop fully, counselors require the nurturing of fellow human beings and the giving of nurturing in return. A major source of nurturing is to love and be loved—something that is needed throughout life. It is through loving relationships that people develop friendships and celebrate life. Jourard (1964) observed that "being the recipient of love from another appears to be a highly inspiriting event. There have been many informal observations of people, previously limp, lackluster, dispirited people, who increased in zeal, muscle tone, integration of personality and in resistance to illness, once they were told they were loved by some significant other person" (p. 87). Without love, humans cannot develop optimally—in fact, they are unlikely to develop at all.

Developing Friendships

It is difficult to overestimate the importance of invitations sent to and received from fellow human beings. Through sharing the company of others, and through countless inviting acts, counselors establish intimate relationships. A student of one of the authors explained the creation of friendships by using the analogy of a cup being gradually filled with appropriate and caring acts. When the cup overflows, a friendship is formed.

There are many different types of friendships. Some are casual, temporary interludes, and others are deep, long-lasting relationships. Invitational counseling suggests that both types of friendships are important to a fulfilled life. Friendships, as with all human functions, can be either beneficial or destructive. Sometimes friends can be destructive by tempting or coercing others into criminal, unethical, or personally injurious behaviors. Conversely, positive friendships are the springboard for mutual support, which enables people to face challenges and overcome barriers to development. People cannot fully experience life and successfully cope with its many difficulties without the benefits of friendship. Nor can they celebrate life without friends to share it.

Celebrating Life

Life can be a celebration. This celebration does not simply consist of the clamor and activity of a Mardi Gras. It is a meaningful celebration of the deeper significance and richness of life. More specifically, celebrating life is a particular disposition that, although not usually conspicuous or extravagant, contributes to a variety of developmental processes. Those who are dependably and consistently inviting with themselves and others are most likely to develop friendships and celebrate life.

As with other aspects of living, celebration sometimes involves risk. Reaching out to others is occasionally met by resistance and rejection. Professional helpers understand this hazard. They realize that some clients are reluctant to risk associations. For some clients, reaching out may inspire terror. Nevertheless, these counselors gently persist, because they understand the value of reaching out and being in the company of others to share human experiences and emotions. As a means of helping clients feel comfortable, counselors sometimes disclose their own personal joys and tragedies. This ability to self-disclose in an appropriate and caring fashion, without burdening others, is an important aspect of inviting others personally.

Self-Disclosing

In *The Transparent Self* (1964, 1971b), Jourard explained the value of self-disclosure. He pointed out that every human being at every point in life must make the decision to allow others to know one fully and openly, or alternatively to hide behind a mask or pretend to be someone one is not. To hide or pretend is to encourage social dysfunction and alienation. It is important to allow others to share one's sorrows as well as one's happiness, one's fears as well as one's anger. Jourard expressed the hypothesis that individuals can attain health and fuller functioning insofar as they gain the courage to be themselves among others. Self-disclosure can be a powerful process that enables individuals to come closer together, share understandings, and relate on the most personal level.

Being Professionally Inviting with Oneself

In no other profession does the personality and behavior of the professional make such a difference as it does in counseling.
Scott Meier and Susan Davis
The Elements of Counseling
(2nd ed.), 1993, p. 60

❧

Counseling is an expanding profession that requires an understanding of worldwide changes that influence human welfare and development. Counselors as well as other professional helpers are responsible for being informed about social forces, technological advances, medical discoveries, vocational patterns, and other trends that have an impact on their performance. This responsibility is met by counselors' practice of being professionally inviting with themselves, a process that includes the responsibility for continuing education, a willingness to explore new counseling theories and practices, and a commitment to stay active professionally.

Continuing One's Education

Like other professionals, counselors pursue years of academic training to acquire their beliefs, knowledge, and skills. These years of formal study usually conclude with a graduate degree in counseling. However, most professional counselors realize the importance of continuing their studies, recalibrating their vocabularies, updating their skills, mastering new techniques, learning new research findings, restructuring their beliefs, and finding fresh ways to improve their professional functioning.

Continuing one's education takes many forms. It may mean reading current and classic literature on counseling, enrolling in a refresher course at a university, attending professional conferences and summer workshops, entering the world of computer technology, or taking a sabbatical or research leave. It may also mean conducting research, either quantitative or qualitative, and presenting one's work at local, state, provincial, national, or international professional meetings. Preparation for such meetings is an excellent way of being professionally inviting with oneself while at the same time sharing one's work with colleagues.

It is especially important to continually educate oneself professionally in order to identify outdated approaches to professional helping. In the fast-moving field of counseling, those who do not keep up-to-date professionally will be obsolete in short order; the sad part is that they may not even know it. To keep abreast, it is vital to continue one's education and participate actively in the counseling profession.

Participating in the Profession

Today's professional counselors work in a wide range of settings that include education, mental health, family, corrections, and gerontological practice. These counselors are united by their membership and participation in professional organizations such as the American Counseling Association and its associated divisions. It is difficult to imagine a professional counselor who does not actively support and participate in the organizations that have spearheaded and promoted the counseling profession.

Being an active participant in one's profession consists of a full range of involvement from membership in organizations to holding office at the local, state, and national levels. The counseling profession is fortunate to have had exceptional leaders in its short life span. Through such leadership, counselors have developed a credible profession. All counselors have this same leadership obligation. It is achieved by joining professional organizations, achieving certification and licensure, volunteering for committee work, reading and writing for professional journals, holding elected office, and performing a host of other professional services. By being active in these organizations, counselors stay in tune with the developments that have an impact on their practice. By keeping up with professional developments and social trends, counselors are in a strong position to explore fresh possibilities and pursue new directions with themselves and their clients.

Exploring New Directions

Many counselor educators have written about future trends that will have an effect on the counseling profession (Schmidt, 1993; Walz, Gazda, & Shertzer, 1991; Wilson & Rotter, 1982; Wrenn, 1973). Some of these trends are presented in the final chapter of this book. Counselors who are professionally inviting with themselves are willing to prepare for future realities. This preparation is an ongoing process that may include attending innovative training institutes, sharing informal "what works for me" sessions with colleagues, and visiting and observing creative counseling programs.

Attending meetings and workshops, and corresponding and networking with colleagues, are only examples of how counselors keep abreast of professional issues. With technology advancing so rapidly, there is also a merging of knowledge. Professionals from different fields are coming together to share common interests and explore similar directions. Counselors in the future will work closely with urban planners, sociologists, law enforcement officers, and medical, educational and other professionals to enrich the places, programs, processes, and policies that impact on human existence and development.

As with all development, professionalism consists of various activities and experiences that allow individuals to progress through successively higher levels of functioning. Learning as a lifelong process is fundamental to invitational counseling. Counselors who realize this make a lifelong commitment to be professionally inviting with themselves. This commitment strengthens their capability to be professionally inviting with others.

Being Professionally Inviting with Others

You can know me truly only if I let you, only if I want you to know me. If you want me to reveal myself, just demonstrate your good will . . . your will to employ your powers for my good, and not for my destruction.

Sidney Jourard
The Transparent Self
1964, p. 5

૪.

By being personally inviting with oneself and others, and *professionally* inviting with oneself, a counselor is in an excellent position to be professionally inviting with others. This quality includes cooperation, collaboration, and contribution, which together facilitate the adoption of a "wide-angle" approach to helping. The first of these, cooperation, demonstrates a willingness to work with others for mutual gain.

Cooperating

It is imperative for counselors to work cooperatively with other professionals. The importance of supportive relations in the workplace was documented in the work of Dworkin, Haney, Dworkin, and Telschow (1990), who reported that teacher illness increased as job stress increased, except in schools where the leadership was viewed as caring and supportive. Counselors who cooperate with their fellow professionals constantly search for common ground and mutual goals. An example of this cooperation can be seen in the experience of a school counselor and a community social worker.

The counselor and the social worker were interested in presenting a parent education program to parents of low-income families. The counselor was leading parent education groups at school in the evenings, but some parents, particularly those who lived in public housing projects from another part of town, had no transportation to come to these meetings. In discussing this dilemma, the counselor and the social worker decided to take the meetings to the housing projects and train selected parents to be co-leaders (with social workers) of future parent groups. The social worker cooperated by finding a suitable facility at the housing project, recruiting parents as potential co-leaders, and scheduling the training. The school counselor co-led the training sessions with the social worker, and several parents were trained for the program.

As we can see in this example, cooperation often means breaking down traditional boundaries of professional fields. Counselors understand that collaborating with other professionals enhances the professional development of all those involved.

Collaborating

Through collaborative efforts, counselors expand their knowledge and skills to include new learning and innovative practices that might otherwise be undetected and undeveloped. Collaboration takes many forms and can be as simple as two people setting up a room for a meeting or deciding to present a joint program. The underlying principle is the same: by working together, both can succeed. Successful helping relationships require collaboration between the client and counselor to focus on particular developmental issues or critical concerns, identify appropriate goals, clarify each other's role, and explore alternatives and options. For example, it sometimes happens that when a client asks a question, makes a statement, or appeals for advice, he or she has already arrived at a possible solution. The client is checking on the appropriateness of the decision. By rephrasing the concern and handing it back to the client, the counselor demonstrates respect for the client's self-directing powers. This will not happen without a collaborative relationship.

Contributing

Counselors who practice invitational counseling derive satisfaction from the contributions they make to the welfare of those who seek their assistance. These counselors measure their success by the extent to which their efforts make institutions, procedures, and programs more receptive, accommodating, and sensitive to people's needs. Sometimes these contributions are found in individual and group counseling services. Other times, they take the form of correcting injustices, cleaning environments, restructuring programs, or creating new opportunities.

Being professionally inviting by cooperating, collaborating, and contributing embraces ideals found in many existential, humanistic, and spiritual orientations. The altruistic posture of Eastern philosophies, the Judeo-Christian beliefs of kindness and love for one's neighbors, and humanistic concepts such as social interest, empathic understanding, and the creative self are all related to this concept. Counselors who extend themselves in cooperative, collaborative, and contributing ways are in an optimal position to advance human welfare.

Summary

This chapter has described four spheres of invitational counseling: (1) being personally inviting with oneself, (2) being personally inviting with others, (3) being professionally inviting with oneself, and (4) being professionally inviting with others. Being personally inviting with oneself is a prerequisite to being personally inviting with others. Counselors who care for themselves emotionally, intellectually, and physically are in an excellent position to reach out personally to others in these same areas. Being personally inviting with others provides a life support system for the counselor. This system consists of people who cherish the counselor and who are cherished in return. The point was emphasized that all the professional success one could imagine will not make up for a lack of success with loved ones. Being professionally inviting with oneself incorporates a desire to change and a willingness to risk. This desire and willingness are exemplified in the efforts counselors make to explore professional change and continue lifelong learning. Being professionally inviting with others is the ultimate goal of invitational counseling. To accomplish this goal, counselors are encouraged to use a rich assortment of cooperative, collaborative, and contributive strategies.

This goal of contributing in so many different ways is best achieved if one has a clear process in mind. Invitational counseling consists not only of the elements, levels, and spheres presented thus far; it also entails a clear process. This process will be explained in Chapter 5.

Opportunities for Further Reading

ABURDENE, P. & NAISBITT, J. (1992). *Megatrends for women*. New York: Villard. This book attempts to answer the question, "What trends do women need to know about to be empowered now and in the future?" It is also a book for men who live and work with women.

ANGELOU, M. (1970). *I know why the caged bird sings*. New York: Random House. Angelou, in this autobiographical narrative, presented a story of childhood suffering. Some of the incidents Angelou depicted are wonderfully funny, but it is a painfully involving memoir of the African American experience.

COVEY, S. R. (1989). *The seven habits of highly effective people*. New York: Simon & Schuster. This motivational book presents effective habits for both personal and professional success in life. Covey emphasized the need to restore the "character ethic" in North American society.

EMERY, S. (1978). *Actualizations: You don't have to rehearse to be yourself*. Garden City, NY: Doubleday. Emery sought to enable the reader to recognize the conditions that add to, or detract from, living. Particular attention is given to the creation of inviting environments in which relationships become "joyful, nurturing, satisfying" adventures in mutual growth.

HEILBRUN, C. G. (1988). *Writing a woman's life*. New York: Ballantine Books. This book is a unique and persuasive call for women to establish their own identity, seek freedom beyond parameters defined by men, and celebrate life to the fullest.

JOHNSON, S. M. (1977). *First person singular: Living the good life alone*. Philadelphia: Lippincott. Johnson gave unusual emphasis to the value of friendship and saw it as perhaps even more important than the passion of love. The book contains some beautifully written passages on loneliness and the need for friendships.

MCGINNIS, A. L. (1979). *The friendship factor*. Minneapolis: Augsburg Publishing House. This work presents many ideas for inviting others personally. At the heart of each personal relationship is the friendship factor—an essential ingredient of friendship is caring.

PECK, M. S. (1978). *The road less traveled: A new psychology of love, traditional values, and spiritual growth*. New York: Simon & Schuster. A bestselling book that explores the essential ingredients of life from a uniquely spiritual perspective. Peck, a psychiatrist, has provided a readable guide to the journey of life.

PIRSIG, R. M. (1974). *Zen and the art of motorcycle maintenance: An inquiry into values*. New York: William Morrow. Hidden beneath this story of a man's search for himself are rich insights into some of the most perplexing human dilemmas. This book deals with people and explores what living is all about. Perhaps most important, the book encourages a special appreciation of planet earth.

CHAPTER FIVE

Dimensions of Invitational Counseling

ఎ

The truths of relationship, however, return in the rediscovery of connection, in the realization that self and other are interdependent and that life, however valuable in itself, can only be sustained by care in relationships.

Carol Gilligan
In a Different Voice
1982, p. 127

ఎ

Does a teachable process exist to accomplish the goals of invitational counseling? Can invitational counseling be divided into analyzable stages? Are identifiable choices embedded in the process? Are there steps that will help counselors apply this process? This chapter answers these questions by presenting a three-stage sequence for invitational counseling. In addition, the four choices of sending, not sending, accepting, and not accepting receive detailed attention. This chapter will also present steps to assist counselors in assessing situations, seeking involvement, selecting appropriate strategies, assigning and assuming responsibilities, and evaluating and following up with relationships.

As these stages, choices, and steps are analyzed, it is important to think in terms of inviting *patterns* of behaviors rather than single inviting acts. Invitational counseling is the total of all behaviors, strategies, and interventions selected by counselors on behalf of their clients. Like the fluid swing of a master golfer, which integrates athletic ability and learned techniques, invitational counseling is made up of specific stages, steps, and choices that, when combined, disappear into invisibly appropriate practice.

Invitational counseling does not happen by chance. First, it is the product of beliefs and behaviors working together. Second, it is an orientation of disciplined character. As Erich Fromm stated, "I shall never be good at anything if I do not do it a disciplined way; anything I do only if 'I am in the mood' may be a nice or amusing hobby, but I shall never become a master of that art" (1956, p. 108). Invitational counseling requires disciplined effort.

Stages

A number of counselors have proposed models that contain stages in the counseling process (Brammer, 1988; Egan, 1994; Gazda, Asbury, Balzer, Childers, & Walters, 1991; Ivey & Simek-Downing, 1980). These models usually include an introduction/facilitation stage, an exploration/transition stage, an action/decision-making stage, and a closure/follow-up stage. Invitational counseling is similar to these models in that it proposes a preparation stage, an initiating/responding stage, and a follow-up stage. Each stage contains four parts.

Preparation Stage

The preparation stage consists of four parts: (1) having the desire, (2) expecting good things, (3) preparing the setting, and (4) reading the situation. Achieving each of these is essential to moving effectively into subsequent stages.

Having the desire. It may seem obvious that counselors must want to help before they can be a beneficial presence in the lives of their clients, but sometimes the most obvious factors are overlooked. As Glinda, the Good Witch of the North, pointed out to Dorothy in the film *The Wizard of Oz*, Dorothy had always had the power to go home; she just didn't *want* to hard enough. Wanting to hard enough is an essential first step in invitational counseling. With a clear understanding that the intentional desire to help is fundamental to successful counseling, counselors are able to implement all other stages and procedures of the process.

The desire to help is essential; but the counselor's desire should always be tempered with a proper regard for one's professional skills and resources. Having the desire is not enough if appropriate counseling skills are missing or personal and professional resources are lacking. It is essential that the desire to help is consistently filtered through the counselor's own energy level and time restraints, as well as by the level of his or her professional expertise.

Expecting good things.   The word *efficacy* appears frequently in contemporary professional literature, designating the belief that one can make a positive difference in human affairs. If counselors do not have this perception, then why would they seek to help others at all? Invitational counseling is based on an optimistic view of people and their relatively boundless potential. Every inviting act, no matter how small or in what area, has limitless impact. Counselors who accept invitational counseling keep a positive outlook about the potential of helping relationships and maintain an optimistic vision about the long-range effects of their work.

Counselors sometimes overlook the positive things they accomplish because they may not become aware of them for weeks, months, or even years. In fact, some beneficial results may never be known. For this reason, counselors who practice invitational counseling work to maintain a special faith in themselves, their clients, and the efficacy of their relationships. These counselors understand that it is seldom that one inviting act, or even one inviting person, makes a monumental difference. It takes a great number of inviting acts and many inviting people to achieve optimal living.

Preparing the setting.   Although having the desire and expecting good things are essential to invitational counseling, it is equally important to make the process as attractive as possible. This requires time and effort in preparing the setting. Having friends over for dinner provides an illustration.

Inviting friends into one's home for dinner is an enduring tradition. As such (in addition to having the desire and expecting good things), the invitation is usually accompanied by considerable preparation. Choosing the menu, setting the table, preparing the food, and straightening the house are all done to prepare a setting in which the dinner party will be successful.

To increase the likelihood of success, hosts and hostesses take time to consider their guests' likes and dislikes, schedule the dinner at a convenient time, and plan activities that will make the evening enjoyable. Guests return the thoughtfulness by arriving on time, dressing appropriately for the occasion, and showing their appreciation during the evening.

As with dinner hosts, counselors who take the time to prepare the setting have a head start in developing successful counseling relationships. This includes scheduling sessions at times convenient to clients, collecting appropriate information or materials beforehand, providing clients with professional disclosure statements, and arranging a facilitative environment for the counseling session. Physical factors such as lighting, temperature, the size, arrangement, and proximity of furniture, the nature of decorations, the degree of privacy, and sound levels all have an important impact on the success or failure of the counseling process. Appendix B offers suggestions for preparing the counseling setting.

Reading situations. Reading situations—also called sensitivity, empathy, interpersonal perceptivity, and social intelligence—is the ability to understand and predict what others are feeling and what they are likely to do. Research on interpersonal communication indicates that differences exist among professionals and nonprofessionals in their sensitivity to various signal systems in the environment and in their sending and receiving abilities through various verbal and nonverbal channels (Rosenthal, Archer, Koivumaki, DiMatteo, & Rogers, 1974). This ability to enter another person's perceptual world is essential to invitational counseling, for it helps to form a bridge between the sender's and receiver's perceptions. Because sharing perceptions is critical, it is important that counselors use all their senses in reading situations. For example, counselors who listen with only their ears may not be able to receive nonverbal messages or sense what their clients are not saying. By listening with all senses, counselors increase the likelihood that they see things as others do.

An example of reading situations was provided by a Moroccan waiter who approached one of the authors in a small cafe in Tangiers, Morocco, and asked for the order in English. When asked how he knew the author spoke English, the waiter replied, "North Americans smell different."

Reading situations requires specific skills that are presented in most counseling textbooks. Many contemporary counseling texts pay primary attention to these communication skills (Brammer, 1988; Egan, 1994; Ivey, 1991; Pietrofesa, Hoffman, & Splete, 1984). These skills include attending, listening, clarifying, questioning, probing, structuring, summarizing, interpreting, compromising, and confronting, which will be addressed in Chapter 6. Without appropriate skills, counselors would find it difficult to move toward the second stage of the inviting process: the initiating and responding stage.

Initiating/Responding Stage

While the preparation stage is essential in the inviting process, it is the decisions made during the initiating/responding stage that create the opportunities for clients' self-maintenance and self-actualization.

The initiating/responding stage involves verbal behavior, such as voice tone and rate of delivery; nonverbal behavior, such as facial expression, body stance, and eye contact; personal appearance, one's clothing, hair styling, and makeup; physical space, which includes physical contact (touching); and the external environment, temperature, appearance, and degree of privacy. This stage requires that counselors (1) choose carefully, (2) act appropriately, and (3) ensure reception.

Choosing carefully. To choose their actions carefully, counselors work to obtain "you and me" and "here and now" information about their clients. By gathering immediate data and staying in the present tense, the counselor is in an excellent position to encourage the client to explore present perceptions and future opportunities.

In choosing carefully, counselors keep in mind that their invitations to explore options are most likely to be accepted and acted upon successfully when (1) the invitation seems safe to accept, (2) there are repeated opportunities to accept, (3) the invitation is clear and unambiguous, and (4) the invitation is not too demanding in intensity or duration. The counselor influences all four of these factors.

Initial invitations should be simple, short-term, and not too demanding. For example, asking a client to describe his or her present work situation is a much more simple and short-range invitation to self-disclose than asking the person to present his or her family frustrations and aspirations. Gradually, as trust develops, invitations can be more complex, intimate, and long-range.

Acting appropriately. It is one thing to choose with care what one is going to do, and quite another thing to do it. Choosing carefully is important and requires skill and feeling, but the proof is in acting appropriately. Individuals often have good intentions but fail to act on them. Even the smallest appropriate action counts for more than the greatest intention never acted upon.

Choosing carefully and acting appropriately offer the greatest likelihood of guiding the client-counselor relationship through the initiating/responding stage. As early as 1960, Lippitt and White demonstrated that "guiding suggestions" are characteristics of a democratic relationship: "What is most important to you?" "Have you considered . . . ?" "What else could you have done?" "What other choices do you have?" The major characteristic embedded in each of these guiding suggestions is a respect for the client's own self-directing powers, coupled with the counselor's cordial summons to take advantage of these powers. From the invitational perspective, the best way to help people is to invite them to do what they can and should do for themselves.

One way to assist clients in exploration is to include observations and reflections: "You've tried several approaches, and you feel stuck," or "You feel your choices are limited." These comments are likely to encourage self-reflections by clients. In some cases, counselors and clients establish specific formal agreements where realistic plans of action are made and acted upon. For example, Goldberg (1977) suggested the establishment of contracts between counselors and clients. These contracts clearly state what the understandings are between the counselor and client, what each will be doing, and what each can expect of the other in the therapeutic relationship. If such formal agreements are used in invitational counseling, they are always enacted with the client's full awareness and cooperation.

Ensuring reception. Frequently people send messages that are never received. Notes are misfiled, comments go unheard, questions remain unanswered, phone messages are misplaced, and gestures escape unnoticed. These are everyday examples of messages sent but never received. Invitations are like letters—they can get lost in the mail.

Because some messages are misdirected or misunderstood, it is vital that the counselor ensure that the content of the message is received *and* acknowledged. This is clearly the counselor's responsibility, but too often this responsibility is neglected. When an invitation is sent but not received, or received but misunderstood, the counselor sometimes mistakenly assumes that the invitation has been accepted or rejected. These breakdowns in communication can be avoided if the counselor ensures that accurate reception has occurred. This assurance of reception is important in any field. For example, in military services throughout the world, the receiver of a communication must repeat the message verbatim before it is considered sent. For example, "Aye, aye, Captain, four degrees port rudder," acknowledges the message. Acknowledgment is also important in the classroom where the teacher gently but firmly inquires, "Johnny, what did I ask you to do?" Unless the content of messages is received and acknowledged, it may remain meaningless. Even worse, confusion and misunderstanding may arise. When breakdowns in communication occur, it is important for the counselor and client to consider how the misunderstanding happened and how it can be successfully addressed.

Clients and counselors have been known to leave a counseling session with the counselor thinking, "That went well. She will do that task successfully." At the same time, the client is thinking, "That was good. I'm glad the counselor is going to do that for me." Ensuring that the content of the invitation has been received, and acknowledging who is responsible for what, are vital in counseling. When this goal is not achieved, misunderstandings and hurt feelings often result. When this happens it is very difficult to move comfortably to the follow-up stage of invitational counseling.

To ensure good communication, it is vital that the counselor take a few minutes immediately after each individual or group counseling session to record what took place. This documentation helps to record observations regarding progress of the process, behavior of clients, length of time spent at each phase of a session, and primary nature and theme of the session. It is also useful in case there is a need to inform supervisors of progress or to document standards of accountability (Meier & Davis, 1993). Of course, confidentiality for clients is essential, so caution is needed when keeping these records (Schmidt, 1991, 1993).

Follow-up Stage

Invitational counseling is the process, in part, of hearing and accepting the essential aspects of what is being communicated by the client, and reflecting these essential parts to the client. During the initiating/responding stage, counselors are mirrors of reflection. In the follow-up stage, counselors go beyond reflection to (1) interpret responses, (2) negotiate positions, (3) evaluate the process, and (4) reinforce trust.

Understanding responses. When the counselor's invitations are sent and received, they become the property of the clients receiving the invitations. Clients have the options of accepting invitations, not accepting them, ignoring them, modifying them with a counter proposal, or tabling them until another time. What is critical at this point is the counselor's interpreting of the client's response.

When a client indicates acceptance of an invitation, is the entire invitation accepted or just part of it? Does the client understand the responsibilities stated in the invitation? For example, when a client agrees to a behavioral contract suggested by the counselor, it is essential that the client understand the obligations and consequences involved in the agreement. Without this understanding, the contract is unlikely to be acted upon successfully.

If a client indicates rejection of an invitation, was it in fact a rejection, or was it nonacceptance? The two responses are quite different. If rejection did take place, was the entire invitation rejected, or just part of it? Will future invitations also be rejected? For example, a client's spouse might be reluctant to participate in marriage counseling not because he or she dislikes the counselor, distrusts counseling, or wants the marriage to fail, but because he or she feels the process makes one appear weak or dependent. Rather than pressuring the spouse into marriage counseling, the counselor might ask for an individual session to share feelings and concerns about the counseling process.

Negotiating. In invitational counseling, counselors and their clients who encounter difficulties work to negotiate a way around these roadblocks. Too often, human relationships are damaged or even destroyed because people are either unable or unwilling to negotiate their differences. Sadly, these disagreements often begin as minor concerns, but they become inflated by vested personal or professional interests that prevent people from putting in as much as they are taking out of their relationships. This is understandable in light of the nature of self-concept explained in Chapter 2. The self-serving quality of the self sometimes hinders a person's ability to reassess values, suspend judgments, accept perceptions, and negotiate differences. Counselors who find that some clients have difficulty accepting responsibility in counseling may first want to help them work on their self-perceptions and assist them in strengthening their negotiating skills.

Most counselors seek to maintain direction and purpose in the counseling relationship, but there is little to be gained by holding doggedly to a plan that a client cannot or will not accept. It is much more productive to find acceptable alternatives, even if these do not fulfill long-range goals. Counselors often discover that client acceptance and completion of an alternative plan frequently lead to the acceptance and completion of the original one.

Evaluating the process. Formal or informal evaluation is unavoidable in any human endeavor. Dinner guests comment on menus, voters choose candidates, judges rule on evidence, teachers grade students, students evaluate teachers, managers get bonuses, parents monitor children, and audiences applaud performances. Proper evaluation of the counseling process helps the counselor gather and assess valuable information for future sessions.

Some counselors comment that they are so busy "doing" that they do not have time to evaluate what they do. Still, counselors are responsible not only for what they do, but also for demonstrating that what they do makes a positive difference. Evaluation is particularly important in school counseling, where tight budgets and reduction in personnel demand that school counselors document the value of their work. In all counseling settings, this level of evaluation requires both informal and formal means of assessing the counselor-client relationship.

Informally, counselors and their clients might evaluate the outcome of counseling by analyzing their progress on particular goals during their counseling sessions. During this informal evaluation process, counselors are as encouraging as possible. They look at the gains made rather than the distance still to travel. Important qualities of counselors are to be optimistic themselves and to invite optimism in their clients.

With the approval of the client and with all ethical constraints in place, the counselor might also check with significant people in the client's life who can verify progress or lack of it. Such persons could include spouses, parents, peers, employers, teachers, or friends. Conversations with these individuals can frequently provide valuable information about a client's progress.

Formally, counselors can utilize standardized tests and interest inventories, behavior rating scales, biofeedback techniques, physical measurements, and other means to assess a client's progress. Invitational counseling applies these techniques with the caution that they are always used for the benefit of clients. Tests that unjustly discriminate and surveys that violate rights to privacy are two examples of inappropriate methods of evaluation. Invitational counseling requires methods that conform to ethical standards of the counseling profession and adhere to published principles and practices of assessment and evaluation.

Assessment is an important aspect of counseling. To provide clients with optimal services, counselors use a wide range of instruments and techniques that enable them to make decisions about interventions. In schools, for example, counselors use standardized tests and inventories to help students understand their academic strengths and weaknesses, assess vocational interests, and measure aspects of personality so that students can attain greater self-understanding (Schmidt, 1993). School counselors also use observations, interviews, and surveys to gather data by which they, students, parents, and teachers can make reasonably informed decisions about educational plans and career choices.

Other formal means of evaluating their performance include documentation on professional activities in which counselors participated, supervision they received, and service they performed for the organization. These formal methods of evaluation add to the credibility of informal sources. Whether informal or formal procedures are used, it is essential that evaluation take place.

Because invitational counseling often involves a marriage of remedial relationships with developmental processes, evaluation is not the final goal. The purpose of invitational counseling is to form an alliance that will achieve even more beneficial sequences of development. One successful sequence generally follows another as trust in the relationship is reinforced.

Reinforcing trust. As Dorothy noted in *The Wizard of Oz,* "To get to a place you have never been, you must go by a road you have never taken." In invitational counseling, a single invitation is a small step in a long walk. As trust develops, it provides the impetus for the client and counselor to continue their journey. Successful human relationships require countless inviting actions, each based on ever-growing trust.

The level of trust that exists between people within any interaction is related not only to each individual's past experiences but also to the intensity of the immediate relationship. This trust level is influenced by past experiences, the nature of the undertaking, and the dependability that each person brings to the relationship. Without a reasonable level of trust, the client will not self-disclose, explore new options, or take the risks necessary to find new ways of being.

The inviting process is cyclical; one sequence leads to another. While the three stages outlined here are highlighted for the sake of analysis, it is necessary to state again that invitational counseling consists simultaneously of many separate activities, each created according to this overall process. In this sense, counseling can be viewed as an overarching invitation for people to see themselves as able, valuable, and responsible, and to function accordingly.

Apparent in each of the previous stages is that decisions are continually made that affect the counseling process, positively or negatively. These decisions can be grouped under the four choices introduced in Chapter 1.

Choices

Every human interaction involves at least one of four basic choices, each with accompanying risks. The first two choices—sending or not sending—lie in the realm of the inviter, and as noted in an earlier section on ensuring reception, these choices are particularly important for the counselor. The second two choices, accepting or not accepting, are in the domain of the invited, and therefore are especially important to clients. Of course, human interactions are complex, and all four of these choices are available to all parties in any given relationship. For this reason, it is important for counselors to understand the dynamic association that exists among the four choices and how it influences their decisions in the process of helping others.

Sending

Sending any invitation inevitably contains risks. The sender faces risks of rejection, postponement, misunderstanding, ignominy—even acceptance. Yet, risk taking is necessary if one is to live life well. As noted in an earlier book, "The greatest hazards in life are to risk nothing, send nothing, accept nothing, be nothing" (Purkey & Novak, 1984, p. 48). This concept was enriched by a graduate student in counseling at the University of North Carolina at Greensboro who wrote: "It is better to invite and be rejected, than not to invite and be dejected." Risks are inevitable in counseling for both the counselor and client.

Counselors take risks when they encourage their clients to explore present options and future opportunities. They face the possibility that their efforts will be misunderstood, rejected, or ignored. Clients take risks by self-disclosing aspects of their lives that leave them vulnerable. As Jourard (1971b) explained, self-disclosure is fraught with risk.

Human beings are sometimes indecisive about whether or not to become involved with others: "Should I or shouldn't I?" Invitational counseling has a partial answer to this age-old question. When the evidence for sending or not sending is about equally divided, it is probably better to send. Few things in life are as sad as a missed opportunity. When an invitation is extended, there is no guarantee that it will be accepted, but if it is not extended, there is the absolute assurance that it has no chance of being accepted, no matter how beneficial the invitation might be in theory. As an illustration, one of the authors was chatting with a colleague who had joined the faculty three years before. In the course of the conversation, the author expressed how glad he was that this colleague had become part of the faculty. The colleague responded by saying, "I have been here for three years and you are the first person to say that to me. I appreciate it more than you know."

Of course, at times it is inappropriate or uncaring to invite. For example, if a friend has a drinking problem, one does not encourage a happy hour, or if someone is trying to lose weight, one does not send a gift of candy. Paradoxically, the most inviting thing to do in such situations is not to invite.

Not Sending

In *Education and Ecstasy*, George Leonard (1968) noted, "Many a liberal educational reform has foundered on lack of specific tools for accomplishing its purposes—even if a tool may be something as simple as knowing precisely when to leave the learner entirely alone" (p. 18). A similar statement is appropriate here: in some situations, doing and saying nothing may be the most caring and appropriate thing a counselor can do.

Examples of uncaring or inappropriate behaviors include providing an answer for a struggling client who could have found it without help, or being overly friendly or protective of a client. The skills used by counselors to make caring and appropriate choices regarding sending or not sending are related to the skills described earlier in this chapter. Because these skills are also important in accepting or not accepting invitations, it is helpful to understand the nature of these choices as well.

Accepting

To the degree that clients accept the opportunity to participate in the helping process, to that degree counseling will be successful. Yet, as with sending, accepting also involves risk. By accepting, the client is saying, "I trust you." When trust is demonstrated by accepting behaviors, the relationship is enriched. Accepting an invitation is a special way of sending one in return, beginning a chain reaction.

Having stated the importance of accepting, it is necessary to recognize that not accepting can also be a most caring and appropriate process. It is folly to think that all opportunities should be accepted, and it is irresponsible to do so. Knowing when not to accept is an essential part of the inviting process.

Not Accepting

Saying no to others can be a great way of saying yes to oneself. Sometimes, the most appropriate and caring response is *not* to accept an invitation. For example, at the end of a party there comes a time to go home, even though the exhausted host encourages guests to stay longer. Because of time, manners, appropriateness, care, commitment, taste, and countless other factors, many invitations are declined.

As noted earlier, the counselor should recognize the difference between rejection and nonacceptance. When a client declines a counselor's invitation, it does not necessarily mean that the counselor has been rejected or that all future invitations will be rejected. For countless reasons, clients are sometimes unable or unwilling to accept even the most beneficial opportunities. The rejection may be a means of eliciting an alternative message that requires a different commitment. In invitational counseling, the key to success is to continue the inviting process as long as there is mutual desire and reasonable hope of success. At times clients do not accept even the most attractive opportunities because they fear the responsibilities of acceptance, cannot engage at the particular time or place, or simply do not know how to handle the situation.

A counseling student at the University of North Carolina at Greensboro pointed out that one of the major problems young people face is how to turn down an invitation without being disinviting. He noted:

> When I was growing up I remember one girl in particular who I asked to a school dance, only to find myself in the embarrassing position of being tersely turned down. Being turned down to a school dance was certainly not a new experience for me, but the way it was done was particularly hurtful. It was not that she disliked me. I believe it was the only way she knew how to decline an invitation . . . or I'm an ugly ogre. I prefer the former explanation.

Sometimes clients will not accept an invitation in order to verify its sincerity. Even then, their intention may not be to reject. They may be seeking to determine whether the invitation is authentic, or to see if the relation is strong enough to survive the initial rejection. Through negotiation (explained earlier in the stages of the inviting process), counselors can assess the reasons for nonacceptance.

A central part of negotiating is the counselor's ability to handle rejection. The inviting process has room built in for rejection. The client's right to decline is absolute. Invitational counseling depends on communication, not manipulation.

As with the other three choices, nonacceptance involves risk—perhaps the greatest risk of all. People who continuously reject invitations risk the possibility of living lonely, isolated lives. When this occurs, they often mask their loneliness by pretending they *prefer* isolation. While this pretense is a temporary defense against further hurt, continued nonacceptance increases the likelihood of permanent isolation. Such people can benefit from professional counseling even though they have difficulty in seeking it. Those who could benefit most from professional help are often the last to seek it. For them, isolation is a final protection against further hurt.

Most experienced counselors realize that those who seek counseling are often resistant to the very help they seek. Counselors who are sensitive to this phenomenon will be patient and consistent in encouraging these clients to make adjustments, seek opportunities, and choose more beneficial directions in their lives.

Awareness of how and when to invite—or not—and how and when to accept—or not—can be a vital learning process for clients. It is equally important for counselors. In addition to basic choices, invitational counseling supports the assumption that every individual is entitled to a degree of privacy, even in counseling. In invitational counseling, this is known as "honoring the net."

Honoring the Net

Counseling is a profession noted by its genuine acceptance of those who seek assistance. A colleague, Bill Stafford, said it well: "Counseling is viewed by those embracing the invitational stance as being among the most personal and intense of human interactions. It is an experience into which neither client nor counselor should enter lightly" (1992, p. 202).

An essential component of invitational counseling that clarifies the responsibility of the counselor and the integrity of the helping relationship is called the net. The net is a hypothetical boundary that exists between the client and counselor; a boundary that, as in tennis, establishes the territory of each participant. A way of understanding the net is by considering the role of self-disclosure in counseling. While self-disclosure is encouraged, the client should remain in control of what he or she will or will not disclose. There is a certain etiquette involved in invitational counseling, with rules to be followed by both counselor and client. The counselor determines the rules under which invitations are sent; but the client determines the rules of acceptance. It is important to establish where the boundaries are and to stay on one's own side of the net. There are things that clients may choose to do or not do, disclose or not disclose. This privacy is the perfect right of anyone in a democratic society.

Counselors who embrace invitational counseling work to honor the net between themselves and their clients. However, there are occasions when the client may feel comfortable and trusting enough to lift the net. "The client needs to be assured that he or she may partially lift the net if the client chooses" (Stafford, 1992, pp. 211-212). While such self-disclosures are encouraged by the counselor, invitational counseling requires that clients be allowed to retreat behind the net when the risk becomes too great or when the pace of self-disclosure becomes too uncomfortable. Invitational counseling also requires that ethical and professional boundaries be respected at all times.

In practice, counselors consistently monitor their clients' participation in the helping relationship. They know when clients become less active, withdrawn, or in other ways uncomfortable with the direction of the session, and they alter the direction or slow the pace down to allow the client time to retreat or reassess his or her position. This is important in both individual and group counseling. The net is always there, regardless of the structure of the relationship.

Honoring the net requires that the counselor be aware of what is transpiring within the counseling relationship. Most important, the counselor is careful about the timing of the choices presented to clients. Timing becomes a critical ingredient that affects both the stages and choices available in invitational counseling. When counselors become thoughtless or careless they may function at an unintentional level. To ensure that the timing of their actions, choices, and interventions is correct, counselors maintain a high level of intentionality.

The stages and choices of invitational counseling are particularly helpful for establishing individual and small-group counseling relationships. Counselors in institutions such as schools, colleges, hospitals, and others benefit from a structure to move beyond individual and small group settings to a larger setting in the institution, thus benefiting the overall group. The next section presents steps for counselors to use in these larger arenas.

Factors

The following factors suggest ways to apply invitational counseling in large settings. In some cases counselors may want to help the institution adjust to the individual needs of a particular client. In others, counselors may see a need to address concerns of a larger group. This is done by assessing all the factors that affect inviting relationships, including (1) the "Five P's"; (2) involving all parties; (3) assigning responsibilities; and (4) evaluating the results.

The Five P's

In invitational counseling, five factors—people, places, policies, programs, and processes—are highly significant for their separate and combined influence on human existence and potential. The combination of these five factors provides a perspective that offers an almost limitless number of opportunities for professional service.

What clients do is always enmeshed within and influenced by their existing ecosystems. As Hobbs (1982) explained, human problems and promises do not reside within individuals, but rather within individuals' ecosystems of which the person is only one part. In

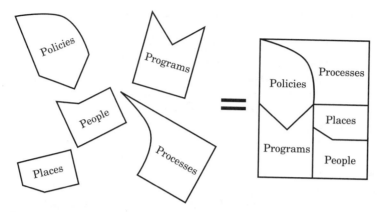

FIGURE 5-1 Five Factors of Invitational Counseling

invitational counseling it is important to take people, places, policies, programs, and processes into full account. As Figure 5-1 illustrates, the challenges facing counselors and their clients can often be related to the process of combining the pieces of a puzzle.

People. Decisions that have tremendous effect on people's lives are too often made by those in authority for reasons of efficiency, effectiveness, and conformity that reflect lack of respect for people. These decisions are often designed for the convenience of a few at the inconvenience of many. Examples include a "no food or drink" rule in a waiting room (to keep the room neat and clean), school regulations that allow only three minutes between classes (to reduce misbehavior) or five minutes for the buses to load (for the convenience of drivers). Invitational counseling is based on proper regard for the value of systems, regulations, and policies, but people come first. It advocates altering, wherever possible, those places, policies, programs, and processes that directly or indirectly inconvenience people or inhibit their development.

An example of the importance of people in the inviting process was observed by one of the authors while working as a consultant for a large hospital. An elderly male patient had been placed on a wheeled stretcher and moved into the hospital hallway. As he lay there, a burly hospital electrician, complete with leather belt and dangling tools, came striding down the corridor. When the electrician spotted the frail patient, he struck up a friendly conversation. After a few words, the electrician asked the patient if there was anything he could do for him. The man replied that he felt cold and would appreciate a blanket. The electrician walked over to the nurses' station, got a blanket, and tenderly covered the patient. At that moment the electrician was as much a health provider as any person in the hospital. Places, policies, and programs are important, but it is the people that create inviting relationships. The importance of people in invitational counseling will be expanded in later chapters.

Places. Invitational counseling also focuses on physical environments, the places that add to or subtract from respect and trust for people. Individuals are connected to their physical environments, and counseling takes place best by taking into account the physical surroundings. For example, consider the problem of "burnout," the process whereby professionals change in negative directions. As Pines and Aronson (1981) noted: "Burnout is not a function of bad people who are cold and uncaring. It is a function of bad situations in which once-idealistic people must operate. It is then that situations must be modified so that they promote, rather than destroy, human values" (p. 61).

Invitational counseling requires a continuous assessment of the places where people live and work to determine their influence on people and, where possible, to improve environments. An often overlooked part of professional helping related to places is the need for a reasonable degree of privacy. A professor known to one of the authors once commented that a successful counselor needs "two big ears, one small mouth, and a little privacy." While the need for privacy is almost self-evident in the counseling relationship, it is sometimes overlooked because the physical environment has not been structured to meet this need.

An assessment of the physical environment will identify variables that can be modified, adjusted, and improved. For example, visitor parking at universities, hospitals, and clinics is sometimes located some distance away, whereas parking for faculty and staff adjoins the buildings. A more equitable assignment of parking space may improve the mood of those who visit these institutions.

Another example of how physical environments contribute to human welfare may be seen in residential group care facilities. A fresh coat of paint, new curtains, improved lighting, carpets, or rearrangement of furnishings can produce highly beneficial results. One secretary reported that when the tall counter and plate glass that divided her office were removed and replaced by an attractive receptionist's desk, she felt as if she had been let out of prison.

Improving the physical environment may not always lead to immediate benefits, but it is important that the total setting be continuously assessed, alternatives explored, and necessary improvements made in the places where people live and work. Counselors who are alert to the total physical environment have a significant advantage in creating helping relationships.

Policies. People and places are influenced by the regulations, codes, orders, mandates, plans, rules, and edicts created by those in authority. Sometimes policies are created that, although well-intentioned, place undue restrictions on individuals or groups. Examples might be a cafeteria policy requiring that an identical amount of food be served to each patron (whether he or she weighs 75 pounds or 275!), a nursing home that requires "lights out" at 9:00 P.M. regardless of the personal desires of the people who reside there, or an elementary school principal who demands silence from children during their lunch time. Such insensitive, uncaring, or inappropriate policies limit opportunities for people to contribute to their own well-being as well as that of others.

On occasion, policies contribute to human difficulties. An illustration is the case of a nursing home resident who often exhibited difficult behaviors and was very cross, particularly when she first got up in the morning. A contributing factor was found to be the bed check policy, which required checks at various hours of the night. This would awaken the older adult who was then unable to return to a sound sleep. Altering the bed check policy and advising nurses to be extra quiet at night when they entered residents' rooms, coupled with providing ear plugs for this particular resident, resulted in restful nights and beneficial effects on her behavior. The policies that people create add to or subtract from the quality of life and the overall effectiveness of professional helpers.

Counselors who understand how policies affect people and who use this understanding to develop procedures that facilitate human functioning and development are more likely to experience success in their work. Still, policies are seldom made in isolation. They are inseparably tied to the programs established, adapted, and implemented by organizations and institutions.

Programs. Organizations routinely develop programs as part of their overall service. Special education classes in schools, work release programs in prisons, social activities in retirement centers, food and nutritional services in nursing homes, infant care training in hospitals, and salary incentives in industry are all examples of programs designed to contribute to the goals and objectives of the respective institutions. Counselors who employ invitational counseling are aware of the importance of programs, not only within their own institutions but also in the larger community. They strive to become knowledgeable about existing community programs that contribute both to their clients' welfare and to the welfare of larger groups. Moreover, these counselors are sensitive to the ways in which programs are created, implemented, and administered.

It sometimes happens that well-intentioned programs harm individuals or groups because they focus on narrow goals and objectives and neglect a wider perspective of human needs and conditions. For example, programs that label and group participants can negatively affect the positive purposes for which these programs were originally created. Although some classifications may be necessary, there is a danger in programs that label, group, and segregate human beings. As Hobbs (1975) warned: "Categories and labels are powerful instruments for social regulation and control, and they often are employed for obscure, covert or hurtful purposes: to degrade people, to deny them access to opportunity, to exclude 'undesirables' whose presence in society in some way offends, disturbs familiar customs, or demands extraordinary efforts" (p. 10). Invitational counseling requires that professional helpers closely monitor programs that add to or subtract from the goals for which they were designed.

Policies and programs go hand in hand in identifying beneficial relationships and systems designed by organizations, such as schools, hospitals, and businesses. These elements also are interconnected with the methods and processes used by these organizations to implement, establish, and enforce policies and programs.

Processes. The context of counseling is reflected in the various processes chosen and applied by professional counselors in their helping relationships. Invitational counseling assumes that as important as *what* is done in the name of counseling is *how* the relationship transpires. Counselors who apply invitational counseling are consistently cognizant of the processes established by themselves and their agencies and how these positively or negatively influence quality of life. Sometimes processes are so embedded in a counselor's repertoire of behaviors, or in an institution's procedures, that little thought is given to how they may affect others. As noted earlier, actions that include little thought often fall in the domain of unintentional functioning.

Invitational counseling promotes the notion that successful relationships exist when counselors are in tune with their clients and select methods of relating that are acceptable to the client. As an example, the counselor who selects the process of group counseling to assist a person who is excessively shy and extremely uncomfortable in self-disclosing may place the client in a potentially harmful situation. Careful assessment of the client's perceptions would avoid this likelihood and enable the counselor to select a more appropriate process.

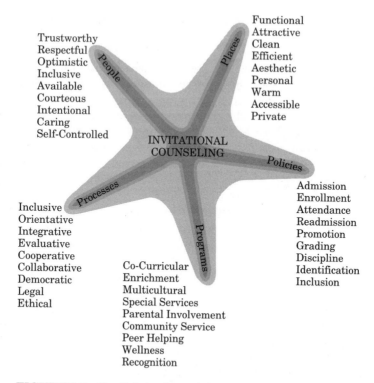

FIGURE 5-2 Starfish Analogy of the Five P's in a School Setting

The Five P's also lend themselves to a conceptualization of institutions that counselors can use to educate colleagues, clients, and other groups about the impact of external and internal elements on the function of people and organizations. Figure 5-2 uses a starfish to illustrate the Five P's in a school setting with examples of personal characteristics and institutional qualities associated with each factor. By adapting this illustration to their particular work settings, counselors in hospitals, prisons, mental health centers, and other locations can demonstrate how these factors have a combined influence on their institutions.

Combining the Five P's. Counselors who adopt invitational counseling think in terms of the Five P's: people, places, policies, programs, and processes. They understand how the dynamics of the Five P's influence the welfare and development of people. They accept the principle that emotional disturbance is a symptom not only of individual pathology but also of a malfunctioning human ecosystem. The following example underscores this principle.

One of the authors had the opportunity to serve as a consultant to an elementary school counselor and a teacher. The school counselor had been working with a young boy who had been referred by his teacher because of inappropriate behaviors, particularly in the cafeteria. The counselor had worked with the boy individually and in groups, but little improvement was noted. While the counselor-student relationship seemed healthy, and certain classroom behaviors had improved, the boy's actions in the cafeteria continued to be deplorable. He was often loud and boisterous, throwing food at other students, running around the cafeteria, and getting into fights.

In reviewing the people aspect of this situation, the consultant, counselor, and teacher agreed that people have a right to eat lunch in a peaceful setting without being bothered by others. It was also agreed that the student would benefit from a calm and appropriate lunch period.

The consultant and counselor asked the teacher to describe what occurred in the cafeteria, the place where the students ate lunch. The teacher described how students went through the lunch line, selected their food, paid the cashier, and sat at designated tables to eat their lunches. All students ate in the cafeteria.

The teacher described the policies and processes for ordering lunch and eating in the cafeteria. As the cafeteria workers prepared the lunch trays, students passed through the line and made choices about the vegetables, main courses, and desserts they wanted. This procedure was particularly difficult for the child in question. He often hesitated in responding to the cafeteria staff's questions. They in turn became frustrated with his indecision. The cafeteria workers would wait a few seconds for his answers and then just give him one of the choices. The boy would get angry at them for making his decisions in the same way the workers would get upset with his indecision and belligerence. When this happened, the teacher reported that the boy would take his tray to the lunchroom, sit at the table, pick at his food, and eventually get into trouble.

After examining the people, places, policies, programs, and processes involved, the consultant, teacher, and counselor agreed on the following intervention. A conference between the young student and the teacher was scheduled so that the teacher could express concern that sometimes the student was not enjoying his lunch time. At this conference the teacher explained to the student that each person has the right to enjoy a relaxing lunch and that disruptive behaviors were not helpful to him or others. The teacher explained that students were welcome to eat in the cafeteria as long as they allowed other people to enjoy their lunch. If the student decided not to do this, then the teacher would find a quiet place in the school where he could enjoy his lunch alone.

The teacher also conveyed to the student her understanding of how difficult it is to make decisions on the spur of the moment, such as deciding what to eat while moving through the cafeteria line. Therefore, every morning the teacher would give the student a copy of the menu and ask him to circle the items he wanted for lunch. He was asked to give the circled menu to the cafeteria workers. They proceeded to fill his order based on the items he had circled. The cafeteria staff was also requested to greet the young boy, as well as all the others who moved through the serving line, pleasantly. Meanwhile, the counselor continued seeing the student in group counseling sessions to focus on self-concept development, decision-making skills, and conflict resolution.

Subsequent follow-up by the consultant indicated that the student had no further difficulty in the cafeteria. The success of the teacher, counselor, and student in handling the situation was related to their ability to employ a wide-angle perspective. The counselor focused on the student initially, but better results were achieved when places, policies, programs, and processes were also assessed.

Assessment of the Five P's

Invitational counseling encourages assessment of the Five P's that influence human functioning. When counselors and clients move toward resolution of concerns or toward the development of more enhancing and enriching relationships, they incorporate into this process an evaluation of the Five P's. Adequate assessment of these factors allows counselors and their clients to target specific strategies accurately, thereby increasing their likelihood of success. The following questions are examples of assessment using the Five P's. Who are the people involved and what can be done to include them in the effort to improve a given situation? What is known about the environment—the place—in which change might occur? Are there guidelines and policies that are interfering with change, or could be developed to facilitate change? What programs can be used to improve the situation, or are programs contributing to the problem? Are the processes and procedures in place beneficial, or do they need to be changed? By asking these and other assessment questions, counselors and their clients place themselves in position to assess the total situation.

Involvement of All Parties

Every time a concern arises about an individual's development, such as inappropriate behavior that is hindering relationships, that concern is of interest to everyone involved. No human condition is experienced in isolation, without affecting other people, groups, organizations, or institutions. Therefore, when problems emerge and concerns are raised, they are important at some level to everyone, in much the same way that the Five P's of invitational counseling imply that *everything counts* and *everyone matters*.

Because everyone matters, counselors seek opinions and encourage participation of everyone involved. For example, with the assessment process described earlier, a school counselor would seek to include teachers, teacher assistants, cafeteria workers, custodians, bus drivers, administrators, students, and parents in evaluating and planning a more inviting school. When counselors work with individual children, adolescents, or adults, they make every effort to include family members in the helping process. Whenever individuals struggle with behavioral adjustments or important decisions, the struggle affects everyone with whom they interact.

Research supports the involvement of others in the counseling process. Studies have shown that schools that invite parental participation, keep families informed about students' progress, and encourage parents to become actively involved in their children's education are more likely to achieve student success (Epstein, 1991). Similarly, businesses and institutions of higher learning are now embracing the philosophy of Total Quality Management (Deming, 1986), which encourages cooperation, collaboration, and a team spirit to enhance employee involvement (Paxton, 1993). Invitational counseling reflects the belief that the more people who are involved in solving problems, and the more input these people have in decision-making processes, the more likely success will be achieved.

The 5-P Relay

One method for encouraging the involvement of all parties is called the 5-P Relay (Purkey, 1991). The 5-P Relay was adapted from the Pass It On exercise developed by Doug MacIver (1991) at the Center for Research on Elementary and Middle Schools at Johns Hopkins University. A description follows of the 5-P Relay as it could be applied in a school setting. Counselors who wish to facilitate a relay in their own institutions will need to add their own creative juices and adapt the 5-P Relay to the unique characteristics of the organizations in which they work. The idea is to encourage creative thinking during a nonthreatening, fun-filled activity.

Preparation.   A large room such as a cafeteria, media center, or gym will serve as the location. Create five stations—one for each P (People, Places, Policies, Programs, Processes)—around the area. Five tables will be needed; one for each station. (In schools with more

than 50 staff members, two identical 5-P Relays can be run simultaneously, in two sets of five stations.) Identify each station with a
large sign: People Station, Places Station, Policies Station, Program
Station, and Processes Station. At each station, place five large sheets
of newsprint and label each sheet with one of the following headings:
Goals, Procedures, Obstacles, Overcoming Obstacles, and Action Plan.
All five stations will need five sheets of newsprint with the five headings. In addition, each station will need felt-tip pens, extra newsprint,
and a roll of masking tape.

Process.   Usually, a three-hour time period is scheduled for the
relay and is divided accordingly:

15 minutes: During an orientation period this description is distributed to all participants and read aloud as everyone follows along.
Questions are answered until everyone understands the purpose of the
activity and their role.

15 minutes: Teams are formed randomly by having everyone
count off by fives. After everyone has counted off, they are assigned to
the five stations. "All the number ones please go to the station marked
People. All the number twos please go to the station marked Places.
All the number threes please go to the station marked Policies. All the
number fours please go to the station marked Programs, and all the
number fives please go to the station marked Processes." After these
five teams are formed, everything is ready for the activity.

15 minutes: Instruct each team to brainstorm at least three do-
able *goals* for their particular *P.* They should write these goals on
newsprint with their heading (People, Places, Policies, Programs, or
Processes). The goals they choose should enable the institution to
become a more personally and professionally inviting place. It is important that the goals they list be *specific* and *measurable.* Once each
team has written the goals for their *P,* it prioritizes its goals, with 1
being most important, 2 the next, and so forth. The groups mark these
priorities next to each goal they have written. At the end of this
15-minute activity a *bell rings* (any sound system will do, and
timekeepers should be creative in the ways they keep people moving).

5 minutes: At the sound of the bell, each team immediately leaves
its station, leaving its list of goals, and moves to the next station (that
is, the People team moves to the Policies Station, Policies team moves
to the Processes Station, Processes moves to the Programs Station,
Programs moves to the Places Station, and Places moves to the People
Station). After this move each team should be at a new station looking
at a set of goals, written by a previous team.

15 minutes: Each team reviews the list of goals at their table and
writes *procedures* to accomplish each of the goals starting with the

highest priority. On a piece of newsprint, the group writes the heading "Here's How to Do It," and proceeds to list ways to accomplish each goal. At the end of this period, the *bell rings*.

5 minutes: Each team leaves its table and moves to the next station in the same order as before.

15 minutes: Each team studies the goals and procedures at its new station left by the two previous groups, and makes a list of *obstacles* (barriers) that might prevent these goals from being accomplished or these procedures from being established. At the end of this period, the *bell rings*.

5 minutes: Each team leaves its lists and table, and moves to the next station.

15 minutes: The teams study the set of goals, procedures and obstacles and makes a list of ways to *overcome the obstacles*. At the end of this period, the *bell rings*.

5 minutes: Each team leaves its table and moves to the next station.

15 minutes: Each team now reviews the goals, procedures, obstacles, and ways to overcome obstacles left by previous teams. Now they make a list of *suggestions* on ways to evaluate whether or not the goals have been accomplished. "How will we know when each goal is achieved?" Teams will list methods to use in measuring outcomes and results. At the end of this period, the *bell rings*.

5 minutes: Each team leaves its table and moves to the next station. At this point each team should be back at the home station, where they first started the relay. Every participant has had an opportunity to be involved in each of the stations, as illustrated in Figure 5-3.

15 minutes: Each team studies its lists of goals, procedures, obstacles, ways to overcome obstacles, and methods of evaluation and prepares an *action plan*. This plan should include clear time lines, assignments and responsibilities for staff members, and an evaluation process. At the end of this period, the *bell rings*.

35 minutes: All participants come together in a large group and each team places its action plan on the wall where everyone can see it. A spokesperson for each team gives a brief report to the entire group. After the meeting these plans are typed, signed by team members, duplicated, and distributed to all the participants.

Follow-up.   After the 5-P Relay, each of the five teams (People, Places, Policies, Programs, and Processes) remains intact for the school year. Each team selects a captain and meets at regular intervals during the year to assure that its goals are being accomplished. In addition, the five team captains meet on a regular basis to report

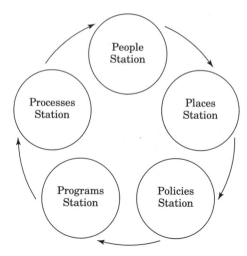

FIGURE 5-3 5-P Relay

progress and share ideas. Accomplishments should be shared periodically with the entire organization.

The 5-P Relay is one method for assessing influential factors in a large institution and involving everyone in decision-making. What is significant about the 5-P Relay is its inclusion of everyone who has an investment in the organization. The essential point is to involve as many people as possible in the assessment process and in the action plans that are selected. Once actions have been selected, the next step is to encourage commitment from all parties and assign appropriate responsibilities. Because everyone has an investment in seeing that identified goals are attained, they also have a part to play in achieving these goals.

Management of Interventions

Counselors who apply invitational counseling realize that their most effective role is one of managing interventions. As an example, imagine a school counselor has been counseling a middle school student about her school attendance. Frequently, the student has been leaving home but not coming to school. Eventually, the counselor and student may reach a point in their relationship where they want to set up specific strategies that encourage school attendance. Optimally, the counselor will include the student's parents, guardians, or adult caregivers who can take a role at home by encouraging their child to share what is going on at school. It also involves the classroom teacher who has an investment in seeing that the student succeeds. The counselor will examine aspects of the school and classroom (places, policies, programs, and processes) that might adversely affect this student's attendance, and design methods to remove these barriers. Classmates of the student might also be involved in group processes, to assure the student that they want her at school. This type of involvement can be extended to include the school's assistant principal who makes a point to greet the student every morning, the cafeteria staff who award a special treat at the end of a successful week of school attendance, and the physical education teacher who invites the student to be an equipment handler for the department. No invitation is too small, and no one person's involvement is too trivial, to ignore. All these strategies contribute in addressing concerns, resolving conflicts, creating healthy environments, and encouraging optimal development.

Mandates rarely result in productive relationships. Rather, counselors use their skills of negotiation and persuasion to win people's commitment. In some instances counselors find that written agreements help solidify the helping process. Usually these agreements are simple in form and content. The purpose is to have the client and others who may be participating sign their name and thereby document their commitment. Whatever the process used by the counselor to seek commitment and assign responsibilities, it is appropriate to continually ask for feedback: "Are you comfortable with this? Do you understand your responsibilities? What do you need to help us with this?" Once everyone has accepted his or her role to implement the strategy, the intervention commences.

Limitations

Although invitational counseling has the potential for wide application in various agencies, educational settings, and other institutions, it has two major limitations. First, invitational counseling is intended for populations that are functioning basically within the expected, normal range of behavior. Certainly, the assumptions and basic beliefs of invitational theory have merit for populations with unusual characteristics, but the process itself assumes that the person or persons involved are in touch with reality, are able to communicate, and have reasonable capability to change and control their behavior. Therefore, people who are hindered by psychosis, suffer from severe and constant depression with biological etiology, have extreme mental limitations, or have other abnormal conditions will need other appropriate interventions in conjunction with invitational counseling.

A second limitation of invitational counseling is that it is predicated on the belief that change in the human condition usually takes time. The self-concept is a stable characteristic that has taken a lifetime to form. Change requires time and effort. Crisis situations that call for immediate action and demand quick change to avoid tragedy may benefit from invitational counseling, but these situations require special interventions to address unique and sometimes life-threatening circumstances.

Brief therapy, as seen in the next chapter, is compatible with invitational counseling when a single or short-term goal is the focus. In these instances, counselors and clients can benefit from structured models that look for specific information, identify clear goals, implement reasonable strategies, and evaluate progress. Brief counseling relationships with specific aims allow counselors and clients to eventually look at the broader picture, encompassing people, places, policies, programs, and processes.

Limitations notwithstanding, each of the steps of the inviting process emphasizes the involvement of many people. This is because invitational counseling is an inclusive approach that values group processes. The communication skills required stress both individual and group proficiency. Some of these skills are presented in Chapter 6.

Summary

This chapter presented a three-stage sequence and explained how it can be integrated into a counseling relationship where the various parts become a seamless whole. The stages of invitational counseling are similar to other counseling models that contain introduction, exploration, and action phases.

Four choices of interacting, each with its opportunities and risks, were presented. These were sending, not sending, accepting, and not accepting. In addition to these four choices, the integrity of the individual (honoring the net) was stressed. Counselors who use the inviting process realize that there is an inviolable boundary that one should not cross without the permission of the person being helped.

Chapter 5 concluded with a series of steps that counselors may use to apply invitational counseling beyond individual relationships. Every concern clients have, every struggle they face, is connected to a larger social structure. The steps proposed by invitational counseling to expand the helping relationship include the assessment of influential factors, involvement of all parties, assignment of responsibilities, and implementation of strategies. Invitational counseling has limitations, and these were briefly discussed.

Opportunities for Further Reading

BENJAMIN, A. (1981). *The helping interview* (3rd ed.). Boston: Houghton Mifflin. In this book Benjamin described the helping interview as a conversation between two people, a conversation that is serious and purposeful. Whether the interviewee comes willingly or comes against his or her will, the ultimate question for the interviewer is always: "How can I best help this person?"

CARKHUFF, R. R. (1987). *The art of helping* (6th ed.). Amherst, MA: Human Resource Development Press. Carkhuff provided a practical guide for developing and improving listening and communication skills while encouraging human development. Carkhuff's presentation of empirically based helping skills is clear and succinct.

EGAN, G. (1994). *The skilled helper: A model for systematic helping and interpersonal relating* (5th ed.). Pacific Grove, CA: Brooks/Cole. This text stresses the importance of method, technique, and skill in professional counseling. It presents an expanded and clarified three-stage model of helping. Stage I explores and clarifies the problem situation. Stage II sets goals based on an understanding of the situation. Stage III designs ways to accomplish goals.

GAZDA, G. M., ASBURY, F. R., BALZER, F. J., CHILDERS, W. C., & WALTERS, R. P. (1991). *Human relations development: A manual for educators* (4th ed.). Boston: Allyn & Bacon. This fourth edition presents an overview of the helping process and the communication skills required to help others. It is a particularly useful training manual for both classroom teachers and counselors.

HACKNEY, H., & CORMIER, L. (1994). *Counseling strategies and interventions* (4th ed.). Boston: Allyn & Bacon. Hackney and Cormier have presented a clear explanation of counseling skills that are needed in invitational counseling. The authors point out that an effective counselor is one who has both personal qualities as well as professional skills.

IVEY, A. E. (1994). *Intentional interviewing and counseling: Facilitating client development in a multicultural society* (3rd ed.). Pacific Grove, CA: Brooks/Cole. Using the premise that intentionality is an essential characteristic in effective counseling, Ivey outlined several communication, observation, and other skills that enable counselors to become more intentional in their professional functioning.

PATTERSON, L. E., & EISENBERG, S. (1983). *The counseling process* (3rd ed.). Boston: Houghton Mifflin. In this third revision, Patterson and Eisenberg outlined basic tenets and skills inherent in the process of professional counseling.

PIETROFESA, J. J., HOFFMAN, A., & SPLETE, H. H. (1984). *Counseling: An introduction* (2nd ed.). Boston: Houghton Mifflin. This book provides a wonderful overview of the theory and practice of counseling. The authors focused on the counselor, the counseling process, and some basic issues embedded in professional functioning.

PURKEY, W. W., & NOVAK, J. M. (1995). *Inviting school success: A self-concept approach to teaching, learning, and democratic practice* (3rd ed.). Belmont, CA: Wadsworth. Purkey and Novak presented a perceptually based, self-concept approach to professional helping that focuses on inviting and disinviting signals that exist in schools and result in student success or failure.

CHAPTER SIX

Development
of Proficiency

ॐ

Marco Polo describes a bridge, stone by stone. "But which is the stone that supports the bridge?" Kublai Khan asks. "The bridge is not supported by one stone or another," Marco answers, "but by the line of the arch that they form." Kublai Khan remains silent, reflecting. Then he adds, "Why do you speak to me of the stones? It is only the arch that matters to me." Polo answers: "Without stones there is no arch."

I. Calvino

Invisible Cities

1972, p. 82

(translated by William Weaver, 1974)

ॐ

The levels of functioning, stages, and factors considered when applying invitational counseling provide the structure for addressing a wide range of developmental and remedial concerns. This structure is useful only when the counselor is equipped with sufficient skill to establish and maintain a professional helping relationship.

In preparing counselors to become proficient helpers, counselor educators have emphasized skill development and training (Cormier & Cormier, 1991; Ivey, 1994), yet research on the efficacy of many counseling skills has produced inconsistent results at best. What the research does suggest is that a genuine caring relationship is of primary importance in effective counseling (Sexton & Whiston, 1991). There is evidence that counselors who skillfully use interactive processes in empathic relationships, while demonstrating positive regard and focusing on the client's concerns, can be successful. Sexton and Whiston (1991) concluded: "The most crucial aspect of counseling

113

technique and intervention seems to be the skillfulness of the counselor implementing the intervention" (p. 343–344). Proficient use of invitational counseling requires counselors to be skilled and, at the same time, aware of research findings related to the efficacy of specific techniques.

The skills commonly used in invitational counseling are the same competencies expected in other models of counseling. When considering the array of skills that many approaches to professional counseling offer, some caveats about their use are warranted. Because invitational counseling is founded on the perceptual tradition, counselors who adhere strictly to a phenomenological philosophy may be uncomfortable with an emphasis on skills that appear to manipulate, control, and direct the helping relationship. For these counselors, the goal of counseling is to facilitate perceptual change through genuine acceptance, empathy, and unconditional regard for the person. At the same time, however, invitational counseling is an action-oriented approach. It provides a structure by which counselors and clients actively search for alternatives, solutions, and other possibilities for improving life. Thus, skills commonly used in most other approaches may also be useful in invitational counseling.

The usefulness of these skills is related to how appropriately the counselor applies them. Any skill has the potential to be either beneficial or lethal in the process of establishing relationships. The skills presented here are to be used openly, without threat or deception, for the client's best interest. In every instance, these skills are used to help clients examine their perceptions, and to make decisions about themselves and their relationships with others. Counselors who employ invitational counseling work to develop basic communication skills and use them appropriately.

Skill Development

It is easy to underestimate the level of skill required to be a professional counselor. The competencies called for are often perceived as common behaviors used in everyday communication. Counselors understand the complexity of these common behaviors, however, and appreciate the talent required in counseling relationships.

Effective Communication

Many authors have identified and described the skills used in effective relationships (Brammer, 1988; Carkhuff, 1987; Cormier & Cormier, 1991; Egan, 1994; Hackney & Cormier, 1994; Ivey, 1994). These skills are described briefly here. (For more detailed descriptions, the reader is encouraged to study the sources listed above and at the end of this chapter.)

Attending.   In the initial phases of the counseling relationship, as well as throughout the helping process, attending behaviors greatly facilitate client-counselor interactions. Attending behaviors include eye contact, vocal patterns, posture, and body movements. How well a counselor attends to what a client says often determines the degree of success their relationship will achieve. Although cultural differences should be considered when discussing attending skills, it is generally accepted in North American society that friendly eye contact, a warm and steady gaze, congruent voice patterns, forward-leaning posture, squaring shoulders with the client (forming an intimate "box"), and selected body movements are important ways of expressing interest in what a client is saying. Attending skills contribute to a counselor's ability to understand what clients are saying as well as what they are *not* saying. Seeking to understand what is happening, what is not happening, what is being felt, and what has ceased being felt, requires good attending skills.

As with many communication skills, attending sounds simple enough. Yet, most people in everyday conversations are distracted by visual stimuli, unexpected noise, their own thoughts, and countless other diversions. Attending consistently to what another person is saying takes concentration. Proficient counselors make a special effort to develop an attitude and habits that facilitate undivided attention to their clients. By attending with a high degree of consistency, counselors increase their ability to listen fully to what others are saying.

Listening.   One of the greatest gifts a person can give another is to yield interest and truly listen to what the other is communicating. The art of listening is influenced by a counselor's desire to understand the perceptual world of the client. Such understanding is validated by the client's affirmative or negative responses, either verbal or nonverbal, during the counseling session.

Listening skills are manifested by *paraphrasing* and *reflecting* client messages. Paraphrasing is the counselor's restatement of the essence of what a client said by using similar, but usually fewer, words and phrases. Paraphrasing demonstrates the counselor's reception of the content of client statements. It has at least three purposes: (1) to help crystallize the client's comments by bringing them into clearer focus, (2) to let the client know he or she is being heard, and (3) to check the accuracy of the counselor's perceptions. When paraphrasing is on target, the counselor is likely to see a lot of client head-nodding.

Reflecting, a skill closely related to paraphrasing, is a process that shows an understanding of the client's underlying *feelings*. The primary purpose of reflecting feelings is to help the client attain a clearer understanding of his or her emotions. At the same time, reflecting feelings can help counselors check their degree of accuracy in interpreting client statements. For example, if the counselor says, "I sense that you are very angry with your father," and the client responds, "Not really angry, more like annoyed," the reflecting skill and feedback from the client help to facilitate the counseling process.

The accuracy of paraphrasing and reflecting is usually measured by clients' acceptance and acknowledgment of counselor statements. For example, when counselors accurately express clients' feelings, by paraphrasing or reflecting, clients usually show appreciation in ways such as saying, "Yes, that's *exactly* how I feel!" In contrast, when counselors paraphrase or reflect client messages inaccurately, non-acceptance or nonrecognition usually results: "No, that's not it at all." Through paraphrasing and reflecting, the counselor can check the accuracy of his or her perceptions.

Counselors in training sometimes comment that the skills of paraphrasing and reflecting appear to be simple when they read about them. In practice, however, budding counselors soon develop an appreciation of the complexity of these skills. As Brammer (1988) and others have cautioned, inaccurate or inappropriate use of listening skills can destroy rather than facilitate counseling relationships. Their accurate and appropriate use will greatly assist in the clarification of clients' concerns.

Clarifying. In counseling sessions, clients often share a significant amount of information in a brief period of time. Because it is essential for the counselor to understand accurately what the client is conveying, skills that clarify information and disclose points of view are crucial.

Clarification means that at the initial session the counselor explains the nature of the helping relationship and the parameters of the counselor's role. For example, the counselor might express that he or she is not a problem solver, a detective, a cheerleader, or a soothsayer. The counselor's role is to serve as a valuable resource for the client to handle concerns, find solutions to problems, and enrich life. At this initial session, the counselor also provides a professional self-disclosure listing his or her training, counseling orientation, and if applicable, a fee schedule.

In counseling sessions, clarifying behaviors take many forms and often are used as paraphrasing and reflecting skills. Sometimes counselors' paraphrased and reflected statements are not accepted by clients. At these times counselors and clients need to work together to review information so that there is some agreement on the issues and concerns expressed. Clarification also calls upon a counselor's questioning skills. These skills can either be inquiries or statements that directly or indirectly seek additional information or elicit feelings from clients.

Questioning. Questions can either encourage or discourage the counseling relationship. When questions encourage the client to elaborate on a point, share opinions, and join the counselor in equal partnership within the helping relationship, they facilitate the process. If on the other hand questions are asked in rapid-fire format, limit responses from the client, or probe too deeply or too quickly, they may discourage and thwart the relationship.

Basically, there are two types of questions—open and closed—and both are useful in the counseling process. In addition to being either open or closed, questions are asked directly or indirectly. As a result, questions can be categorized in any of four ways: (1) a direct open question, (2) a direct closed question, (3) an indirect open question, or (4) an indirect closed question.

Open questions are nonjudgmental inquiries that invite clients to freely explain or expand upon a particular issue or point. These questions are useful in clarifying clients' perceptions, values, and situations. An example of a *direct* open question in marriage counseling is, "What leadership roles do you and your spouse assume in your marriage?" In contrast, a direct, but closed, question would be, "Who is the leader of this marriage?" An example of asking an open question *indirectly* is, "In most relationships, such as your marriage, partners assume different leadership roles. Describe your role." A closed *indirect* question on the same subject might be, "Do either of you tend to influence the marriage more than the other?" As seen in these examples, questioning does not always take a single form.

Closed questions are more limiting than open questions, but they too are useful in counseling. Generally these questions are used to seek specific information, bring the session back into focus, or regain direction in the relationship. For example, the question "What are some ways that you and your spouse enjoy leisure time together?" may redirect the focus of a session toward positive aspects of a relationship. Either closed or open questioning can facilitate the counseling process. Sometimes, however, it is necessary to probe at a deeper level.

Probing. As a counseling skill, probing is used in several ways. One involves asking repeated questions about the same issue for the purpose of "probing" for more information. Other times probing is more than gathering information; it is a quest for deeper meaning or feelings that have not yet surfaced in the helping relationship. Occasionally clients present information at a surface level, and counselors find it necessary to ask questions beneath that level of verbal interaction. When counselors search for information that lies beneath the level of current interaction, their questions tend to be open and aimed at subjective information a client appears reluctant to disclose. It may be that feelings are at a level of sensitivity that prevents the client from dealing with them, even privately. Yet these feelings are so powerful that they cannot be ignored if the client is to benefit from the counseling relationship. Encouraging clients to express deeper feelings can help them to bring ill-defined or suppressed emotions into focus. As noted in earlier chapters, when counselors who employ invitational counseling decide to probe into what a client is sharing, they are careful to respect the net.

An example of probing is illustrated by a session one of the authors had with a graduate student who was experiencing great difficulty relating to one of her professors. At one point in the session the counselor said, "I sense that feelings you have about your professor are very strong, even painful. Perhaps they are related to past experiences in your life with someone who was very close to you." The woman then began crying and self-disclosing many deep emotions about her relationship with her father. During this self-disclosure she became aware for the first time of how much the professor reminded her of her father, even his physical appearance.

By becoming aware of how perceptions of past experiences influence present functioning, and by bringing them into focus, clients are in a better position to make adjustments in their perceptions. Counselors who appropriately probe beneath the more superficial levels of verbal interaction can assist their clients in gaining insights and strengthening their abilities to make adjustments in their own lives. Probing, questioning, and other skills are connected to the structure of the overall counseling relationship.

Structuring. The decisions counselors make in choosing the types of questions or levels of interaction influence the direction of the counseling relationship. By analogy, the counselor does not try to drive the client's car or choose the client's destination, but he or she can provide road maps, arrange traffic signs, flash direction signals, and set the speed limit. This ability to "direct traffic" is demonstrated by the effectiveness with which counselors structure their sessions with clients.

Communication skills not only facilitate counseling relationships but also help to structure these relationships. Structuring skills are used by counselors to set the course of the relationship, identify goals for change, manage time requirements, and keep the counseling sessions on task. In addition to the proper use of communication skills, structure is accomplished through such factors as creating an inviting physical environment and establishing an agenda for each counseling session. By structuring, counselors set the tone of a helping relationship and influence its direction and speed. Proper structuring also involves summarization.

Summarizing. A skill that helps counselors maintain consistency in direction is summarizing. This skill is used to synthesize information, ideas, and feelings so that a common focus can be achieved and maintained by both the client and counselor. Summarizing can be done at any point in the counseling process: during the introductory phase, throughout the interactive process, as well as in the concluding stage.

In the beginning of a counseling session it is useful for counselors to summarize the interactions and decisions that occurred in previous meetings. Communicating this information helps the client understand where the counseling relationship begins and what direction the session will take. In addition, this summary is a clear message to the client that he or she has been heard and that what was shared was important enough for the counselor to remember. The counselor also summarizes at various points during a session to tie together statements of content and feeling to give the session a reasonably clear focus. At the conclusion of a session, summarizing is useful in highlighting what was addressed and decided. It is also useful for outlining what is to be done through homework assignments and in future counseling sessions.

Summarization depends on the counselor's attending, listening, and clarifying skills. Without these, a counselor's summaries of content, ideas, or feelings would be less than accurate. Accuracy is important in all communication, but it is essential in professional counseling, particularly when counselors interpret what clients are expressing verbally and nonverbally.

Interpreting. Beyond paraphrasing, reflecting, clarifying, and summarizing, a further communication skill is the ability to interpret statements, behaviors, and events to a client. Unlike earlier skills, which are designed to help counselors understand, accept, and reflect their clients' perceptual worlds, interpretation is a means of offering clients alternative ways of perceiving the events around them. As Ivey (1994) and others have noted, the skill of interpreting is closely related to a counselor's theoretical orientation. Counselors who employ invitational counseling base their interpretations on the assumptions of the perceptual tradition and self-concept theory.

Processes that explore alternative perspectives, consider new insights, and accept new meanings are facilitative in two ways. First, interpretation in counseling allows clients to explore, consider, and accept new possibilities in a secure, nonthreatening setting. As mentioned in Chapter 2, individuals tend to cling to their perceptions as a drowning person clings to a straw. It is no easy matter for people to let go of perceptions that have guided their behavior over the years. However, once a client understands that the present course of action is not the only course available ("What else can you do?" "What choices do you have?"), he or she can begin to look at other possibilities and opportunities.

Exploration helps clients to expand their own frames of reference, which in turn enables them to mobilize their self-directing powers. By considering different interpretations of events and imagining future activities, clients prepare themselves to explore and accept new alternative actions. Assisting the client in recognizing more appropriate and caring ways of perceiving and behaving is a fundamental goal of invitational counseling. Often this goal is achieved through the process of compromising.

Compromising. Sometimes even the most beneficial opportunities for growth are not accepted. When this happens, it is helpful to negotiate particulars so that other possibilities can be considered. For example, counselors sometimes use behavioral contracts to specify what behaviors clients will alter and what the result of changing those behaviors will be. In using behavioral contracts with clients, counselors sometimes find it necessary to renegotiate parts of original agreements that may have required too much change too soon. Counselors who negotiate effectively and compromise appropriately demonstrate respect for their clients.

Compromising calls upon the abilities, insights, and knowledge of *both* counselor and client. It requires a collaborative, cooperative posture by both parties and exemplifies the "being with" stance so essential to invitational counseling. On occasion, however, compromise is not achieved. If this situation persists, the counseling skill of gentle but firm confrontation may be in order.

Confronting. When a client's resistance to change contradicts the goals and objectives he or she has described to the counselor, it may be appropriate for the counselor to confront this discrepancy. Later in this chapter, confrontation will be considered as part of a larger process for managing conflict. Here, the discussion of confrontation will be limited to its use as a skill for moving the counseling relationship forward.

Clients often resist opportunities to make alternative interpretations of events, accept new perceptions, alter habitual behaviors, or make fresh decisions that will improve their lives. When this resistance continues and progress is not being made in the counseling relationship, the most appropriate and caring thing the counselor can do is to gently but firmly confront clients regarding the situation. A useful technique is to ask the client to replace his or her "I can't" statements with "I won't." For example, a client's statement that a choice "is impossible" might be reworded "It would be very difficult." This change in wording can help clients to reconsider the situation and recognize their own self-directing powers. Such confrontation, when done appropriately and caringly, communicates the inconsistencies between what clients are doing and what they say they are doing, or what clients say they want to happen and what they are willing to do to make it happen.

Confronting is also useful in pointing out inconsistencies between a client's verbal and nonverbal behavior. Such inconsistencies are illustrated by the client who says she is happy but whose eyes show that she is on the verge of tears, or the client who states he does not need anyone but whose hands reach out in an imploring manner. Similarly, trying to smile when one is unhappy often results in a lopsided smile, with one corner up and the other down. Confrontation is appropriate when a client's verbal and nonverbal behaviors communicate divergent messages. What clients express with their bodies is often more revealing than what they say with words. Some clients wear so much psychological body armor (clenched jaw, hunched shoulders, furrowed brow, crossed arms and legs, and other signals of stress) that it is possible to imagine them clanking as they enter the room. Confronting clients with their contradictory signals can help them face themselves fairly, and possibly resolve painful contradictions.

A further use of confrontation is when clients insist on negating themselves and their abilities. When a client continues to make negative self-statements, the counselor can simply ask for specific reasons for such negative self-verbalizations. One effective technique is to ask the client how he or she thinks other people react to these negative self-statements. This causes clients to reflect on the origins, logic, and impact of such self-debasing comments.

Finally, confrontation can be used to encourage clients to negotiate so that more acceptable avenues can be agreed on: "You don't want to practice this activity in assertive behavior? Okay, what activity are you willing to do that will help you improve?"

This process of confronting, compromising, seeking, and reaching agreement enables the counseling relationship to proceed toward a successful conclusion.

Group Leadership

While much of the work counselors perform is through individual counseling, group processes are recognized as an effective and efficient means of addressing concerns, solving problems, learning new skills, and acquiring new information (Gazda, 1989; Gladding, 1991). Group process is advantageous for several reasons. First, groups offer clients and counselors a social setting in which they can share concerns, support one another, and practice new behaviors in a safe, nonthreatening atmosphere. Second, clients in groups can learn about and share common perceptions held by other members. Clients can examine perceptions different from theirs and determine whether or not to alter their own views. A third advantage of group process is that counselors can rely on peer support to encourage clients to examine behaviors, select alternative goals, and plan new ways of obtaining their objectives in life.

Groups are also action-oriented. Unlike one-to-one relationships, which tend to be verbal in their content, group processes open up the possibility of using games, role-play, group exercises, and other methods to have clients experience and practice the changes they desire in their lives. These structures provide a more realistic setting for problem solving and decision making.

One additional advantage of group procedures is that they are an efficient use of a counselor's time. This advantage is particularly important in organizations where counselors serve large populations and are expected to provide a wide range of remedial, preventive, and developmental services. Organizations such as schools, colleges, industries, prisons, and churches benefit from the use of group processes. Counselors who use group methods need to be proficient in all of the communication skills mentioned earlier, because these skills transfer to group processes. In addition to these skills, counselors use leadership techniques that are particularly useful in groups. The following is a brief summary of these skills. For more extensive study of group leadership techniques and skills, please consult Capuzzi and Gross (1992), Gazda (1989), Gladding (1991) and other references.

Facilitating. Success in group work is particularly related to the leader's ability to bring the group together on common issues and goals, and move the group toward solutions and plans that will facilitate change. To accomplish these ends, a group leader uses behaviors and techniques that can generally be called facilitating skills. With these skills, leaders help group members find common ground and agree to reasonable, workable plans of action. Group leaders also encourage open communication while ensuring respect for individual members. Facilitative skills contribute to a group leader's ability to assist groups in identifying concerns, selecting alternative options, reaching a successful closure, and providing support.

Supporting. Counselors have limitless opportunities to provide support in their groups. Frequently, when groups first come together, individual members are reluctant to participate and share their feelings. By planning appropriate ice-breaking activities and modeling accepting behavior for the group, the counselor demonstrates supportive behaviors that elicit openness and participation. Support is shown in various ways. Verbal behaviors can be used to gently assure members that the group is a safe, confidential place to discuss concerns they might otherwise keep to themselves. Physical signals, such as eye contact or placing a hand on an individual's shoulder, are additional ways that counselors illustrate their concern and support.

Sometimes, a group counselor may need to support a member who is under fire from others in the group. Peer pressure can be useful in groups, but only when the counselor has clear control and uses supportive skills in a timely fashion. Too much support may tell the group member that it is all right to continue behaving in a nonproductive manner or that he or she is too weak to function without the counselor's defense. Too little support may be interpreted as the client's not being wanted in the group, or could result in a member being abused by others. In all cases, the support shown by a counselor should help the client feel a part of the group, and sense that he or she is protected from harm.

Protecting. Because counselors often use group process to delve into personal areas of people's lives, the protection of individual members is paramount. No member's gain should come at the expense of another member's loss. The counselor is obligated, professionally, ethically, and morally, to protect the integrity of each member of the group. In seeing that this protective climate is created, the counselor must impress on each member the importance of valuing everyone in the group, respecting differences in perception, and honoring confidentiality. In a successful group, this becomes a visible code that each member expresses through his or her behavior.

Comparing and Contrasting. An essential goal for group counselors is to bring the group together so that members bond with one another in what is called group cohesion. Two skills that help this process are comparing and contrasting. By comparing similarities among group members (also referred to as linking), counselors show that many of the concerns people have are based on common ground. For example, a counselor might say: "So Joe's problems with his boss are similar in a way to Mary's fights with her mother. They both relate to how Mary and Joe feel about the orders they are given."

The skill of comparing or linking common concerns also helps the counselor move group members from a concrete level of sharing basic information about themselves to a more abstract notion of universality, a central group mechanism identified by Yalom (1985). This process of universalization "counteracts the sense of isolation and uniqueness that people in conflict and suffering often feel" (Capuzzi & Gross, 1992, p. 95).

While pointing out similarities helps bring group members together, it is equally important to show the unique value of each person's perspective. For this reason, counselors also illustrate contrasting elements that allow group members to maintain their individuality. Returning to the example above, the counselor might also say: "While we see similarities between Joe and Mary's problems, there are also differences, because having disagreements with one's mother is not the same as being in conflict with one's boss." Taken together, comparing and contrasting can be powerful skills that enable groups to see similarities and differences and be accepting of other points of view.

Blocking. Sometimes, groups get off track or onto subjects that do not facilitate growth. When this happens, it is the counselor's responsibility to block nonproductive discussions and bring the group back on focus. This responsibility may sound contradictory to invitational counseling, but it is not. By blocking a nonproductive direction, the counselor encourages the group to move back to its purpose of identifying concerns, setting goals, and formulating plans of action. What is important when a counselor decides to block group discussion is that the purpose is made clear to the group and the blocking is done without harm to individual members: "What we are talking about sounds interesting, but I am not sure it relates to the concern that Bob has raised. Tell us again, Bob, what the concern is about." Abruptness, sarcasm, or behavior that belittles the point of discussion are obviously inappropriate and uncaring. The counselor simply needs to lead the group back to its goal.

Modeling. In all cases where group counselors use specific skills to move a group toward closure, it is essential that they model these behaviors themselves. By observing a group leader as he or she models appropriate behaviors, group members are able to incorporate these skills into their own repertoire, which moves them closer to sharing group leadership.

An example of modeling in action would be the counselor's calm understanding and acceptance of the client's fears and anxieties. The client's anxiety is balanced by the counselor's composure. In this way the client can model the counselor's confidence that together they will cope effectively. This may be the first step in the client's learning how to handle anxiety in appropriate ways.

Sharing Leadership.   The most proficient group counselors are ones who begin visibly leading the group in the early sessions and whose leadership as the group progresses becomes less discernible to the untrained eye. Successful groups are ones in which members realize the goal of helping one another. To do this they need to take some degree of leadership during the group process. Collaboration and cooperation are two characteristics of inviting processes, so it follows that these qualities would be encouraged in groups. They are also important characteristics found in instructional leadership, a group process recently being used by professional counselors, particularly in educational settings.

Instructional Leadership

All of the preceding group skills are also useful in instructional relationships such as classroom guidance activities, psychological education, parent education groups, and teacher in-service programs. These types of services are most often used by counselors in schools, colleges, and other educational institutions. However, contemporary counselors in nontraditional educational environments also use large-group leadership skills in programs such as personnel orientation in business and industry, wellness programs in health-care facilities, and many others. In addition to the skills listed above, counselors who present large-group instructional activities will find the following behaviors helpful.

Preparing.   Successful instructional programs demand adequate preparation of materials and time. Counselors who instruct large groups are successful when they choose their objectives carefully, plan appropriate activities, and schedule a reasonable time frame for the lesson. When counselors choose developmentally appropriate objectives, use stimulating materials and media, and begin and end the lesson in a time span that encourages optimal learning, their presentations are likely to be successful.

Presenting. Once a counselor has prepared an instructional activity, the next skill is to present it in a way that the group receives the information successfully. Specific skills used in making successful presentations include these (Schmidt, 1993):

1. Starting the presentation on time and using time efficiently.
2. Stating the purpose of the presentation clearly.
3. Giving clear instructions and directions.
4. Encouraging participation of all audience members.
5. Using appropriate group management skills.
6. Facilitating the session with listening, questioning, reflecting, clarifying, and summarizing skills.
7. Respecting the individuality of all group members.
8. Affirming and reinforcing members' willingness to contribute.
9. Providing effective feedback to the audience.
10. Using evaluative measures to assess the outcome of the presentation.

Soliciting feedback. To create relationships in which people accept information and attain skills, counselors seek ongoing feedback from participants. In this way, they encourage a free exchange of ideas about the information presented. When presenting to large audiences, professional counselors are open to views of the audience, which sometimes express conflicting opinions. Skilled counselors use these responses not to highlight the conflict but rather to establish a common ground where the group, with its diverse views, can come together. Other times, when no disparity of views exists, a counselor uses feedback to ensure that the audience is receiving the information as planned. In this way, the counselor is careful not to continue with the presentation without knowing that the audience is receiving the intended message.

Evaluating. Counselors who present to large audiences want to know whether the content of their presentation has been received and whether audience members are satisfied with their participation. To assess their presentations, counselors design evaluation methods, and by gathering information from their audiences, they are able to adjust their programs to meet the needs of future groups. Evaluation processes contribute to the research and measurement procedures counselors use to assess their overall effectiveness.

Research and Measurement

The focus of this book does not permit a full treatment of the many research and measurement skills that counselors employ to evaluate themselves, their clients, and their counseling relationships. Yet, it is important to emphasize that invitational counseling is far more than simply "good" feelings or "nice" interactions. It is a professional human service where research is an essential component. Consequently, research skills are as necessary in invitational counseling as they are for other approaches of human service.

The evaluation of effectiveness has been a difficult philosophical and methodological issue for the counseling profession. Regardless, demands by consumers as well as concerned professionals have made it imperative that counselors be concerned with the measurement of their professional performance. In meeting this need, counselors should become familiar with research, measurement, and accountability models such as those outlined by Pietrofesa, Hoffman, and Splete (1984), Fairchild (1986), Marzano, Pickering, and McTighe (1993) and others. More than a decade ago, Vacc and Bardon (1982) compiled and edited a range of articles pertaining to assessment and appraisal issues in counseling. In a special edition of the journal *Measurement and Evaluation in Guidance,* they presented a resource guide for program evaluation, test utilization, and other areas of evaluation.

Some counselors continue to resist research, measurement, and accountability processes because they are "too busy," "lack the time," or possibly are afraid of what the outcomes might show (Schmidt, 1993). While these reasons for not conducting research are understandable, they do not free counselors of the responsibility to demonstrate how they are spending time and whether or not their services are producing beneficial results. Practitioners of invitational counseling need to know: (1) What goals have been attained in this relationship? (2) What has changed in the client's life as a result of counseling? (3) How satisfied is the client with progress made in counseling? The proper use of research and measurement skills enables counselors and clients to determine their degree of success or failure in ameliorating concerns, mobilizing abilities, and improving human existence. These research and measurement skills include standardized assessment techniques, self-monitoring and self-reporting procedures, structured interviews, biofeedback analysis, and behavior-management methods.

Assessment and Measurement. As noted earlier in Chapter 5, assessment techniques, such as personality profiles, achievement tests, interest inventories, and attitude surveys, can provide data by which counselors and clients are able to determine whether any traits, attitudes, or interests have been influenced during the course of the counseling process. Self-report instruments, self-concept measures, and self-monitoring procedures—such as behavioral frequency counts—can also assess perceptual or behavioral changes. Survey information gathered by behavior rating scales or other questionnaires is useful in verifying behavioral changes identified as goals in the counseling process. Some assessment procedures can assist clients both in identifying behaviors to monitor and alter as well as in measuring how successful they are in reaching their behavioral goals. For example, some counselors use biofeedback—the process of self-monitoring one's physical condition such as heart rate and blood pressure—to help clients learn about their responses to problem situations.

Biofeedback assessment helps people monitor their physical responses to behavioral events. Behavioral management charts the occurrence of specific behaviors to determine increases and decreases in their frequency. A client who wishes to lose weight might set a goal to eat only three meals a day and allow a predetermined maximum number of calories at each meal. By charting calorie intake at mealtimes and keeping a daily weight chart, the client can evaluate progress in managing eating behaviors.

In counseling, clients and counselors usually set specific goals to achieve within a designated time frame. Effective counselors help their clients determine specific goals to reach as an integral part of the helping relationship. Measuring the degree to which the outcomes of the counseling relationship are obtained is important. In schools, for example, counselors should be able to document how their services have benefited students as well as the quality of school life.

Counselors design different ways to assess the outcomes of counseling depending on the circumstances. Some common methods are self-reports by clients, observations reported by others (such as teachers, parents, spouses), behavioral rating forms, and physical changes such as weight loss, blood pressure changes, and general wellness. In choosing outcome measures, counselors are careful to include clients in the decision. Together they select processes and instruments that are reliable and valid.

Follow-up Research.   Invitational counselors also depend on follow-up activities to research their efficacy as professional helpers. By maintaining contact with clients beyond the attainment of specific goals, counselors are able to establish long-term helping relationships as well as to collect valuable data on outcomes. Successful remedy of concerns does not automatically signal the end of a counselor-client relationship. Invitational counseling encourages follow-up activities in which counselors evaluate their own effectiveness and seek to help clients recognize opportunities, mobilize strengths, and explore new goals that will move them to higher levels of personal and professional functioning.

The preceding research, assessment, and measurement skills are used by counselors who embrace a wide range of approaches in their helping relationships. When combined with the stages, choices, and steps outlined in Chapter 5, these skills can assist both counselors and clients in examining their level of personal and professional functioning. Sometimes, the issues raised by clients with their counselors can be resolved in a brief period of time. In these instances, invitational counseling, like other approaches to counseling, takes the form of brief therapy.

Brief Therapy

Professional counseling is both an educational and therapeutic process. In invitational counseling, this process attempts to help the client identify areas of life that tend to detract from his or her development and satisfaction or areas that could be enriched to improve situations and relationships. In most cases, brief therapy endeavors to focus on one developmental issue or to remedy one existing concern over a relatively brief period of time, or in a few sessions. This philosophy corresponds to recent developments in the counseling profession that encourage an "orientation that is only minimally concerned with how problems arose or even how they are maintained" (Huber & Backlund, 1992). In general, brief counseling is more interested in how people can enhance immediate situations and resolve pressing difficulties.

Brief therapy is advocated in contemporary counseling literature (Amatea, 1989; Lopez, 1985; O'Hanlon & Weiner-Davis, 1989), and is particularly valuable in institutions that rely on educational processes. For this reason, invitational counseling is a suitable approach to use when limited sessions are necessary for helping a client make a decision or alter a behavior. An adaptation of Lopez's (1985) four-step model of brief therapy is one example of how invitational counseling could be applied.

Ask the client to describe in concrete terms what he or she wants to change. In this step the counselor explores with the client those "disinviting" aspects that may be hampering development. At this stage the Five P's may be helpful, and the client is asked to narrow down his or her most critical concerns.

Examine what the client has done thus far. Most people know when they have a concern or when they are facing a barrier and they make attempts to resolve these dilemmas. Sometimes they try positive approaches without success, but other times they resort to negative behaviors. In this step, the counselor helps clients look at all these attempts to see whether any have further use and might be altered to be more successful.

Clearly identify a goal. As noted throughout this text, counseling must be intentional if it is to be successful. Therefore, the counselor and client need to identify clear and measurable goals that will indicate their success in the helping relationship.

Develop and implement strategies. Since invitational counseling is founded on the premise that people are encouraged or discouraged by the messages they send and receive, it is essential that the counselor and client create positive, beneficial strategies aimed at reaching the identified goal. One way to begin is by assessing the Five P's and addressing areas of concern with initial, low-risk strategies.

With an uncomplicated structure like this four-step approach, counselors take a pragmatic course and encourage short-term relationships with their clients. The brief nature of the therapy serves several purposes. First, it demonstrates to clients that they are not "sick" or "disturbed." They are healthy people who with minimal support and encouragement can resolve their own concerns. Second, brief therapy is an efficient use of the counselor's time because it seeks expeditious results. In such relationships, counselors are more accountable to their clients and the institutions that employ them. Finally, short-term approaches to counseling encourage independence and foster self-responsibility and self-reliance.

Because invitational counseling relies on the perceptual tradition, the same caveats given earlier about using counseling skills apply to brief therapy. As with counseling skills, brief therapy is always practiced with the best interest of the client in mind. Efficiency is a wonderful virtue, but not if it compromises the integrity of the helping relationship by manipulating, controlling, directing, and accelerating it to extremes under the guise of facilitating a client's development.

At times, of course, clients require extended periods of time with a counselor. Counselors and clients may see the need for long-term relationships, especially when dealing with several interrelated issues. The principles of invitational counseling remain beneficial in these instances, particularly when the helping relationship involves normally functioning, healthy individuals who have reached crossroads in their lives, have come up against barriers that are thwarting their development, or feel the need to enrich their existence in specific ways.

This chapter has emphasized specific skills that counselors use in individual and group counseling and instructional leadership. For counselors who have responsibility for addressing concerns of large populations, such as in schools, colleges, and industries, special skills are helpful in enriching the overall atmosphere of the organization and the general functioning of people being served or working there. One area in which counselors have become more and more involved in recent years and that requires special skill is in helping individuals and groups manage conflict.

Conflict Management

Conflict, or the potential for conflict, exists in every corner of life and within every organization and institution in which people learn, work, and live. This can be advantageous, for without some degree of conflict life would be repetitious, monotonous, and stagnant. Conflict can be beneficial when it helps people address important issues, increases involvement, improves problem-solving capabilities, encourages creativity, strengthens relationships, and increases productivity. When conflict gets out of hand it encourages the opposite of these benefits; it becomes a destructive force that debilitates and damages people.

In keeping with its theoretical foundations, invitational counseling offers a five-step approach to conflict management in which conflicts are resolved at the lowest possible level and with the least amount of energy (Purkey, 1992b). Vital to invitational counseling is that conflict be managed in the most respectful and humane manner possible. To accomplish this, counselors can practice the process themselves and share it with their clients. The process is called the Five C's: concern, confer, consult, confront, and combat. The process begins with the lowest C, concern, and moves upward only as necessary.

Concern

The first level of intervention for individuals who face frustration, annoyance, and perhaps conflict is to determine whether the situation is truly a matter of concern. Limitless situations face those who live and work in homes, schools, mental health clinics, hospitals, prisons, and other settings. Many situations involve real or imagined conflicts. Addressing all these challenges and conflicts equally is impossible. Therefore, the initial step in managing any troublesome situation is to assess its importance. To do so, those experiencing conflict ask themselves some essential questions.

First, can this concern be safely overlooked without resulting in undue stress for oneself or others? Many situations and events that cause concern have little impact on overall performance and satisfaction in life. For example, many marriage partners can identify with the sudden and amazingly furious battle that will spring up over the most insignificant action, such as leaving the tie off the bread wrapper, slurping coffee at the breakfast table, or forgetting to empty the trash. Yet, these episodes can be annoying to the point where people become consumed by them. At these times, counselors do well to ask themselves or their clients: "Would it be wise to pay less attention to this situation? What would be the risk if you ignored it altogether? Can it be reconceptualized into something less bothersome? Is this really worth worrying about?" Following this logic, the counselor might pose the question whether this conflict might resolve itself without any intervention. At no time, however, should the counselor minimize concerns or trivialize feelings.

A related question is whether this is the proper time to be concerned about a bothersome situation. Timing is an important element in dealing with conflict. Sometimes people mishandle events not because they pay too much attention to them, but because their actions are poorly timed. An example is the client who complained that whenever he raised a particular concern with his wife about their relationship, she became upset and stormed out of the room. In examining this with the client, the counselor noted that he always brought up this concern soon after his wife arrived home from work without giving her time to relax and cool down from a hectic day at the office. Together the client and counselor explored opportunities for discussing this concern at times when his spouse might be more receptive. By searching for a better time, the client was able to avoid conflict with his wife that was unrelated to his primary desire—finding ways to enrich their marriage.

Another question to ask in the initial, concern phase of conflict management is whether or not sufficient resources and information are available to successfully address and resolve the situation. Frequently, when the client attempts to find solutions, he or she discovers that necessary resources, financial support, and adequate information are simply not available. If resources, support, and information are lacking, the counselor may need to assist the client in adjusting to the present situation or focusing on ways to rectify these deficits before addressing the initial concern.

Sometimes conflicts are the result of unrecognized prejudices and biases. Identifying and confronting these feelings is a first step in resolving these apparent conflicts. For example, a client may express great hostility toward a particular group of people. An analysis of the content of prejudices, coupled with an exploration of where these prejudices came from, might point the way to overcome them and move beyond them.

Related to prejudices and biases are matters of ethics, morality, and legality that counselors and their clients may mishandle, thereby raising the potential for conflict. These matters should be fully explored to identify the actual concern and ensure that intolerance or other negative factors are not the problem. This first step is also essential for counselors to examine their own biases and prejudices. To the degree that the counselor can set aside his or her own biases, prejudices, and intolerance, he or she can practice invitational counseling.

By handling conflict at this lowest, concern level, counselors and their clients will find that a majority of difficult situations can be resolved expeditiously. Sometimes, however, problems become sufficiently troublesome that they require some action to be taken. At these times, the Five C's approach suggests a second step: conferring.

Confer

To confer is to initiate an informal and private conversation with another person. It begins by signaling the desire for a positive interaction (smiling, using the person's preferred name, making eye contact, shaking hands, and so on). Then the person briefly explains, in a nonthreatening way, the nature of the concern. For example, if a client conveys to the counselor that a particular conflict with a family member is an important concern, but attempts to resolve it indirectly have been unsuccessful, the counselor may encourage the client to confer directly with this family member.

Many of the counseling skills used by professional counselors help them model conflict management for their clients. Counselors who apply invitational counseling use informal exchanges with their clients to strengthen positive interactions. By demonstrating respect for the client and helping to identify the concern, the counselor models the process of conferring. The process of conferring includes these elements: (1) ameliorating the concern through informal, private, one-to-one discussions; (2) establishing that each person has a clear understanding of the nature of the concern; (3) determining whether or not both parties know *why* this situation is a concern; (4) agreeing on *what* both parties want to happen for the concern to be resolved; and (5) determining where there is room for compromise.

For a surprisingly large number of real and imagined concerns, the issue can be successfully handled at a nonthreatening, conversational level. This is accomplished by the client's simply requesting what he or she wants. Because some clients have difficulty asking for what they want, they can be assisted by assertiveness training (Alberti & Emmons, 1978). Should the issue or concern persist, the next step is to consult.

Consult

Consultation is a more formal, structured interaction than conferring. For example, when counselors schedule a consultation, they plan an agenda (sometimes in writing) of items that need to be covered. While more formal than conferring, consultation still requires respect for all parties involved. Consultation uses the five goals listed above in a more formal process that includes (1) an introduction phase of identifying the concern, (2) an exploration phase of seeking alternative ways of handling the conflict, (3) an action plan in which the participants accept responsibilities, and (4) an evaluation phase during which the parties contact one another and express their satisfaction or discontent with progress being made to resolve the situation.

Consultation is an important aspect of the work of most professional counselors (Brown, Pryzwansky, & Schulte, 1991; Hansen, Himes, & Meier, 1990). It is a process that is used for dispensing information, providing instruction, and problem solving (Schmidt, 1993). The last of these purposes, problem solving, is the one closest to conflict resolution, and therefore the one most helpful at this point.

In problem-solving consultations, the relationship is triangular: there is a consultant, a consultee, and a problem situation. In using this model to resolve conflict, the person who initiates the consultation takes the role of consultant and the other person in the conflict becomes the consultee. The conflict situation is the third angle of the triangle and represents the situation contributing to the disagreement. At times, the conflict situation may involve other people (friends, relatives, coworkers, and so on). Figure 6-1 illustrates this type of consultation. In the consultation, the consultant works to reach agreement with the consultee on an action plan that will be implemented to resolve the conflict situation. For problem-solving con-

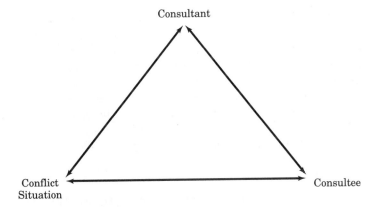

FIGURE 6-1   Problem-Solving Consultation

sultations to be successful, all parties, including others who have a vested interest in the conflict situation, must know what is expected of them and they need to know what consequences might result if the conflict continues.

Sometimes, when action plans are formed and participants understand and accept their responsibilities, they fail to follow through. When this happens and the conflict remains unresolved, it is time to confront this deadlock.

Confront

Confrontation may seem like an incongruous term in invitational counseling. In practice, however, sometimes the most inviting thing an individual can do is to confront gently, yet firmly. In resolving conflict, anyone may choose to confront as a way of moving a relationship in a positive direction. A counselor might confront a client about his or her failure to follow through on an agreement. A client might confront a family member about financial concerns. Again, confrontation is used only with genuine respect and regard for the person or persons involved, and only after concern, confer, and consult steps have been unsuccessful in resolving the issue. At these times, a counselor may ask the client: "You agreed to your part of the plan and you did not do it. How can I help you keep your agreement?" Or, a client may say to a relative: "You told me you were going to help with the rent, but you haven't. Please write a check to cover your share."

During confrontation it is imperative to stay focused on each person's responsibilities and not on what other people have done that prevented follow-through on an agreement. Self-responsibility is the key; blame and excuses are counterproductive. Here the goal is to renegotiate another plan for action (or the same one if it still has potential of success), and try again to resolve the conflict.

Even though invitational counseling takes an optimistic posture in managing and resolving conflicts, there are times when confrontation is insufficient. In spite of sincere efforts, the conflict continues. Now it is time to consider the fifth step: combat. Before moving to this high level of conflict resolution, the individuals involved should ask themselves:

1. "Have I been sincere in all my efforts to resolve this conflict at the lowest level possible so that everyone benefits?"
2. "Do I have clear evidence that demonstrates my earlier efforts?"
3. "Do I have sufficient authority and desire to follow through on consequences?"
4. "Is the concern of such magnitude that it requires this final step?"

If all answers to these questions are affirmative, the individual might now reluctantly move toward combat.

Combat

At this high level of conflict management, the word *combat* is used as a verb rather than a noun. The goal is to combat the situation, not an individual or a group of people. Using the word *combat* to describe this highest step stresses the seriousness of the concern. Combat appears when all other steps have failed to resolve the conflict. This level now moves to logical consequences.

Logical consequences are meaningfully connected to the original concern. For example, when a child leaves toys laying about the house, a logical consequence, by agreement in the family, is that after a period of time a parent or adult caregiver picks up the toys and places them in a 24-hour holding closet. The logic is that if the child does not want to lose access to the toys for a 24-hour period, he or she will be responsible for them. In this way, continuous conflict about toys being left around the house is avoided.

The combat level is one of high stakes. Counselors and their clients should work to avoid this final step because it requires a great deal of energy that might be better spent in finding productive ways to enhance and enrich people's lives. All too often, when people face conflict they move immediately to the combat stage, thinking that brute force will be expeditious. In the larger scheme of things, however, when people seek solutions through combat they elicit resentment and bitterness that fuel future discord. The use of force is seldom proportionate to what it accomplishes. By handling conflict at the lowest possible level, counselors and their clients "save energy, reduce hostility, and avoid acrimony" (Purkey, 1992b, p. 116).

What Counselors Can Do

Counselors who apply the Five C's successfully do so only when the basic assumptions and elements of invitational counseling are part of the process. These include the tenets of optimism, trust, respect, and intentionality. In applying the Five C's, counselors might consider the following ten guidelines for conflict management.

1. *Welcome the existence of conflict.* Not all conflict is bad for individuals or organizations. It is sometimes helpful and healthful for conflict to occur because it presents an opportunity for learning, growth, and creativity. Counselors who constantly take the position that *all* conflict is to be avoided may be inhibiting their clients' development and hindering organizations.
2. *Show a sense of humor.* Because conflicts are often challenging and stressful, a view of the lighter side can sometimes ease the strain and give people a breather. Appropriate humor, when well timed, can be the catalyst that moves a situation toward resolution of the problem.
3. *Clarify the nature of the conflict.* Too often conflicts persist and expand because people are unable to agree on the nature of the concern. Counselors have the responsibility of helping people in conflict clarify the issues so that there is minimal chance of misunderstanding.
4. *Listen with understanding.* As with all counseling relationships, conflict resolution requires a high degree of empathic understanding. It is not enough to hear what another person is saying; it is vital to understand how the other person sees the problem, and accept those perceptions.
5. *Suggest procedures and ground rules.* Since much of the conflict management done by counselors is performed in

group settings, it is important that counselors outline group procedures and set ground rules to help the group conduct itself in a helpful manner. These procedures and ground rules help to create an atmosphere of respect and tolerance among group members.

6. *Accept feelings of self and others.* Emotions sometimes run high in conflict situations. Although counselors want to maintain some control of the emotional atmosphere, they also want to genuinely accept the feelings conveyed in conflict situations.

7. *Keep an open posture.* One aspect of optimism that is helpful during conflicts is the ability to remain open and fair throughout the proceedings. Counselors and clients who deal effectively with conflict work to keep an open mind and listen fully to the ideas suggested by others.

8. *Open channels of communication.* When counselors maintain an open posture, they invite communication. Equally important, they value the participation of everyone affected by the conflict. In schools for example, this could mean including students in conferences with parents and teachers.

9. *Propose experimental solutions.* In all conferences and consultations, regardless of the setting, every participant brings an area and level of expertise. One area of expertise that the counselor brings is the knowledge of solutions that have been successful in previous and similar conflict situations. Clients, too, bring a lifetime of experience that may offer solutions. Proposing these ideas as experimental solutions is part of the problem-solving process. These ideas are offered as suggestions, not mandates.

10. *Seek feedback.* Throughout relationships that attempt to manage conflict, counselors seek information on how things appear from the client's point of view: "How do you feel about our sessions?" "Are there other ways you are willing to try?" These and other comments provide valuable feedback from clients.

The skills and procedures presented in this chapter offer a limited menu of the many techniques and strategies used by professional counselors to manage conflict. All of these are common to most approaches to counseling. They become invitational counseling when they are combined with an awareness, understanding, application, and adoption of invitational theory.

In Search of Proficiency

Take seriously your responsibility as a listener. . . . To listen
intently, to listen consciously, to listen with one's whole intelligence is the least we can do in the furtherance of an art that is
one of the glories of mankind.

Aaron Copeland
What to Listen for in Music
1939, p. 163

ཟ

Because invitational counseling is an expanded model for professional
helping, it seeks to move beyond one-on-one or small-group counseling
to address the totality of environments in which humans live and
work. One way to address this larger goal is through use of the Invitational Helix (Purkey & Novak, 1993). The helix follows the
pioneering work of Stillion and Siegel (1985), who first suggested that
a hierarchy exists within invitational theory. This hierarchy consists
of a twelve-step, three-level model beginning with an introductory
level, moving to an intermediate level, and ending at an advanced
level of functioning. The helix has a twofold value: (1) it allows counselors to quickly identify the level and stage of invitational functioning
for any individual or organization, and (2) it serves as a dependable
guide for individuals and organizations who seek to incorporate and
advance invitational functioning in their settings. Figure 6-2 illustrates the helix.

Introductory Level

The first level of the helix consists of four steps that reflect initial
exposure to invitational theory and offer counselors practical ideas for
implementing basic invitational strategies. What distinguishes these
efforts as introductory level is that they are usually unrelated to one
another and are usually easy to implement. Counselors who function
at this beginning level perform helpful deeds, practice basic attending
skills, are nice to people, create pleasant physical environments, plan
celebrations, call people by name, and generally do things that establish a supportive atmosphere.

While beneficial, these efforts will not by themselves result in
substantive change in people's lives or significantly indicate the

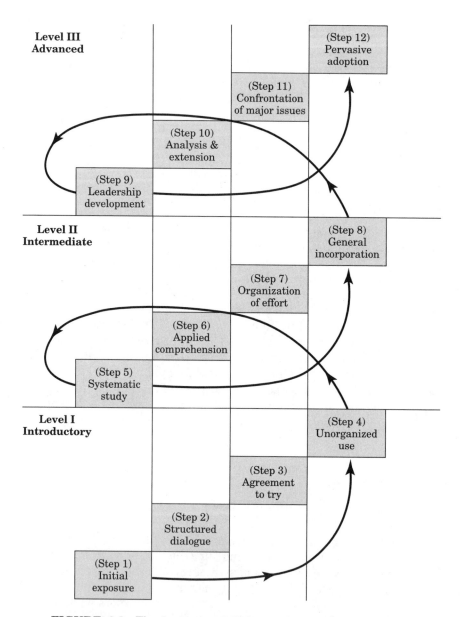

FIGURE 6-2 The Invitational Helix: A Systematic Guide for Individual and Organizational Development (© International Alliance for Invitational Education. Used with permission. Purkey, W. W., & Novak, J. M., 1993. The Invitational Helix: A systematic guide for individual and organizational development. *Journal of Invitational Theory and Practice, 2*(2), 59–67.)

presence of invitational counseling. They are, however, a good starting point in that they pave the way for more essential changes to occur. As seen in Figure 6-2, initial exposure is the beginning of the introductory level.

Step 1: Initial exposure. Most counselors are constantly searching for approaches that may help them better assist their clients. At this first step, a counselor may simply become aware of invitational counseling through reading an article or book (such as this one), viewing a videotape, or attending a conference or seminar. This awareness is expanded and elevated when counselors use this initial exposure to seek more information about invitational theory and its application in counseling.

Step 2: Structured dialogue. Counselors who move to this second step become involved in some type of structured interaction or dialogue. This dialogue might be in the form of a workshop, retreat, or other organized study. Here, counselors learn the basic assumptions and principles of invitational theory and are encouraged to recognize and appreciate inviting practices already in place. This appreciation leads to an agreement to try some invitational strategies.

Step 3: Agreement to try. Now counselors have an opportunity to try out some inviting ways in their work. They agree to apply some suggestions for creating more inviting forces. Through replication or simple modifications, counselors practice their ideas with minimal risk to themselves or others. Sending follow-up notes to clients, rearranging the furniture in their office, rescheduling meetings at times more convenient for clients, and answering the phone more politely are examples of these efforts. At Step 3, these efforts are unorganized and uncoordinated, and continue to be so in the next step.

Step 4: Unorganized use. In this fourth step of the introductory level, counselors accept suggestions, create their own efforts, and adopt these into their daily practice. Although unorganized and uncoordinated, these efforts usually have a beneficial impact on people and institutions. Counselors who have an interest in invitational counseling begin at the introductory level and usually experience initial success. By experiencing this success and sharing it with others, these counselors prepare themselves to move to the intermediate level of invitational counseling.

Intermediate Level

The second level of invitational counseling is characterized by more intense study, sophisticated application, assessment of the Five P's, and formal incorporation of invitational practices into one's personal and professional life. Steps 5 through 8 of the helix describe this intermediate level.

Step 5: Systematic study. After counselors have been introduced to invitational theory, their knowledge is strengthened by serious study and participation in learning activities. These activities include systematic study under the direction of an experienced and knowledgeable practitioner, participation in workshops and conferences, and involvement in the development of invitational theory through associations such as the International Alliance for Invitational Education (IAIE), the Invitational Education Special Interest Group of the American Educational Research Association (AERA), or the Invitational Counseling Professional Interest Group of the American School Counselor Association. (See Appendix A.)

Step 6: Applied comprehension. As counselors become knowledgeable about invitational theory, they seek an association with other professionals who share their interest in invitational counseling. At this step of the helix, counselors who adopt this approach are able to give an in-depth explanation of invitational counseling and answer questions about its application in their personal and professional functioning.

Step 7: Organization of effort. Step 7 is characterized by counselors having a clear understanding of invitational counseling coupled with the ability to apply it in their professional practice. This ability includes the competence for leading organizations through an examination of present practices toward a clarification of future goals. As explained in Chapter 5, one strategy to use toward this end is an assessment of the five factors: people, places, policies, programs, and processes. Counselors who reach this step of the helix are able to facilitate the Five P's assessment process in helping organizations, such as schools, hospitals, businesses, and others, apply invitational theory to practical concerns.

Step 8: General incorporation. The examination of present practices and clarification of future goals is now incorporated into a larger plan for organizational development. Counselors who employ invitational counseling understand that at this level of practice the concepts and strategies have power and impact that move beyond individual helping relationships. That is not to devalue individual counseling; rather, it is a recognition of the extended benefits available to the population at large when invitational practices are adopted by a majority of the people who make up an organization or association. Counselors who accept this role are in the vanguard, scheduling assessment meetings, seeking feedback about strategies attempted, and making special efforts to help others learn about the process.

Advanced Level

Counselors who have taken leadership roles in their institutions and have been instrumental in helping others learn and employ invitational concepts have reached the advanced level of practice. Their goal at this level is to have invitational theory pervade the attitudes of individuals and the cultures of organizations. As one can imagine, achieving this goal takes sustained effort. At this level, counselors practice at the highest point of professional performance, ethically, intellectually, and artfully. They continue to lead organizations, conduct and review research about invitational theory, extend these findings in more research, confront major issues and contradictions, and advocate invitational practices in all aspects of society, even beyond their professional arena.

> *Step 9: Leadership development.* At this advanced level, counselors take leadership roles in conducting workshops, keynoting conferences, and advancing the development of invitational theory. In the process, these counselors continue to learn new concepts and hone their own professional skills.
>
> *Step 10: Analysis and extension.* At this step, leaders in invitational counseling critically analyze invitational theory, particularly new and emerging concepts. This analysis also includes critical comparisons and contrasts with other counseling theories and approaches. While many similarities may be found with existing models of counseling, it is equally important for leaders in invitational counseling to understand and describe the uniqueness, complexity, and value of their approach to helping.
>
> *Step 11: Confrontation of major issues.* Today's counselors work in a variety of settings and help clients with a wide range of concerns. Some of the challenges facing people and organizations require major rethinking, restructuring, and reconceptual-

izing of relationships, programs, and institutionalpractices. Invitational counseling offers a philosophy and structure by which people within organizations can become empowered to initiate positive change. At the same time, invitational theory can be used to consider larger, more complex issues, such as racism, sexism, and homophobia. These principles can be used to encourage an appreciation of cultural contributions and the nature of democratic values. They can also be used to cultivate human decency by helping organizations respect the individual abilities, worth, and responsibilities of all people.

Step 12: Pervasive adoption. This final step of the helix brings together all the others in an orchestrated effort to employ invitational theory in all aspects of life. Counselors who reach this level are reflective in their professional practice and maintain high regard for themselves and others. They consistently examine the appearance of environments, evaluate the benefits of programs, assess the appropriateness of policies, and scrutinize the application of processes in their own work and that of their organizations. They understand the deeper significance of the four basic assumptions of invitational counseling, introduced in Chapter 1 and repeated here: (1) people are able, valuable, and responsible, and should be treated accordingly; (2) helping is a cooperative, collaborative alliance in which process is as important as product; (3) people possess relatively untapped potential in all areas of human development; and (4) this potential is best realized when people design places, policies, processes, and programs that intentionally invite themselves and others, both personally and professionally, to the celebration of life.

Summary

Incorporated into invitational counseling are many of the counseling skills found in most, if not all, professional helping relationships. As with other counseling models, invitational counseling involves the use of skills thought to be proficient in establishing helping relationships. The skills that are most important are those that convey empathy, warmth, and positive regard toward the client (Sexton & Whiston, 1991). These include attending, listening, reflecting, and clarifying, among others. Invitational counseling encourages the use of these and other facilitative skills that help clients set goals, explore concerns, and take action in their lives. These skills include questioning, structuring, and confronting. In addition, this chapter explored the importance of group leadership and evaluation processes.

Chapter 6 also presented an invitational approach to conflict management. Invitational counseling recognizes that in all human relationships there is potential for conflict. Some conflict is beneficial—when it encourages self-examination, strengthens relationships, and enhances learning.

Finally, this chapter offered a systemic guide, the Invitational Helix, for counselors and others to follow in appraising their own and others' understanding and application of invitational theory. The helix provides 12 steps to assess levels of knowledge, understanding and practice of invitational counseling. The next chapter presents an expanded view of professional helping and shows how invitational counseling fits this broad perspective.

Opportunities for Further Reading

DERLEGA, V. J., & CHAIKIN, A. L. (1975). *Sharing intimacy: What we reveal to others and why.* Englewood Cliffs, NJ: Prentice-Hall. Derlega and Chaikin offered an insightful description of the process by which people allow themselves to be known by others. Of particular value is the way the authors emphasized appropriateness and demonstrated that nondisclosure of one's self, or too much disclosure too soon, are related to symptoms of mental disorder.

GAZDA, G. M., ASBURY, F. R., BALZER, F. J., CHILDERS, W. C., & WALTERS, R. P. (1991). *Human relations development: A manual for educators* (4th ed.). Boston: Allyn & Bacon. This text provides an overview of the helping process and a description of the communication skills needed to help others effectively. It is a useful manual for classroom teachers and counselors. Training exercises are included.

JUNG, C. G. (1974). *The undiscovered self.* New York: Mentor Books. In this classic book, Jung explained the predicament of the human being in an uncertain and restless world. He offered a solution to pressures through understanding the inner self.

KELLEY, H. H. (1979). *Personal relationships: Their structures and processes.* Hillsdale, NJ: Erlbaum. Kelley demonstrated that the outcomes (benefits and costs) that participants in a relationship experience depend on the joint activities they undertake. Moreover, Kelley emphasized responsiveness, which is the degree to which people take into account, in making choices, the consequences of those choices for their partners.

LEHR, J. B., & MARTIN, C. (1992). *We're all at risk: Inviting learning for everyone.* Minneapolis, MN: Educational Media. Lehr and Martin provided a manual of activities for educators and helping professionals that fits beautifully with the introductory level of the helix presented in this chapter.

MAYEROFF, M. (1971). *On caring*. New York: Harper & Row. This brief book deals with two interlocking themes: a generalized description of caring, and an account of how caring can give comprehensive meaning and order to one's life.

NODDINGS, N. (1984). *Caring: A feminine approach to ethics and moral education*. Berkeley: University of California Press.

NODDINGS, N. (1992). *The challenge to care in schools: An alternative approach to education*. New York: Teachers College Press. Both of these books by Nodding offer the reader a unique view of how schools can create empathic environments in which all students can learn.

PURKEY, W. W., & NOVAK, J. M. (1988). *Education: By invitation only*. Bloomington, IN: Phi Delta Kappa Educational Foundation. Purkey and Novak asked the reader to imagine a school that intentionally invites everyone to realize their relatively untapped potential. They then described a visit to this imaginary school.

PURKEY, W. W., & STANLEY, P. H. (1994). *The inviting school treasury: 1001 ways to invite student success*. New York: Scholastic Press. A practical guide for creating myriad invitational processes in a school setting, this book offers suggestions that are easily adapted to a variety of professional arenas.

CHAPTER SEVEN

Integrating Approaches to Counseling

֍

Those writing about invitational theory often speak of taking an inviting stance. This term seems well chosen, for it is the stance that serves to bring together parts and pieces of the total gestalt of the counseling process.

William B. Stafford
"Invitational Theory and Counseling"
Advancing Invitational Thinking
1992, p. 216

֍

Carl Rogers (1980) explained that people "do not like to live in a compartmentalized world—body and mind, health and illness, intellect and feeling, science and common sense, individual and group, sane and insane, work and play. They strive rather for a wholeness of life, with thought, feeling, physical energy, psychic energy, healing energy, all being integrated in experience" (pp. 350–351). This chapter presents this view of an integrated experience as an expanded perspective for professional counseling. In addition, it identifies four elements of compatibility that may be considered when integrating various approaches into the practice of invitational counseling.

With its attention to environmental and institutional factors, invitational counseling is different from counseling approaches that focus strictly on relationships. The intention is not to diminish the importance of relationships but to extend this importance to larger arenas. This means that when counselors work in schools, hospitals, businesses, and other settings, they attend to every aspect of those organizations in creating systems, promoting activities, and delivering services for the benefit of everyone. Organizations, like human beings, are more than the sum of their parts, and are best understood when counselors achieve and maintain a holistic view of their mission.

Over the years, professional counseling has engendered many different theories of counseling, each with its own unique view of human development and the helping relationship. Invitational counseling, while maintaining its own unique stance, has similarities and differences with existing theories. These require understanding by counselors who wish to employ invitational counseling in their professional setting. To assist with this understanding, the next section presents a brief review of professional counseling and its multiple definitions.

Professional Counseling

Professional counseling has been defined extensively in the literature, but not consistently. Over the past half-century many authorities have attempted to define counseling, and their efforts have resulted in a wide variety of views. As illustration, Good's (1945) early definition of counseling as "individualized and personalized assistance with personal, educational, vocational problems" (p. 104) is compared to Gladding's (1992) more inclusive description of counseling as "a relatively short-term, interpersonal, theory-based, professional activity guided by ethical and legal standards that focuses on helping persons who are basically psychologically healthy to resolve developmental and situational problems" (p. 9). These and many other definitions of counseling offer a full spectrum of viewpoints regarding the nature of professional helping.

The variety of definitions can be attributed to three interrelated variables that influence the functioning of professional counselors. These variables are (1) the theoretical beliefs of the counselor, (2) the focus and content of the counseling relationship, and (3) the professional setting. Counselors who agree with the tenets of invitational counseling might use these variables in assessing their definition and implementation of counseling processes. A brief consideration of each variable follows.

Theoretical Beliefs of Counselors

A review of definitions of counseling in classic works by Arbuckle (1965), Shertzer and Stone (1974), Stefflre and Grant (1972), and others demonstrates the influence various theoretical orientations have had on the meanings given to counseling. From his client-centered perspective, Carl Rogers (1952) described counseling as the process by which the basic nature of the self is relaxed in the safety of the relationship with the counselor and where previously denied experiences are perceived, accepted, and integrated into an altered self. In contrast, Shaffer's (1947) behavioral view maintained that counseling should be defined as a learning process that enables the client to acquire skills to control his or her behavior. Shertzer and Stone (1974) combined self-concept and behavioral views in their definition: "Counseling is an interaction process which facilitates meaningful understanding of self and environment and/or clarification of goals and values for future behavior" (p. 20).

Counselors of a psychodynamic orientation have provided yet another definition of counseling. King and Bennington (1972) described an essential goal of counseling as one "to reduce the anxiety of the client to manageable limits in order for the ego to function in a more discriminating and effective manner" (p. 187). Adlerian theorists defended the primary goal of professional counseling as "behavior change within the existing lifestyle" and differentiated it from the goal of psychotherapy for which "a change in lifestyle is the desired outcome" (Sweeney, 1981, p. 144). Throughout the counseling literature, definitions of counseling are as varied as the beliefs of its practitioners. Each definition is a reflection of the basic assumptions held by the various authorities, and each emerges from the unique focus and content of the counseling relationship espoused by individual theorists.

Focus and Content of Helping Relationships

The focus and content of the helping relationship as reflected in the various counseling perspectives and approaches have further complicated the formulation of a precise or consistent definition of counseling. For example, early trait-factor theory (Williamson, 1972) described the purpose of counseling as one that "emphasizes choice of school or work. This is not restricted to the initial choice of a career but to successive stages of development of the individual, including the intangible problem of value commitments" (p. 137). Other definitions of counseling have focused on the client's needs, his or her development, and the importance of responsible decision making to bring about some desired change. Pepinsky and Pepinsky (1954) emphasized, in their definition of the counseling process, the goal of helping clients change their behaviors to resolve identified concerns and problems. Similarly, Belkin (1976) wrote about counseling as a problem-solving process. These and related definitions of counseling have stressed the resolution of problems.

Counseling has also been viewed as a goal-setting and planning process. Smith (1955) described counseling as a "process in which the counselor assists the counselee to make interpretations of facts related to choice, plan or adjustment which he needs to make" (p. 156). Likewise, Cottle and Downie (1970) stated: "Counseling is the process by which a counselor assists a client to face, understand, and accept information about himself and his interactions with others, so that he can make effective decisions about various life choices" (p. 1). Bordin (1968) viewed counseling as "interactions where one person, referred to as the counselor or the therapist, has taken the responsibility for making his role in the interaction process contribute positively to the other person's personality development" (p. 10). In all of these definitions, the dominant theme is that counseling should help people achieve goals. Some of these goals may be remedial; others are developmental.

More recent definitions have reflected the counseling profession's movement toward a balance between remediation and development. Contemporary views also emphasize the collaborative nature of the counseling process. Egan (1994) put it this way: "Counseling is a peculiar kind of service. It is a collaborative process between helper and client. The problem-management and opportunity-development model described in this book is not something that helpers do to clients; it is a process that helpers and clients work through together" (p. 6). Similarly, Pietrofesa and others (1984) defined counseling as "a relationship between a professionally trained, competent counselor and an individual seeking help in gaining greater self-understanding and improved decision-making and behavior-change skills for problem resolution and/or developmental growth" (p. 6). These current definitions are perhaps most analogous to invitational counseling.

How counselors perceive the purpose of the helping relationship influences their definition of that process. The focus and content of counseling, while heavily influenced by the counselor's theoretical views, are also related to the professional setting where counseling occurs and to the specific counseling services offered in that arena. Clearly, what counselors do, with whom, and where, are critical elements in how they define themselves and their work.

Professional Settings

Counselors function in a variety of settings: family clinics, mental health centers, schools, industries, hospitals, retirement villages, court houses, child guidance clinics, military installations, religious institutions, recreational facilities, correctional centers, and private practice, among many others. These diverse locations contribute to the difficulty of achieving a consistent understanding of counseling. Years ago, Orr (1965) observed: "Counseling cannot be precisely defined. It is not a single activity nor is it the province of any one profession" (p. 3). Today, Orr's statement remains understandable, given the variety of responsibilities of professional counselors and the many settings in which these responsibilities are met.

In addition to working in a variety of settings, counselors confront such an array of human concerns that finding a specific definition of their professional service is extremely difficult. Orr (1965) summarized the arduous task of defining professional counseling:

> The breadth and diversity of counseling may be suggested by such characterizations as the following: It is the *art* of helping people to help themselves. It is the applied *science* of psycho-socio-biological pathology. It is the *process* of solving human problems in a professional setting. It is a *relationship* between a trained helping-person and other persons with problems from which the latter draw strength, confidence, and insight in the process of working out their own solutions to the difficulties. (p. 3)

The professional helper who employs invitational counseling would add to Orr's description that it is also the *development* of programs, policies, places, and processes that contribute to the quality of life for all people.

Although there remains a variety of perceptions about the nature of professional counseling, there is also common ground. Of all the descriptors used to characterize professional counseling, the one term that is most often used is the word *process*. From the many definitions of counseling, *process* either appears or is implied in almost every one. Counseling is viewed by most theorists as a process of assisting others in making decisions and acting upon them. Because process is so central to the theory and practice of counseling, it is necessary to consider it more closely.

Counseling as a Process

A process can be defined as a systematic and continuous series of actions taking place in a definite manner and directed toward an identified goal. By this description, professional counseling is certainly a process. It can be viewed as a series of purposeful actions, directed toward a goal or objective. Each action within the counseling relationship can be defined both as a process in and of itself as well as part of the total practice of counseling. Numerous processes are reported in the counseling literature. Four common examples of processes used in counseling are accepting, understanding, exploring, and evaluating.

Accepting behaviors, stressed at numerous points throughout this book, are vital to the establishment of the initial counseling relationship and to the facilitation of the counseling process. Counselors accept their clients for their unconditional worth. They also accept clients to increase the probability of opening and maintaining lines of communication and to understand a client's perceptions and feelings.

To relate to others effectively, counselors not only accept their clients but also seek to understand their feelings and resonate with them; to empathize with their perceptions and respond to their feelings. Professional counselors seek to move beyond the accepting and understanding phases of their relationships to assist their clients with a deeper appreciation of themselves and the world. To do this, counselors encourage their clients to explore their feelings, experiences, and behaviors.

Personal and professional development obtained through counseling culminates in the evaluation process. This occurs throughout the helping relationship, but particularly during the action phase in which alternative behaviors are chosen and practiced by the client. Both the counselor and client evaluate the counseling process by their private thoughts, verbal agreements, and observable behavior changes.

To accept, understand, reflect, explore, and evaluate experiences and perceptions is vital in all counseling models, but without *intentional* movement to enrich experiences or alter perceptions, invitational counseling would have no reason to exist. Counselors who employ invitational counseling work with their clients in identifying behaviors, environments, systems, policies, and programs that can be acted upon to bring about healthy changes in their lives. Figure 7-1 illustrates how the essential elements of the counseling process expand to embrace influential factors in people's lives. One unexpected product of sharing this action phase together is that, when successful, both the client and counselor move toward higher levels of personal and professional functioning.

Previously it was noted that, of the many theories and models studied by counseling students and followed by practicing counselors, the majority emphasize a process to remedy deficiencies. Relatively few give equal importance to development or prevention. It is useful, therefore, to compare and contrast remedial treatment processes with developmental and preventive ones.

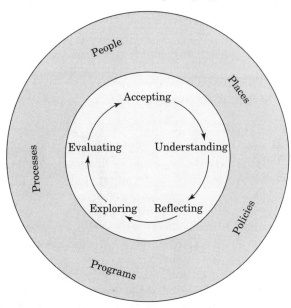

FIGURE 7-1   Counseling as a Process

Treatment

The perspective that the purpose of counseling is to treat some dysfunction, disability, or deficiency in a remedial process begins with the premise that people have problems and come to counselors for help. As an illustration, Downing (1983) pointed out that the majority of counselors have accepted by default the classification system provided by psychiatry. This classification system is essentially negative and focuses on morbidity, psychopathology, neuroses, psychoses, and various mental illnesses. From this remedial perspective, the professional relationship focuses on specific problems and develops strategies that will eliminate them. The counseling relationship ends when problems are resolved.

Much of traditional behavior modification, for example, focuses on specific behaviors that hinder a person from performing adequately or producing appropriately. Similarly, psychoanalysis explores inadequacies and developmental deficiencies that have influenced and continue to influence a person's personality. Psychoanalysts spend many hours, months, and sometimes years helping clients confront past events and relationships that have hampered their ability to function satisfactorily.

Rogers' early client-centered therapy, while viewing the client positively and maintaining an optimistic stance toward self-actualization, also tended to focus on client concerns, problems, and difficulties. In this sense it too was a deficit model of counseling. The contemporary transformation of client-centered therapy to person-centered counseling gives Rogers' approach a more developmental orientation.

Each of the approaches mentioned above, as well as many related counseling theories and therapies, can make valuable contributions to professional helping. They suggest ways to assist people with specific problems and remove barriers to abundant living. Yet all are limited to the degree that they view the counseling relationship as initiated primarily to remedy concerns, remove barriers, and solve problems. Professional counseling can be far more than the identification and remediation of problems. It can be a process for people who are functioning well in day-to-day living but who can benefit from recognizing and realizing their relatively boundless potential in all areas of human endeavor. The rapid growth of community career counseling, where successful individuals seek ways to enrich their lives further, and the popularity of marriage enrichment programs, are examples of counseling processes that focus on a broader spectrum of human development issues.

Development

When establishing helping relationships, most counselors identify those areas that are hindering development and assist clients in removing these roadblocks. However, an expanded perspective of professional counseling does more than assist people with problems. It seeks avenues that enable clients to recognize their potential, make proactive decisions, and develop more positive relations with themselves and others, personally and professionally.

Counselors who define the counseling process in terms of realizing human potential encourage their clients to view counseling in the same way. Just as the skilled basketball player with excellent peripheral vision sees many scoring possibilities that others may miss, the person who is encouraged by a counselor to take a developmental view is more likely to recognize opportunities to enrich his or her own existence as well as that of others.

Analogous to development is the notion of prevention. Preventive helping has some unique elements that warrant special consideration.

Prevention

Because most people live and work in organizations with many layers and facets, invitational counseling advocates processes that monitor the wellness of organizations. When counselors find situations that have the potential to do harm, they seek to intervene. At the same time, counselors who work with individuals and groups make it a point to teach protective strategies. By addressing issues in a preventive fashion, counselors may find that remedial treatment is in less demand.

Prevention activities take many forms. Sometimes counselors observe people's interactions with one another and determine that, if left unattended, these interactions may lead to difficulties in the group. As a result of these observations, counselors plan services to help people examine present interactions and make decisions to avoid future problems. At other times, counselors might design instructional programs, such as classroom guidance in schools, to help people learn about particular situations that hold potential threat to their development. For example, school counselors are often involved in substance abuse prevention programs designed to help students understand the risks involved and make appropriate decisions. Whatever the circumstance, all the helping skills mentioned in this book are as important to prevention as they are to treatment and developmental processes.

In helping clients realize opportunities for potential growth, or identify requirements for safety and precaution, counselors move from a remedial perspective to a developmental and preventive wide-angle view of helping. They use their skills to help clients cope with existing concerns while assisting organizations, institutions, communities, and other groups in preventing problems and encouraging development. Invitational counseling manifests this relationship in its emphasis on people, places, policies, programs, and processes in professional helping. An extension of Figure 7-1 illustrates this phenomenon in Figure 7-2.

An Eclectic Approach

Helpers need a conceptual framework that enables them to borrow ideas, methods, and techniques systematically from all theories, schools, and approaches and integrate them into their own theory and practice of helping.

Gerard Egan
The Skilled Helper
(5th ed.)
1994, p. 14

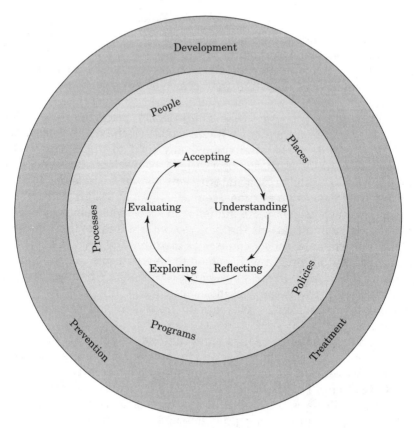

FIGURE 7-2   Benefits of an Expanded Process

As explained earlier, invitational counseling uses a number of approaches and techniques formulated over the years in the helping professions. The incorporation of these approaches and techniques into invitational counseling exemplifies its integrative perspective, which has sometimes been associated with an eclectic orientation, simply defined as an approach that chooses from various sources.

Similarities and Differences

Eclecticism in professional counseling has been praised and condemned for decades. In the 1980s, the debate was renewed in the counseling literature (Brabeck & Welfel, 1985; Patterson, 1985a; Rychlak, 1985), and during that time numerous integrative models of counseling were introduced (Beutler, 1983; Hutchins, 1979; L'Abate,

1981; Lazarus, 1981; Ward, 1983). Contemporary views embrace a systematic eclecticism that is "more than a random borrowing of ideas and techniques from here and there" (Egan, 1994, p. 14). The integrative posture of invitational counseling seems compatible with this perspective. Its expanded outlook is close to the view of Patterson (1985a), who encouraged an integrated practice that "takes as its basic foundation the common elements of all the major theories. These common elements constitute the therapeutic relationship" (p. 350).

Invitational counseling applauds the importance of the "core conditions" as outlined and researched by person-centered therapists (Carkhuff, 1969a, 1969b; Patterson, 1959, 1985a; Rogers, 1957). It also accepts the empirical contributions of the various behavioral and cognitive approaches that have formulated effective techniques useful with specific disorders (Bandura, 1982; Mahoney, 1977; Martin & Pollard, 1980; Masters, Burish, Hollon, & Rimm, 1987; Meichenbaum 1977, 1983). Moreover, the assumptions and beliefs of perceptual psychology (Combs & Snygg, 1959), self-concept theory (Combs & Gonzalez, 1994; Purkey, 1970), the influence of individual psychology (Ansbacher & Ansbacher, 1956; Dinkmeyer, Dinkmeyer, & Sperry, 1987; Sweeney, 1981), and the personal construct theory of Kelly (1955, 1963) all provide important tools for invitational counseling.

While respecting the contributions of various theories and models to the counseling process, invitational counseling also recognizes the philosophic and theoretical differences in these approaches. Stafford (1992) warned that forcing an integration of theories may be incongruous because "not all counseling theories can comfortably fit under the invitational umbrella" (p. 217). Although selective, invitational counseling does seem to provide an overarching structure in which compatible theories and approaches can be organized into a consistent pattern of personal and professional functioning. A fictional case of mild agoraphobia demonstrates how invitational counseling incorporates different approaches into a systematic purpose.

An older adult client is experiencing anxiety about being in a large sheltered workshop. If the client can identify a specific environmental reason for the anxiety, the counselor may be able to employ techniques that systematically alter the physical setting, resulting in an environment that is less threatening to the client. In reducing anxiety, a knowledge of learning theory is useful to the counselor. If the most anxiety-producing stimulus is found to be the noisy work area with loud machines and clanging locker doors, the counselor could initiate a behavioral strategy with the client, beginning with a gradual process of helping her become accustomed to the physical surroundings of the sheltered workshop. At the same time, the counselor could consult with the sheltered workshop director to explore the creation of noise-abatement systems aimed at reducing noise levels.

If a dominant factor is not specific places or policies, but rather a people problem—such as the client's worrying about what others may think about her, or her concern about succeeding with assignments—the counselor might choose a cognitive approach to help the client confront and alter troublesome thoughts. This could be combined with small-group counseling for sheltered workshop participants to form a support group. The group counseling process would focus on how belief systems contribute to anxieties. It would also seek to develop client self-confidence and strengthen peer relationships. Whatever approaches to helping are involved, the counselor views the handling of the anxiety as only the first step of a developmental process designed to help each person thrive in a healthy environment. This wide-angle approach to helping is likely to benefit others in the sheltered workshop as well as the single anxious adult.

One additional quality of invitational counseling related to its expanded perspective is *balance*. Earlier in this chapter, the importance of treatment, development, and prevention in helping relationships was emphasized. Invitational counseling not only notes the different role each of these processes plays, but also emphasizes an orchestrated balance across these three areas, as illustrated in Figure 7-2. To view counseling as a remedy for conflict, anxiety, apathy, or personal misfortune seems to be an unnecessarily narrow definition of the professional helping relationship. At the same time, defining counseling in terms of self-fulfillment without considering barriers to development seems unrealistic. The following examples demonstrate the importance of maintaining this balance.

Marriage counselors who seek to reduce marital conflicts without encouraging those involved toward the development of their relationship may be providing superficial Band-aid solutions that prolong or even increase the pain of an unhealthy marriage. Reducing tensions or removing problems, while helpful, will not necessarily enrich the partnership. It is important to move beyond remediation and toward development. By teaching couples the communication skills needed to reach out toward each other, and by helping them to enrich their lives, the counselor can assist couples in resolving immediate concerns while strengthening their marriage.

When counseling children, it is important to help youngsters discover alternative and socially acceptable ways of handling situations, rather than to simply eliminate problem behaviors. As Herbert (1987) pointed out, problem behaviors have the potential to help the child discover better ways to deal with difficult situations and to focus on assets that can be marshaled toward personal development. The removal of negative forces does not ensure a therapeutic relationship, just as the removal of harmful insects does not ensure a good harvest. The inviting relationship seeks to go beyond remediation of problems and toward the realization of potential.

It is important to pause at this point and specify for whom invitational counseling is intended. In Chapter 5, it was noted that invitational counseling is most appropriate for people who are functioning basically in normal, healthy ways. Many people who are coping successfully and contributing adequately can still benefit from counseling. Highly successful people can seek further enrichment opportunities through the services of professional counselors. Countless individuals make mid-career changes from already profitable occupations, or seek enrichment opportunities upon retirement from successful careers. Invitational counseling is designed to highlight the opportunities existing in each person's life, and to assist clients in their search for ways to take advantage of these opportunities. Simultaneously, the counseling relationship is an opportunity for the counselor as well. This can be thought of as a "doing with" stance.

A "Doing With" Stance

Counselors who adhere to invitational counseling view each helping relationship as potentially beneficial to everyone involved. This is not to imply that counselors themselves actively seek self-enhancement from counseling others. Rather, it means that embedded in invitational counseling is the ideal that when clients alter counterproductive behaviors, make healthy decisions, realize their potential, and approach self-actualization, the counselor also learns and grows as a human being. Combs and Gonzalez (1994) echoed this view when they wrote: "Helping others is a two-way street. One cannot successfully enter deeply and meaningfully into the life of another person without having that experience affect one's self as well" (p. 224). The elements of collaboration and cooperation, highlighted in Chapter 4, emphasize a "doing with" posture.

In contrast to a "doing with" posture, some models of professional helping, particularly early models of behavior modification, conveyed the message of "doing to" others. When counselors function with the purpose of manipulating people to conform to organizational goals or take charge of a client's life, they are operating from a "doing to" stance. There is value in behavioral strategies, analytic understanding, instructional guidance, and other prescriptive techniques, when they are used in a humane context to help people recognize their potential, take control of their lives, and alter self-perceptions. In this way, reinforcement, environmental controls, analytic interpretation, and other techniques are not, in and of themselves, either good or evil. When incorporated into a broader helping role that respects individual integrity and creates an inclusive process of "doing with," these strategies can be beneficial.

Elements of Compatibility

To facilitate the selection of activities and techniques from various counseling models, invitational counseling offers several identifying elements of compatibility that reflect its views and expectations. Although the following elements of compatibility are not inclusive, they are a starting point. Four questions should be asked when considering theories and techniques for inclusion into invitational counseling. Answering these questions can assist counselors in giving reasons for their activities as well as helping counselors to maintain a dependable and consistent stance in their professional practice.

Does the Approach Have a Perceptual Orientation?

Approaches to professional helping that are compatible with invitational counseling emphasize the importance of individual perceptions—particularly perceptions of self-identity, self-regard, and self-efficacy. Approaches that neglect these individual perceptions tend to view human development from an external perspective. Such a viewpoint is incongruent with invitational counseling because it can result in a manipulative "I-it" posture rather than a cooperative "I-thou" one. An orientation based on the perceptual tradition encourages counselors to focus on how clients are perceiving themselves and the world, and to respect the ability and responsibility that people have in choosing the course of their own development.

Human beings are unique in that they have the ability to reflect on and reinterpret their past as well as envision and direct their future. Individuals are not only aware, but aware of their awareness as well. Through this awareness they can reassess their experiences and influence the pattern of their lives. Recognizing the power and responsibility of each person to assert self-control is fundamental to invitational counseling.

Does the Approach Emphasize Self-Concept?

Acceptance of a perceptual orientation goes hand-in-hand with the assumption that self-concept is a dynamic force in human development. Counselors who see self-concept as a mediating variable in individual behavior seek to observe, analyze, and understand human development from an internal point of view. This process is also significant as counselors seek to understand their own feelings. Self-understanding is the basis for a consistent stance in helping and a hallmark of invitational counseling.

Self-concept theory places primary emphasis on the individual's active role in determining a direction for his or her development. The assumption is that the active, guiding moderator of self-concept offers clients and counselors countless opportunities for ameliorating present difficulties while seeking positive enrichment in their lives.

Is the Approach Humanely Effective?

While respect for individuals and their perceptions is a vital measure of acceptability into invitational counseling, the short- and long-term effectiveness of counseling methods also requires consideration. Clients deserve helping relationships that are likely to achieve beneficial results. By definition, any invitation has purpose and direction, and invitational counseling is a goal-directed helping process. Counselors who practice invitational counseling are aware of the intended beneficial effects of both remedial and developmental relationships, and they stand ready to evaluate the effectiveness of their work.

Effectiveness, while necessary, is not in and of itself sufficient— the approach must also be humane. There may be counseling methods in existence that, while measurably effective, tend to belittle, denounce, seduce, punish, or dehumanize. Such methods are counter to the approach presented in this book and should not be considered as invitational counseling, regardless of how effective they may be.

Does the Approach Encourage Applicability?

Because invitational counseling advocates a balance between the resolution of present concerns and the realization of future aspirations, it can be employed in a variety of settings with many different clients. This applicability should be of special interest to counselors who wish to apply their skills across a broad spectrum of developmental, preventive, and remedial activities. Counselors who include individual and group counseling, preventive educational interventions, and consulting activities in their programs are in a stronger position to maintain a balance of services across a wide spectrum of human concerns.

Summary

This chapter presented an expanded view of professional counseling and illustrated how invitational counseling fits this view. Related to this holistic perspective is the belief that counseling is most beneficial when seen as a process that can include aspects of treatment, development, and prevention. For this reason, invitational counseling starts from an eclectic orientation that accepts strategies and techniques from other compatible approaches to professional helping. This chapter concluded with a summary of elements and characteristics of these compatible approaches. These approaches can be used in invitational counseling when they adhere to a perceptual orientation, place emphasis on self-concept, are humanely effective, and incorporate the belief that individuals have the power and responsibility to influence their own development. Counselors who employ invitational counseling evaluate varying approaches according to four questions of compatibility.

Invitational counseling maintains a hopeful vision of people and their ability to make positive changes in their lives. The presence or absence of this vision is particularly significant in choosing approaches to be used by counselors. Compatible approaches support an optimistic viewpoint, respect for people, trust in the human organism, and an emphasis on intentional choice. This evaluation process serves as a framework for counselors to choose from a wide selection of counseling approaches and to adopt appropriate and caring techniques that are beneficial to their clients.

Opportunities for Further Reading

AVILA, D. L., COMBS, A. W., & PURKEY, W. W. (Eds.). (1977). *The helping relationship sourcebook* (2nd ed.). Boston: Allyn & Bacon. This book of readings brings together a collection of original papers of broad relevance to professional helpers. Papers by Carl Rogers, Earl Kelley, Donald Snygg, David Aspy and others explain and illuminate the perceptual tradition in professional helping.

COMBS, A. W., & GONZALEZ, D. M. (1994). *Helping relationships: Basic concepts for the helping professions.* Boston: Allyn & Bacon. This edition of a 1978 text by Combs, Avila, and Purkey offers a clear description of the professional helper from a phenomenological perspective. Self-concept is explained within the context of expanded helping relationships.

COMBS, A. W., RICHARDS, A. C., & RICHARDS, F. (1976). *Perceptual psychology: A humanistic approach to the study of persons.* New York: Harper & Row. Originally published in 1949 under the title *Individual Behavior: A New Frame of Reference for Psychology,* by Donald Snygg and Arthur Combs, this edition updates and expands the perceptual tradition in professional helping. It points out that perceptual psychology is more than an expression of the humanist movement; it is also a frame of reference for the solution of major problems facing humanity.

COREY, G. (1991). *Theory and practice of counseling and psychotherapy* (4th ed.). Pacific Grove, CA: Brooks/Cole. This book is intended primarily for graduate students in counseling. It provides an insightful overview of the major theories of helping and explains how they apply to various human concerns.

GLASSER, W. (1981). *Stations of the mind.* New York: Harper & Row. Glasser integrated reality therapy with brain functioning, perceptual understanding, and behavioral development. He provided a view of how people can learn to be in control of their behavior.

GOOD, E. P. (1987). *In pursuit of happiness: Knowing what you want—getting what you need.* Chapel Hill, NC: New View Publications. This book is based on the concepts of William Glasser's reality therapy. In it, Good presented practical ideas for valuing one's self and establishing beneficial relationships with others.

IVEY, A. E. (1991). *Developmental strategies for helpers: Individual, family, and network interventions.* Pacific Grove, CA: Brooks/Cole. Ivey offered concrete ideas for using developmental approaches in counseling. Many self-assessment exercises encourage the counselor to evaluate aspects of his or her own development in the process of learning to be a more effective helper.

PATTERSON, C. H. (1985b). *The therapeutic relationship: Foundations for an eclectic psychotherapy.* Pacific Grove, CA: Brooks/Cole. This book provides the reader with an understanding that the essence of successful psychotherapy depends on good human relationships. Patterson used both philosophy and theory to propose an eclectic system of counseling and psychotherapy.

PURKEY, W. W., & SCHMIDT, J. J. (1990). *Invitational learning for counseling and development.* Ann Arbor, MI: ERIC/CAPS. A volume of the "Créme de la Créme" series from ERIC, this book offers a synopsis of invitational counseling and includes testimonials from practitioners who employ this approach.

CHAPTER EIGHT

An Expanded Perspective for Professional Counseling

❧

Another great challenge of our time . . . is to develop an approach that is focused on constructing the new, not repairing the old; that is, designing a society in which problems will be less frequent, rather than putting poultices on those who have been crippled by social factors. The question is whether our group can develop a future-oriented preventive approach or whether it will forever be identified with past-oriented remedial functions.

Carl R. Rogers
A Way of Being
1980, p. 240

❧

Because invitational counseling offers an expanded perspective for professional counseling, it is appropriate here to place it in the context of the developing counseling profession, particularly the evolution of present practices and future promises. The counseling profession, like all other professions, has been shaped by historical events that have influenced the roles and functions of practitioners and contributed to its present definition and future potential. An understanding of past events and present conditions encourages an appreciation of the need for an expanded perspective for professional counseling.

This chapter reviews the role of today's professional counselor and presents several scenarios for the future of counseling. To fully understand how counselors have arrived at their contemporary roles, it is necessary to understand the historical development of the profession. The reader who wishes to study historical events and consider future trends in detail is referred to works by Aubrey (1977, 1982), Baker (1992), Gladding (1992), Schmidt (1993), Shertzer and Stone

(1974, 1981), Vacc and Loesch (1994), Walz, Gazda, and Shertzer (1991), Wilson and Rotter (1982), and Wrenn (1962, 1973), among others. Combined, these writings provide in-depth presentations of past events and a glimpse of future trends in professional counseling.

Contemporary Counseling

The early roots of the counseling profession can be traced to the beginning of the 20th century when the introduction of guidance programs in schools and other agencies came as a reaction to conditions in North American society. Aubrey (1977) pointed out that the rapid shift during the late 1800s and early 1900s from an independent, agriculture-based society of small farmers to that of an inter-dependent, industry-based nation of employees resulted in tremendous social changes. These changes produced marvelous technological and industrial achievements, but they were accompanied by undesirable side effects and misery for many people. The creation of guidance programs in schools and other places was an effort to ameliorate some of the undesirable aspects of those sweeping social events and guide students and others into necessary job training and placement.

The social reform movement of the early 1900s, itself a response to the demands and pressures of an expanding industrial economy, provided additional support for the development of the counseling profession. As Roeber (1963) explained, "School dropout rates, exploitation of child labor, a restrictive school curricula, an expanding economy, advances in technology, and a constant surge in individualism are but a few examples of the conditions which contributed to a cultural readiness for vocational guidance, as well as educational guidance, and eventually the emergence of the school counselor" (Roeber, 1963, p. 2). The vocational guidance movement begun at this time gradually developed into a broad concept of assisting young people through the total educational process.

The growth of guidance programs in the 1940s and 1950s was reflected by the founding of the American Personnel and Guidance Association (APGA) in 1952. At that time, the National Vocational Guidance Association (NVGA) joined with the American College Personnel Association (ACPA) and the Association of Guidance Supervisors and Counselors (AGSC), later to become the Association for Counselor Education and Supervision (ACES). This established APGA as an umbrella organization for all guidance and counseling personnel.

Through the 1970s and 1980s, the counseling profession continued to wrestle with the labels and descriptors that best characterized its purpose and membership. This is evidenced by the 1983 decision of the American Personnel and Guidance Association to change its name to the American Association for Counseling and Development (AACD). Following this, a growing number of state associations changed their names by replacing the terms *guidance* and *personnel* with the terms *counseling* and *development*. Although the gradual shift away from guidance and toward counseling was not uniformly popular, many professionals saw the move as beneficial and long overdue. This movement was apparent in 1992 when the name of the organization was again changed, this time to the American Counseling Association (ACA). Today, this national organization encompasses several divisions that represent thousands of counselors who practice in a wide range of institutions, such as schools, mental health centers, hospitals, nursing homes, and prisons. These settings illustrate the broad arena in which today's counselors provide services.

Today's Counselor

Differences in contemporary counselors are apparent not so much by their use of distinct counseling processes or techniques as by their varied work environments. For example, school counselors are primarily concerned with the educational progress and emotional health of students, while family therapists focus on the relationships that influence families and their individual members. The functions of these professional counselors overlap considerably. Sometimes school counselors counsel parents and families in conjunction with educational services, while family therapists counsel family members about educational or vocational concerns that are affecting family relationships. With such overlapping responsibilities and territories, differences in viewpoints are inevitable, particularly when it comes to the question of the relative importance of the counseling process itself.

The counseling process, as opposed to other educational or vocational activities, has not received unanimous support within the profession, particularly in some school programs where other pressing needs such as testing, placement, advisement, and guidance are sometimes seen as more important than counseling. Consequently, practicing counselors from diverse settings continue to debate the merits of their various professional roles and functions.

The diversity of today's professional counselors is demonstrated by the variety of divisions in the American Counseling Association (ACA). The present divisions of ACA include the Association for Humanistic Education and Development (AHEAD), the National Career Development Association (NCDA), the American Mental

Health Counselors Association (AMHCA), the American Rehabilitation Counseling Association (ARCA), the American School Counselor Association (ASCA), the Association for Assessment in Counseling (AAC), the American College Counseling Association (ACCA), the National Employment Counselors Association (NECA), the Association for Multicultural Counseling and Development (AMCD), the Association for Specialists in Group Work (ASGW), the International Association of Addictions and Offender Counselors (IAAOC), the Association for Counselor Education and Supervision (ACES), the Association for Spiritual, Ethical, and Religious Value Issues in Counseling (ASERVIC), the Association for Adult Development and Aging (AADA), and the International Association of Marriage and Family Counselors (IAMFC). In addition to these groups, many professional counselors are members of organizations associated with specific professional practices, including the National Association of Social Workers (NASW), the National Association of School Psychologists (NASP), the American Psychological Association (APA), and the American Association of Marriage and Family Therapists (AAMFT). These organizations represent members from a wide spectrum of work settings.

In the 1980s, ACA (then AACD) helped to create a National Board of Certified Counselors (NBCC) to certify qualified counselors based on documentation of appropriate professional training and experience and completion of a comprehensive examination covering eight content areas of professional counseling. This national certification and identification process has helped to draw counselors closer together. In addition to this national certification process, state credentials such as licensure give visibility and credibility to the counseling profession.

Since the early 1900s, counseling literature and counselor education programs have offered various approaches to assist children, adolescents, adults, and older adults in overcoming obstacles and meeting the expectations of society. Most professional counselors have typically selected certain theories, strategies, and activities to direct their day-to-day functioning, but as responsibilities and roles continue to multiply, counselors have become increasingly aware of the need for a larger perspective for their professional functioning. This need has become apparent as counselors face the challenges brought about by growing technology and emerging moral and social concerns. Every discipline appears to be in the midst of a revolution, and this is particularly true of contemporary counseling.

Faced with rapid advances in technology, the counseling profession, like industry, is finding it difficult to keep up with human acclimatization. This technology has demonstrably advanced the quality of life, but these advancements have been accompanied by difficulties that complicate, impede, or even threaten human existence. Paradoxically, in some cases—as with nuclear weaponry, chemical or biological warfare agents, and other destructive forces— advancements actually place at risk the existence of humans on this earth.

A Modern Paradox

Scientific advancements, such as the discovery of nuclear power, the exploration of space, or the invention of the microchip, are coupled with the fears of nuclear holocaust, war in outer space, or the domination of machines over humans. The spectacular progress of computer technology, for example, while having a revolutionary impact on information processing, carries the corresponding risk of personal isolation, as illustrated by a counselor's complaint that her supervisor was "terminally" hunched over a microcomputer. The use of computers, data banks, and instant retrieval systems by governments, schools, and other institutions, coupled with advanced surveillance technology, also increases the possibility of invasion of privacy and threatens other civil rights as well.

As computers and robots are used to perform tasks formerly done by people, individuals may have less opportunity to work cooperatively —if they are able to find work at all. Instead, each employed person may be paired with a unit of electronic equipment or a robot that works around the clock without weariness or complaint. Lacking human contact, workers may feel a decreased sense of belonging and an increased sense of personal isolation. The same phenomenon may be found in the field of medicine.

In recent years medical achievements have significantly extended the average life span, and they promise to continue to do so. By the end of this century it is likely that the basic causes of many diseases will be understood, and preventive or curative measures developed. Scientists are already using DNA markers to predict whether a person will develop particular diseases later in life. In the immediate future, people who develop heart-lung difficulties will probably receive complete heart-lung transplants along with gene therapy to alter the immune system and prevent rejection of the transplant. Among the most active and exciting medical frontiers is the replacement of damaged body parts with various anatomical and mechanical substitutes. In sum, living well beyond four score and seven years of age will probably become common.

Simultaneously, medical miracles have raised social and moral issues that evade clear-cut answers. Increasing life spans will result in a growing population of older adults. People will live longer, but will they live better? What will be their role in future society? Science can now prolong life by extraordinary means almost indefinitely, to the extent that the meaning of *life* eludes consistent definition. Life and death continually take on new meanings, forcing society to consider complex moral, legal, and ethical questions. When does life begin, when does it end, and who is qualified or responsible for making such determinations? Who has the right to decide when to end life, and who has the right to assist with such a decision? What are the ethical, moral, and legal issues in transplanting major organs from humans to humans, or from other animals to humans? Certainly future counselors will play an important role in assisting people with these and other issues.

Social Transformations

Transformations in society have, for the most part, contributed greatly to an improved quality of life, but they also have created problems. Many of today's jobs and responsibilities will vanish, while worldwide industrial and manufacturing realignment will continue to uproot millions of people from familiar geographic locations and vocational roles. Moreover, unemployment, particularly for the undereducated and unskilled, or for those whose skills have been displaced, will remain a problem, resulting in increased stress, anxiety, and alienation.

A major new social transformation underway for the past several decades is the growing number of women in the worldwide workforce. Women are presently being hired and being successful in many occupations once considered unsuitable or off-limits for females. The result is that dual-career families are commonplace. Moreover, professions that have traditionally depended on female applicants to fill their ranks, such as teaching and nursing, are hurting as many women turn to other professions. As traditional sex roles are successfully challenged, both in the home and workplace, counselors are being called on as never before to help ease tensions and recognize opportunities brought about by changing perceptions and conditions regarding the roles of men and women in society.

One further illustration of the changes brought about by rapid social transformations is the increase in professional specialties. Social progress, educational opportunities, and the need for specialization have resulted in the training of highly skilled professionals to help with complex scientific, medical, educational, industrial, and human relations issues. Paradoxically, the growing trend toward specialization has sometimes resulted in an overprotection of professional boundaries. Rather than working together so that each can offer his or her expertise, professionals occasionally find themselves in competitive postures, protecting domains while hindering human service. For example, competition and resulting conflicts in the helping professions may sometimes be found among clinical psychologists, mental health counselors, social workers, counselors in private practice, school counselors, educational psychologists, and others. Such competition and conflicts seldom result in improved human services.

Other forces within the counseling profession sometimes run counter to its development. The increasing need for competent counselors, combined with the willingness of counselors to provide services in a variety of settings for an endless number of concerns, can result in counselor burnout. Burnout may be found in counselors who have stretched themselves too far or too fast and have neglected the first two corners of the four spheres of invitational counseling described in Chapter 4: being personally inviting with oneself and being personally inviting with others. Their own personal well-being and the well-being of their family and friends have taken a back seat to pressing professional demands. The value of caring for oneself and others personally to ameliorate stress and avoid burnout has been emphasized throughout this book.

Finally, the contemporary emphasis of the counseling profession on self-development requires that this emphasis be balanced with genuine social interest and a deep concern for the human community. What Alfred Adler referred to as a lack of social interest can emotionally paralyze individuals as well as groups (Dinkmeyer et al., 1987). This need for renewed social interest has also been expressed by Aspy and Aspy (1993), Carkhuff (1988), and many others.

The desire to self-discover, self-improve, self-enhance, and self-actualize can receive inordinate attention, as evidenced by the vast array of personal development and self-help books found on today's store shelves. In light of the continuing emphasis on the promotion of oneself, it is critical for counselors to develop all four spheres of invitational practice and strike a healthy balance between self-enhancement and a spirit of oneness with others. To do so, people may want to look beyond popular self-help and how-to guides and look for the essential ingredients to put into their plans for a successful life (Schmidt, 1994). Self-realization can be obtained only when people develop and maintain respect and trust for others and an optimistic view of their value, abilities, and self-directing powers. This balance reduces alienation and fosters a spirit of community.

From this overview of contemporary counseling, it is clear that counselors face a complex, ever changing, ever more specialized technical world. Seldom if ever has society placed greater demands on or held higher expectations for the professional counselor. To fully appreciate the scope of these demands and expectations, one needs to comprehend the range of professional settings that utilize counseling services.

Settings and Services

In recent years, the counseling profession has expanded its practice to include services in a wide range of institutions and organizations. In all of these settings, counselors assist clients with treatment, development, or prevention goals, or a combination of these objectives.

By way of illustration, the following sections give a brief description of some settings in which professional counselors work. These are by no means inclusive, but they depict the diverse organizations that use counseling services.

School Counseling

The emergence of the counseling profession in the early 1900s eventually led to the development of the school counseling profession. Although school counseling began at the secondary level, today's school counselors are found in elementary, middle, and high schools, and comprise a large number of professional counselors. The American School Counselor Association (ASCA), the largest division of the American Counseling Association (ACA), had more than 13,000 members in 1994.

School counselors are responsible for designing a comprehensive program of services that complement the mission of the schools in which they work. These comprehensive programs consist of services for students, parents, and teachers that focus on overall student development. There are three essential areas of development: educational, career, and personal or social issues. Examples of the services counselors use in schools include individual and group counseling, teacher and parent consultation, student assessment, coordination of mental health services in the school, crisis intervention, and instructional guidance. In all of these services the primary purpose is to help with educational planning, career awareness and decision making, self-knowledge and acceptance, and appropriate socialization.

Counseling in Higher Education

In addition to working in elementary, middle, and high schools, counselors are also employed by colleges and universities. In contrast to school counselors who provide a wide range of services and activities to students, parents, and teachers, counselors in higher education tend to specialize depending on the division, department, or program in which they work. For example, professional counselors are employed by colleges and universities in their resident life programs to offer orientation, educational, and other assistance to students who reside on campus. At the same time, counselors are found providing direct services in college counseling centers to assist with immediate personal, social, academic, and career needs. Universities and colleges also employ counselors in their admissions' offices, career placement centers, financial aid offices, and academic advising programs, among others. In each of these situations, the counselor's role and function is defined by specific program goals and objectives.

Lewing and Cowger (1982) identified several functions that describe college counseling. These include academic or educational counseling, vocational counseling, personal counseling, testing, supervision and training, research, teaching, professional development, and administration. According to Gladding (1992), "three of these activities—personal, vocational, and educational counseling—account for over 50% of counselors' time" (p. 354). In this respect, the broad role and purpose of college counseling is a continuation of the services found in elementary, middle, and high school counseling programs.

Agency Counseling

In addition to educational settings, professional counselors work in an array of community agencies from rehabilitation hospitals to church-related centers. In most of these organizations, the counselors have a narrower focus than counselors in educational institutions. Their role is to assist clients with identified concerns; in most instances this role means a treatment mode is used.

Agency counselors (also called community counselors) are found in mental health centers where they complement services provided by psychiatrists, clinical psychologists, and clinical social workers. They provide counseling services for children, adolescents, and adults on a wide range of issues that are disrupting lives or hindering development. Frequently the children and adolescents seen by mental health counselors are referred by school counselors who, because of their obligation to the broader school population, cannot devote the time necessary for long-term or intense treatment.

Agency counselors are also found in hospitals and hospices helping patients and their families cope with terminal illnesses, in clinics that provide substance abuse treatment and prevention programs, in churches to offer counseling that complements the ministry's spiritual guidance, and in family counseling centers to help with marriage counseling, parenting education programs, and family intervention. In all these cases, counselors use the theories and skills common to the counseling profession, but maintain a limited focus related to the primary objectives of the agency.

Counseling in Business and Industry

Today's professional counselors are also employed by businesses and industries to offer services to employees and prospective employees. When counselors are hired by businesses and industry, they usually work in personnel services or human resource development. Their functions can be varied depending on the purposes for which they are employed. For example, some counselors are used to train new employees, provide orientation, and identify any immediate concerns employees may bring to the work site. Other counselors work in employee assistance programs (Gladding, 1992) and provide direct counseling services to workers. Employee assistance programs have been the response by business and industry to keep workers on the job when personal and social difficulties arise. In part, this response is one of economics, because business and industry have found it may be more cost-effective to help an employee through a difficult time rather than firing him or her only to hire and train a new worker. Consequently, many businesses have established programs within their organizations, or have contracted with external counseling centers, to assist employees with difficulties such as substance abuse, family dysfunction, and financial stress (Smith, Salts, & Smith, 1989).

The Future of Counseling

I strongly suspect that we eventually will see the emergence of a new model of professional psychology which will not be like present clinical, school, counseling, organizational, or community psychologies of today. Instead, it will involve broad training intended to permit the professional psychologist to adapt to different settings and to offer interventions, programs, and services based on the needs of the client rather than on the predetermined biases and predilections of the specialty of psychology involved in offering the service. Training will emphasize understanding the importance of knowing a lot about *where* one works as well as *what* one does.

Jack Bardon
"The State of the Art," *American Psychologist*
1976, *31*, p. 785

ᴤ

Predicting the future of professional counseling is a risky business. Today's certainties become tomorrow's fallacies. Yet, a need exists for a visionary perspective for counselors, whether it be called invitational counseling or something else. The position taken in this book is that such vision will require a process of integrating compatible theories and philosophies with acceptable strategies and practices.

As scientific discoveries and technological inventions continue to add to the complexity of everyday living, people's corresponding need to handle new challenges steadily increases. As professional specialization becomes the norm, counselors will become a more active force, influencing places, policies, processes, and programs as well as working with people to facilitate human development. Counselors of the future will need a consistent stance from which to operate as they employ a wide selection of approaches and strategies that affirm people in their present value while inviting them to realize their potential.

Counseling and Technology

Technological influences on counseling are already apparent in the use of videotaping equipment to increase the effectiveness of counselor training programs. Audiovisual and microcomputer technology is being used by counselors in clinical practice as well as in educational settings. Video playback is used in counseling sessions to allow clients to see themselves as others see them. Clients often gain valuable insights by watching their own behaviors in a nonthreatening and nonjudgmental environment. Moreover, video and computer-assisted programs are being used to teach new coping behaviors, provide information about personal development, demonstrate learning skills, and impart other knowledge. Soon, erasable videodiscs will make today's videotape recorders and microprocessors obsolete. These discs will be electronically encoded with sound and images and played on machines the size of present portable tape recorders. Technological advances will strengthen the counselor's technical skill, but they may also add to the danger of neglecting the people in the process.

How counselors utilize new technology may be as important as the technology itself. Improved systems, places, programs, and policies can offer vital assistance to future counseling, but they cannot replace the human qualities that are essential to successful helping. Keeping the *human* in human development will be a challenge for tomorrow's counselors.

An example of how technology can be used to assist, rather than replace, the counselor may be seen in present computer-assisted counseling services. The key term is *computer-assisted,* rather than *computerized.* A computer-assisted program allows counselors and clients to maintain important human interactions while using technology as a tool to store information, present instruction, score inventories, and perform other supplementary and supportive functions. In contrast, a computerized counseling program implies a lack of human contact. According to the assumptions of invitational counseling, the phrase *computerized counseling* is a contradiction in terms. Invitational counseling depends on human qualities and personal relationships.

The challenge to future counselors will be how to accept high-tech advances without neglecting "high-touch" humanity. To become automated and computerized without primary regard for people in the counseling process would lead to a "doing to" rather than a "being with" profession. Invitational counseling requires that technological advances be constantly monitored and properly evaluated.

Social Change and the Human Condition

In earlier sections of this chapter, challenges to human welfare resulting from social movements, scientific discoveries, and advanced technologies were identified. Additional descriptions of these three sources are presented here to illustrate how future counseling services might ameliorate these disinviting side effects.

Scientific discoveries and technological inventions will continue to influence life expectancy as the nation's population ages. Future counseling services will help families and individuals enjoy this additional life expectancy for the optimal benefit of the individual and society. As the average life span is extended, people will require a greater appreciation of developmental concerns in the aging process, including physical needs, medical services, availability of social activities, family and generational interactions, educational pursuits, and other areas related to the continued development of potential.

Geriatric counselors who are prepared to meet the needs of expanding ranks of older adults should have little trouble finding positions. Meeting the requirements of an aging population will offer many new service avenues and opportunities for professional counselors.

Simultaneously, the achievement of longer life spans may be accompanied by longer periods of dying. Medical advancements already can prolong an individual's life even in the most critical of situations. How the critically ill individual, his or her family members, and close friends cope with this side of medical progress will be a concern of future counselors.

When death comes, professional help is often needed for those who have suffered the loss of a loved one. A growing number of hospitals, nursing homes, hospices, and funeral establishments are hiring counselors to provide bereavement counseling services. It is likely that many more will do so in the future.

Changing patterns in industry and business will also call for an increase in counseling and human services. As automation increases, more and more people will be working individually without the benefit of social groups. Increasingly, people are setting up workstations at home, using computers to do correspondence, accounting, bookkeeping, and catalogue sales for large businesses. Lack of social support in the work setting is likely to have negative effects. This will create a need for counselors who can facilitate people, design places, and encourage policies and programs that provide quality social interaction.

An unavoidable result of an ever increasing life span, coupled with ever growing automation, will be the time available for leisure activities. Workdays will be shorter, schedules more flexible, and vacations and sabbaticals longer. As Ferguson (1980) indicated, the industrial transformation in future society will call for a change in attitude, from making a living to making a life. Future counseling services will be called upon to help people make this transformation. Leisure counseling, vocational planning, mid-career advising, and retirement counseling are only a few of the many services counselors will be asked to provide.

Social forecasts predict that societies around the globe will become more culturally diverse. Counselors will need expanded models, such as invitational counseling, to address the needs of culturally divergent populations. As such, the role of counselors will continue to include individual and group processes that assist with personal adjustment, educate people about cultural differences, and create environments in which policies, procedures, and processes accept individual worth in the context of community (Schmidt, 1993).

While cultural divergence has the potential to enrich future societies, socioeconomic disparities threaten their very existence. Poverty and its siblings—malnutrition, inadequate health care, and unequal education—are insidious forces with which future societies must contend. For counselors, proactive models of helping are required to combat these corrupting elements. So many other issues—such as violence, drug abuse, and social depravity—are interconnected with poverty that a solitary approach will not be effective.

Finally, future counseling services will need to encourage a balance between personal feelings and social expectations. This balance will be needed in educational as well as in governmental, financial, corporate, business, and family settings. Counselors will require models that balance the remedial needs of people with their long-range developmental goals. It may serve little purpose to feed a hungry child, for example, if other social, educational, personal, and financial issues in the child's life are not assigned long-term priority.

A Place for Invitational Counseling

Throughout this chapter the counseling profession has been pictured as an expanding field of study and practice. If counselors who work in various settings are to accept this view, they need theories and paradigms that incorporate such a vision. Invitational counseling is one approach that offers this possibility. Regardless of the setting in which a counselor works, invitational counseling provides a framework to establish a broad program of services, develop assessment procedures, create guidelines for service delivery, and implement methods of evaluation.

Invitational counseling is already established as a viable model for counseling in schools (Novak, 1992; Purkey & Schmidt, 1990; Purkey & Stanley, 1991, 1994). This is logical because schools offer an opportunity for comprehensive services across broad populations, including students, parents, and teachers (Schmidt, 1991, 1993). Invitational counseling has promise for use in many other settings, even those that appear to have limited their focus to remedial relationships. Counselors in mental health centers, prisons, and similar agencies will find that the elements, levels, spheres, choices, and styles inherent in invitational counseling are adaptable to their professional practice.

In adapting this approach, counselors will want to focus on the philosophical and theoretical assumptions embraced by invitational counseling. The place of invitational counseling in the future of the profession is best illustrated by its principles and attributes, which have been presented throughout this book. In summary, invitational counselors will establish future helping relationships that

- create optimistic visions of human capability
- are action-oriented by design, but reject the belief that the end ever justifies the means
- respect individual perspectives within the context of social responsibility
- encourage diversity while striving toward common goals for the good of all people
- combine individual, group, and organizational efforts to bring about appropriate change
- demand proficient use of skills in communicating, leading, and assessing outcomes of all relationships
- value the role of professional counselors in a wide range of settings that aim at prevention, development, and the alleviation of human concerns

Summary

This chapter presented an overview of historical and future aspects of professional counseling. Because of rapid changes in the counseling profession in a modern technological society, a need exists for a more encompassing perspective on professional functioning.

In recent years, scientific advancements, educational progress, and other social transformations have increased the pressure and complexity of daily living and enlarged the demand for counseling services. Now more than ever, professional counselors are needed to establish helping relationships with individuals, families, school populations, industrial workers, older adults, institutional residents, members of religious organizations, military personnel, and myriad other groups whose members wish to satisfy immediate concerns while seeking to develop optimally.

The evolution of counseling has resulted in many views of professional helping now being practiced in North American society. Most of the changes in the profession are related to the practice of counseling in seemingly divergent settings with a multitude of different missions. Invitational counseling bridges these differences and offers a common ground for professional practice.

This final chapter concluded with a theme echoed throughout this book: future counselors will strive to integrate their belief systems and personal characteristics with their professional theories and counseling techniques into a developmental approach to human service. This integration requires a philosophy of professional helping that transcends specific approaches and techniques, extends far beyond the counseling center, and focuses on relatively boundless human potential. Thus, a structure for the ever growing body of research findings that tie together seemingly unrelated aspects of professional helping is essential. Invitational counseling provides this structure for present and future counselors.

Opportunities for Further Reading

ARBUCKLE, D. S. (1975). *Counseling and psychotherapy: An existential-humanistic view* (3rd ed.). Boston: Allyn & Bacon. A classic text that provides an existential, deeply humanistic perspective on the counseling profession and the counseling process.

DEAL, T. E., & KENNEDY, A. A. (1985). *Corporate cultures: The rites and rituals of corporate life*. Reading, MA: Addison-Wesley. The major theme of this futuristic book is that strong organizations are those with a cohesion of values, myths, heroes, and symbols that "tie people together and give meaning and purpose to their day-to-day lives" (p. 5). The authors pointed out that we cannot return to the way it used to be because it no longer exists.

FERGUSON, M. (1980). *The Aquarian Conspiracy: Personal and social transformation in the 1980's*. Los Angeles: J. P. Tarcher. What is the Aquarian Conspiracy? Ferguson described it as a growing movement to create a society based on a vastly enlarged concept of human potential. In the 1990s and toward the 21st century this observation remains vital for professional counselors.

JANTSCH, E. (1980). *The self-organizing universe: Scientific and human implications of the emerging paradigm of evolution*. Oxford, England: Pergamon Press. Who among us ever thought of black holes, antimatter, genes jumping between chromosomes, inclusive fitness, or subatomic particles without mass? Jantsch described the information explosion and pointed out that every discipline is in the midst of a scientific revolution.

REICH, C. A. (1970). *The greening of America*. New York: Random House. The question posed in this controversial bestseller is, How can we develop a new consciousness based on the value, ability, and self-directing powers of each person? Though the book was published more than 25 years ago, the question remains important today.

VAILLANT, G. E. (1977). *Adaptation to life*. Boston: Little, Brown. This book presents an in-depth study of a small sample of male college graduates over a 35-year period following their graduation. Most manage life's problems with surprising strength and adequacy.

WALZ, G. R., GAZDA, G. M., & SHERTZER, B. (Eds.). (1991). *Counseling futures.* Ann Arbor, MI: ERIC/CAPS. This edited volume offers many intriguing ideas about the future of counseling. In sum, these ideas support an expanded model for professional counseling.

WRENN, C. G. (1973). *The world of the contemporary counselor.* Boston: Houghton Mifflin. Wrenn presented an excellent analysis of contemporary and future trends that require ever freshening visions of the roles of professional counselors.

APPENDIX A

Development of Invitational Counseling

The concepts that set the stage for invitational counseling came in large part from the writings of Sidney Jourard (1964, 1968, 1971a, 1971b, 1974). In his 1968 book, *Disclosing Man to Himself,* Jourard wrote, "I now believe there is no biological, geographical, social, economic, or psychological determiner of man's condition that he cannot transcend if he is suitably invited or challenged to do so" (p. 59). In this and an earlier book, *The Transparent Self* (1964, 1971b), Jourard argued that each person's physical and psychological health are profoundly influenced by the degree to which a person finds meaning, direction, and purpose in human existence. These findings are related to the invitations given and received during the course of a lifetime. Jourard died in a tragic accident before he could expand on his thoughts, but the seeds he planted gave birth to a set of beliefs that evolved into invitational theory and, later, invitational counseling.

At the time of his death, Jourard was a professor of psychology at the University of Florida. He became acquainted with, and then heavily influenced the thinking of, two young professors at that university, William W. Purkey and Betty L. Siegel. During this time Purkey and Siegel were examining and writing about how human perception and self-concept influence teaching and learning and were presenting their ideas to teachers, counselors, and other educators in workshops around the United States and beyond.

Invitational theory first emerged as a result of a brief book, *Self-Concept and School Achievement* (Purkey, 1970). As Purkey later wrote, "Following the appearance of the earlier book, many people contacted me to ask such questions as: 'Assuming that self-concept does play an important role in school achievement, how can we build a student's self concept?' 'What can our school do to enhance students' self esteem?'" (1978, vi). His answer was to work with Betty Siegel,

John Novak (at that time a doctoral student at the University of Florida), and others to conceive invitational theory. It was an exciting time at the University of Florida during the 1960s, and the work of many talented University of Florida professors and students such as David Aspy, Donald Avila, Walter Busby, Arthur Combs, Sandra Damico, Ira Gordon, Hal G. Lewis, Frank Pajares, Mark Wasicsko, Hannalore Wass, and Joe Wittmer advanced the development of invitational theory. Several events heavily contributed to the development of this approach, including funding from a private foundation and the organization of the International Alliance for Invitational Education.

Historical Events

In the late 1960s Purkey and Siegel applied for and received a grant from the Noyes Foundation of New York. This grant provided fellowships for teams of teachers, administrators and school board members to attend residential summer training programs at the University of Florida. These training programs focused on ways to humanize education. In the process, Purkey, Siegel, and hundreds of workshop participants wrestled with the emerging concepts of invitational education (Purkey, 1992a).

Eventually, Purkey compiled these ideas into an early statement of invitational thought. His book, *Inviting School Success: A Self-Concept Approach to Teaching and Learning* (1978), offered the first view of this emerging theory. About this time, the Noyes Foundation, after eight years of funding these residential workshops, ended its support. Purkey noted that this event "was a major turning point" in a developmental process, because the decision was to continue the workshops with support limited to registration fees. From that period until the present, workshops and conferences have been held at various locations in the United States and Canada in cooperation with numerous universities including Western Carolina University, the University of North Carolina at Greensboro, Lehigh University in Pennsylvania, Guilford College in North Carolina, Brock University in Canada, and the University of Nebraska in Lincoln.

Until 1978 there was no formal structure for this loose-knit group of educators, counselors, and psychologists. At that time, Purkey, Siegel, and colleagues officially formed the Alliance for Invitational Education to encourage collegial relationships and examine, critique, and research the invitational approach. This early alliance was still an informal organization with none of the effects of well-organized associations: no membership list, no officers, no bylaws, and no dues. Nevertheless, through workshops and conferences, the alliance continued to grow. By the summer of 1982, it was apparent that the group had grown so large that some type of organized structure was required.

During a 1982 summer institute at Lehigh University, Purkey and Siegel met with ten leaders of the alliance and forged an organization that included membership dues, a slate of officers, a charter, and a newsletter. Shortly after, a group founded the Canadian Invitational Education Association, and a special interest group (SIG) in the American Educational Research Association (AERA) was established through the work of John Novak. Today the alliance is named the International Alliance for Invitational Education and boasts a membership of more than 1,200 worldwide.

In addition to its longstanding association with AERA through its special interest group, the alliance has worked cooperatively with the National Middle School Association, the National Education Association, the ERIC clearinghouse for counseling and student services (ERIC/CASS), and Phi Delta Kappa by publishing monographs and manuals on invitational education. All of these collaborative efforts have enabled the alliance to network with professional associations and promote the tenets of invitational theory.

The International Alliance for Invitational Education continues to sponsor workshops and conferences and publishes two periodicals, the *Invitational Education Forum* newsletter and the *Journal of Invitational Theory and Practice*. In addition, the alliance distributes tapes, books, and other publications about invitational theory and practice. These efforts have contributed to the expansion of this movement and the credibility of the theory.

Major Publications

In addition to the works mentioned earlier, several books have been published about the invitational approach. Purkey and Novak's second and third editions of *Inviting School Success* (1984, 1995) has had an influence on this movement. Likewise, John Wilson's *The Invitational Elementary Classroom* (1986) was the first book to give specific attention to the application of the invitational model. In 1987, Purkey and Schmidt wrote *The Inviting Relationship: An Expanded Perspective for Professional Counseling,* the first view of the invitational approach beyond student-teacher interactions. These works have been followed by other books including: *Invitation to Friendship* (Schmidt, 1988); *Invitational Learning for Counseling and Development* (Purkey &

Schmidt, 1990); *Living Intentionally and Making Life Happen* (Schmidt, 1994); *Invitational Teaching, Learning, and Living* (Purkey & Stanley, 1991); *Advancing Invitational Thinking* (Novak, 1992); and *The Inviting School Treasury* (Purkey & Stanley, 1994).

All these works are complemented and supported by journal articles, research papers, master's theses, and doctoral dissertations published since the early 1970s. Paula Stanley (1992) has compiled these writings in a bibliography that illustrates the chronological development of invitational theory and practice.

APPENDIX B

Inviting Oneself Personally

Give yourself a celebration. Make a pledge to do something special for yourself, and only yourself, in the immediate future. Give yourself a hot bath, a window-shopping trip, a new outfit, a special hour for yourself, a good book, a favorite meal. At least once a week take yourself out to a movie, concert, dinner, or some other special event. When you celebrate yourself, it's easier to celebrate others.

Rehearse the future, not the past. So often when we make mistakes, we go over them again and again in our minds—in effect, practicing the mistakes. A better way to overcome the mistake is to ask, "How will I handle this concern the next time?" By concentrating on future responses or behavior, we can rehearse the future, not the past.

Practice positive self-talk. Negative self-statements—such as "I could never do that"—can discourage one from perceiving oneself as able, valuable, and capable. Change negative self-talk to positive internal dialogue.

Negative self-talk	*Positive self-talk*
"I could never do that."	"It may be hard, but I'll do it."
"I never do anything right."	"It is only human to make mistakes."
"I can't."	"I will."
"I'm hopeless."	"I am having difficulty, but I will persist."
"No one could like me."	"There are people who will like me for myself."
"I should not have said that."	"I can be more careful with what I say."

Find a way to exercise. Professionals can be more inviting when they maintain their own physical health. Whether it is an organized sport (bowling, tennis, golf) or an individual effort (jogging, walking, weight lifting, swimming), find ways to maintain, protect, and enhance your physical body.

Talk with a friend. A good way to prevent professional burnout is to talk with a friend whose judgment you trust. Sometimes another perspective can help us avoid self-destructive behaviors and thought processes.

Plant a garden. Working in the soil can be a relaxing and rewarding experience, particularly when you watch a plant grow and produce. Even the smallest apartment has room for a window flower box, and a tiny garden can be rewarding with flowers and vegetables.

Build a personal Fort Knox. Start a special file of letters, awards, notes, gifts, and other recognition you have received over the years. When you begin to feel down or burned out, visit your own personal Fort Knox of golden nuggets and restore your spirits. It will renew your faith in your own ability and energize you to help others.

Form positive food habits. When planning your meals or eating out, try meats that are broiled, baked, or roasted rather than fried or sautéed. This way you will avoid excess calories and fat. And leave a little food on your plate. The childhood adage "clean your plate" has probably contributed to the weight problems of many individuals.

Renew a friendship. Call or write an old friend you have not talked with in a long time. Perhaps you can work out a date for dinner, or plan to see a concert, movie, or other special event.

Live with a flourish. Avoid drabness, gain satisfaction from many sources, find ways to enrich your life; stand tall, dress well, eat less, and surround yourself with things you like.

Live a longer life. People live longer when they take responsibility for their physical health. Remove salt shakers from the table, eliminate smoking and other injurious substances, cut your alcohol intake, drink plenty of water, maintain dental hygiene, and fasten your seat belt.

Explore a library. For a relaxing experience, spend several hours browsing in a library. As you wander through the stacks, you'll have a world of knowledge at your fingertips—and it's all free!

Plan an adventure. Visit travel agencies and load up on travel brochures. Dream a little. You will be tomorrow where your ideas of today take you.

Raise your drawbridge. Although too much isolation is not good, some time alone to enjoy stillness, to contemplate and meditate on who you are, where you came from, and where you are going contributes to living and can be both personally and professionally rewarding. The goal is to be at one with the world and with the spirit.

Take a few risks. When chances of success are good, it usually pays to take a few chances. You have to risk life to live it well. Accept new people, ideas, and experiences that widen your perspective on life. One of the saddest things in life is a golden opportunity—missed.

Laugh. Subscribe to a happy little magazine titled *Laughing Matters.* It is published quarterly by Dr. Joel Goodman, Director, The Humor Project, 110 Sprint St., Saratoga Springs, New York, 12866, and it will brighten almost any day.

Be a good physician. Over 85 percent of all the medical attention a counselor receives is self-delivered. Each of us places bandages on cuts and scratches, prescribes medicine (aspirin, vitamins, cold tablets), removes splinters, massages stiff muscles; the list is endless. Healthy counselors work at being good physicians to themselves by taking responsibility for their own well-being.

Inviting Others Personally

Throw a party. Invite friends and colleagues over for an informal get-together; and don't forget the neighbors. The way to have friends is to be one.

Name that tune. When planning a picnic, party, or other social event for friends or group members, give the occasion a lift with a special theme such as "Monte Carlo Night," "Oktoberfest," "Roarin' Twenties," "Home on the Range," or "Hawaiian Luau." A theme costs little or nothing and will make planning easier, increase attendance, and build enthusiasm.

Promote "please" and "thank you." Do what you can to have all directional and other signs around your office, center, or workplace begin with "please" and end with "thank you."

Celebrate birthdays and other special occasions. Birthdays of friends and colleagues and other special events can be marked on a private calendar in readiness for the special occasion. An unexpected happy note, greeting card, or delicious treat can add much to a person's day.

Recognize the indispensable staff. Sometime during the year, perhaps at a holiday season, it is important for counselors to express appreciation to the custodians, secretaries, cafeteria workers, and other staff people for their work. It is important to remember that all staff are part of the "family," and they add a great deal to the success—or failure—of counselors.

Send a welcome back note. We often think to send get-well cards to friends, colleagues, employees, and others when they are ill. It is doubly appreciated when our thoughtfulness is extended to welcome back those who return after an illness, death in the family, or long business trip.

Greet others. Make the effort to say hello to as many people as possible when walking down the hallway. Greeting others and expecting a proper response costs nothing and builds good relationships.

Plan comfortable meetings. A careful check of facilities before an activity begins helps ensure that personal needs are considered. This includes seating, lighting, temperature, materials, rest rooms, and related items of comfort. People participate best when they feel personally cared for.

Listen for the name. When you are introduced to people, listen carefully to their name. Repeat it to yourself three times and use their name as you speak with them; they will appreciate the recognition.

Treat guests cordially. If you have an office in your counseling center, arrange it so you have an informal area to talk with visitors. The informal area could include comfortable chairs, a coffee table, and an area rug.

Send double-strength invitations. As nice as it is to receive complimentary words directly, it is even nicer to hear that kind words about you have been expressed to others. Rather than praising someone directly, praise the person to someone else. The original praise will probably reach the person with double the impact.

Offer refreshments to visitors. Breaking bread together is an ancient sign of peace and friendship. By offering each visitor a beverage or light refreshment, the stage is set for the solution of concerns and facilitation of good feelings.

Keep a "mug" file. Start and maintain a card file on those individuals with whom you have contact, both personal friends and professional colleagues. A single index card can hold a wealth of information about people you know. Each card can contain such personal items as the name of spouse, number and names of children, hobbies, interests, and so on. This card system can help to strengthen your memory and is one additional way to operate at the invisibly appropriate level.

Personalize some pencils. For a few dollars it is possible to order pencils with some special greeting, such as "Season's Greetings to you from Mr. Smith." The pencils can be given before a holiday or other significant day. For example, school counselors can use the idea just before school ends for the summer: "Ms. Reynolds wishes you a great summer vacation!"

Inviting Oneself Professionally

Carpool an adventure. Is a noted lecturer, important conference, counseling workshop, or other activity appearing or taking place in some other part of the country? Join with other counselors, pool your gas money, and attend as a group. At the conference, pick up brochures, handouts, and catalogues to share with colleagues who were unable to go.

Venture an invitation. Is there someone in your professional world whom you admire and would like to know better? If so, be brave! Invite that person to lunch one day. The result may be exciting and bring future professional exchanges. After all, your dearest friend in all the world was once a total stranger.

Keep on schedule. Punctuality is a sign of intentionality. Being on time demonstrates professional caring for yourself and those who depend on your professional involvement. Place a small clock somewhere in your office so that a quick glance will keep you on schedule without distracting you from present conversations or tasks.

Visit another world. Take time to look at another vocational area. For example, visit a business, an industry, a hospital, a school, or other work setting different from your own and see how professionals in these areas do things. You'll collect many good ideas that will work in your own location.

Cool down first. The professionally inviting counselor avoids responding while angry or upset. It is important to let tempers cool down a little before answering, particularly when you are responding in writing. Inappropriate comments exchanged in the heat of battle are difficult to take back.

Manage your time. Develop a system (a checklist of things to do or a schedule of important events to attend) and manage your time accordingly. Budgeting your time helps you expend your energy evenly so that no one area or task consumes all your attention.

Be visible. For a helping professional, visibility is an important part of accessibility. You may benefit by being out of the counseling center as much as you are in it. Whether you counsel in an agency, hospital, school, or other institution, it would be good to eat in the cafeteria occasionally, walk the halls, greet passersby, and visit a colleague at the far end of the hall.

Monitor college offerings. Keep up to date on classes taught at neighboring colleges and universities, particularly in your professional field. By posting these offerings, you can also invite your fellow professionals to take advantage of them.

Obey the "rule of four." If you spend much of your time doing paperwork and other chores that could be done by a volunteer with only four hours of training, then you are violating the "rule of four." Training and using volunteers is an excellent way to cut down on heavy workloads.

Visit an exemplary program. Spend some time with a colleague whose work you have heard about at a conference or through another source. Contact the counselor and ask if you can visit for a day to learn about his or her counseling program.

Feed the feeders. Take time to publicize your program. Write an article for your organization's newsletter or call the local newspaper and ask if their lifestyle or education editor is interested in a story. Informing the public about counseling services is important for your professional identity.

Nourish simple ideas. The next time you have an idea about how to improve your counseling program, write it down. Expand upon it. Write an article about your idea. Share your article with colleagues and incorporate their suggestions. When your idea has developed into a completed manuscript, send it to a state or national journal for publication.

Inviting Others Professionally

Share the consultant. When you schedule an in-service program, invite neighboring systems or related organizations to share the experience. Perhaps the cost of bringing the consultant can be shared as well. It makes good money sense, saves travel time for the consultant, and invites a feeling of professional cooperation.

Make the telephone your ally. Use the phone with professional courtesy. For example, identify yourself when calling others: "Good morning, this is Bob Smith. Is Mrs. Jones available?" By the same token, answer the phone in a friendly, open manner. A counselor who answers, "Counseling Center," could as easily say, "Good afternoon, Counseling Center, Bob Smith speaking. May I help you?"

Brighten up the center. Just because they stuck you in a closet is no reason it has to look like one! Hang posters, get some living plants, and make your office a place where people want to come. A fresh coat of paint does miracles. Moreover, be sure to consider the hallways, lounges, rest rooms, lobby, and other public areas of your facility. They also add to, or subtract from, your counseling center.

Follow through promptly. One of the most significant characteristics of the professionally inviting counselor is that he or she follows through promptly. The most positive action, when long delayed, loses much of its value. In addition, when someone shares a problem, be sure to ask about it later. It is important to follow up your initial involvement with continued concern and interest.

Know your stuff. An organized counselor is better able to share professional information readily. Being able to locate materials easily to share ideas with staff, administration, and clients is a sign of professionalism. Careful record keeping, filing, and organization benefits everyone.

Strangle the paper monster. Unfortunately, counselors are sometimes among those who create forms for others to fill out. Try to keep the methods of communication between you and your clients and fellow professionals as easy and simple as possible. Time is precious. It should be valued highly and not spent on relatively unimportant activities.

Be positive. Counseling is a very demanding and sometimes frustrating profession. It is important to remain positive during difficult times. Constant criticism is destructive. Counselors are in ideal positions to listen to criticisms, frustrations, and complaints with an understanding and sympathetic ear, and at the same time help the staff, administration, and clients find constructive alternatives. A counselor who joins the chronic complainers and feeds the fires of discontent often violates the spirit of the inviting relationship.

Send a professional gift. Need to obtain a special gift for a colleague? Enter a subscription to a professional magazine or journal in that person's name. It is a gift that lasts all year, and perhaps even longer.

Hold a happy hour. Open your center after hours so that folks can drop by to enjoy refreshments and conversation. This time can be an excellent opportunity for the staff to develop a feeling of community as well as to present a mini-session for new ideas. These gatherings may be relaxing, with no business, or they may combine business with pleasure.

Give "expert" advice sparingly. One of the basic tenets of invitational counseling is recognition that every person has the potential to become more capable and self-supportive. For this reason, it is wise for counselors to be reluctant to provide a ready answer. Counseling is a way of helping people find alternatives and solutions and guiding them through decision-making processes to choose suitable courses of action. One of the best ways to help people is to invite them to do what they can and should do for themselves.

Maintain a giveaway library. Keep a fresh stock of books on hand that you cherish by visiting garage sales, library book sales, or flea markets. It is worth the small cost to watch a client's eyes when you say: "Here's a gift; it was written just for you."

Say no slowly. When you must give a negative response to a request, let it come after you have listened carefully and considered the request fully. Failure to hear the person out can hurt more than the negative answer. The secret is to encourage the expression of the request fully before it is decided upon.

Check your timing. Timing is very important in counseling. Too much, too soon, too little, or too late can weaken invitational counseling. When sending invitations, counselors should ask: *What* invitation, from *whom,* is most likely to be accepted by *this* person at *this* time?

Invite explicitly. The more explicit an invitation, the more it lends itself to acceptance. Vagueness creates misunderstanding, and others wonder: "What was meant by that?" Precision and clarity are signs of the inviting relationship.

Float the staff meeting. Move the staff meeting around the building and meet in different environments. This gives a freshness to meetings and a new outlook on problems. It also helps to get everyone involved. And no matter where you meet, remember to arrange for something to eat and drink. The care and feeding of staff members is most important. Even such simple fare as coffee or tea and cookies primes the pump for a successful meeting.

Encourage participation. If you would like more participation in staff meetings, you can encourage discussion of important issues by dividing and subdividing the group. Start with pairs, then groups of four, and later larger groups if possible. It's difficult to remain silent and unresponsive when you're 50 percent of the group!

Invite positive public relations. It's never a matter of whether or not a counseling center has public relations; it's a matter of what kind. To invite positive public relations, make sure that the majority of messages sent to colleagues, clients, and community members are positive.

Be accessible. As a professional person you provide important services. If you set up office hours that are an imposition on other people, or if visitors must ask permission of the receptionist to see you, then few people will feel welcome to use counseling services. Moreover, if you put a "Do Not Disturb" sign on your office door, expect people to become disturbed. Reasonable availability is a hallmark of the professionally inviting counselor.

REFERENCES

ABELSON, R. (1979). Differences between belief systems and knowledge systems. *Cognitive Science, 3,* 355–366.

ABURDENE, P., & NAISBITT, J. (1992). *Megatrends for women.* New York: Villard.

ALBERTI, R. E., & EMMONS, M. L. (1978). *Your perfect right* (3rd ed.). San Luis Obispo, CA: Impact Publishers.

ALLPORT, G. W. (1937). *Personality: A psychological interpretation.* New York: Holt, Rinehart & Winston.

ALLPORT, G. W. (1943). The ego in contemporary psychology. *Psychological Review, 50,* 451–478.

ALLPORT, G. W. (1955). *Becoming: Basic considerations for a psychology of personality.* New Haven, CT: Yale University Press.

ALLPORT, G. W. (1961). *Pattern and growth in personality.* New York: Holt, Rinehart & Winston.

AMATEA, E. S. (1989). *Brief strategic intervention for school behavior problems.* San Francisco: Jossey-Bass.

ANGELOU, M. (1970). *I know why the caged bird sings.* New York: Random House. (Reprinted 1983, Bantam.)

ANSBACHER, H., & ANSBACHER, R. (1956). *The individual psychology of Alfred Alder: A systematic presentation in selections from his writings.* New York: Harper & Row. (Reprinted 1964, HarperCollins.)

ARBUCKLE, D. S. (1965). *Counseling: Philosophy, theory and practice.* Boston: Allyn & Bacon.

ARBUCKLE, D. S. (1975). *Counseling and psychotherapy: An existential humanistic view* (3rd ed.). Boston: Allyn & Bacon.

ARCENEAUX, C. J. (1994). Trust: An exploration of its nature and significance. *Journal of Invitational Theory and Practice, 3*(1), 35–49.

ASPY, C. B., & ASPY, D. N. (1993). The human age in education. *Journal of Invitational Theory and Practice, 2*(1), 5–11.

ASPY, D. N. (1972). *Toward a technology for humanizing education.* Champaign, IL: Research Press.

AUBREY, R. F. (1977). Historical development of guidance and counseling and implications for the future. *Personnel and Guidance Journal, 55,* 288–295.

AUBREY, R. F. (1982). A house divided: Guidance and counseling in 20th century America. *Personnel and Guidance Journal, 16,* 198–204.

AVILA, D. L., COMBS, A. W., & PURKEY, W. W. (Eds.). (1977). *The helping relationship sourcebook* (2nd ed.). Boston: Allyn & Bacon.

AXLINE, V. M. (1947). Nondirective therapy for poor readers. *Journal of Consulting Psychology, 11,* 61–69.

BAKER, S. B. (1992). *School counseling for the twenty-first century.* New York: Merrill.

BANDURA, A. (1982). Self-efficacy mechanism in human agency. *American Psychologist, 37*(2), 122–147.

BANDURA, A. (1986). *Social foundations of thought and action: A social cognitive theory.* Englewood Cliffs, NJ: Prentice-Hall.

BARDON, J. I. (1976). The state of the art (and science) of school psychology. *American Psychologist, 31,* 785–791.

BASSO, K. H. (1979). *Portraits of "The Whiteman": Linguistic play and cultural symbols among the western Apache.* New York: Cambridge University Press.

BAUM, L. F. (Adapted by Horace J. Elias, 1939, renewed 1976). *The wizard of Oz.* Metro Goldwyn-Mayer. Baltimore, Md.: Ottenheimer Publishers.

BELKIN, G. S. (1976). *Counseling directions in theory and practice.* Dubuque, IA: Kendall Hunt.

BENJAMIN, A. (1981). *The helping interview* (3rd ed.). Boston: Houghton Mifflin.

BENNIS, W., & NANUS, B. (1985). *Leaders: The strategies for taking charge.* New York: Harper & Row.

BEUTLER, L. E. (1983). *Eclectic psychotherapy: A systematic approach.* New York: Pergamon Press.

BLAILIFFE, B. (1978, March). *The significance of the self-concept in the knowledge society.* Paper presented at the meeting of the Self-Concept Symposium, Boston, MA.

BLOOM, B. S. (1976). *Human characteristics and school learning.* New York: McGraw-Hill.

BORDERS, L. D. (1989). Developmental cognitions of first practicum supervisees. *Journal of Counseling Psychology, 36,* 163–169.

BORDIN, E. S. (1968). *Psychological counseling* (2nd ed.). Englewood Cliffs, NJ: Prentice-Hall.

BRABECK, M. M., & WELFEL, E. R. (1985). Counseling theory: Understanding the trend toward eclecticism from a developmental perspective. *Journal of Counseling and Development, 63,* 343–348.

BRAMMER, L. M. (1988). *The helping relationship: Process and skills* (4th ed.). Englewood Cliffs, NJ: Prentice-Hall.

BROWN, D., PRYZWANSKY, W. B., & SCHULTE, A. C. (1991). *Psychological consultation: Introduction to theory and practice* (2nd ed.). Boston: Allyn & Bacon.

BUBER, M. (1958). *I and thou.* New York: Scribner.

BUGENTAL, J. F. (1989). *The search for authenticity: An existential-analytic approach to psychotherapy.* New York: Ivington.

BURNETT, P. (1993, March). Self concept, self esteem and self talk:

Implications for counseling children. Paper presented at the meeting of the American Counseling Association, Atlanta, GA.

BURNS, G. (1976). *Living it up, Or, they still love me in Altoona.* New York: Berkeley Publishing Corp.

BUSCAGLIA, L. (1972). *Love.* New York: Charles B. Slack. (Reprinted 1985, Fawcett.)

BUSCAGLIA, L. (1984). *Loving each other: The challenge of human relationships.* New York: Holt, Rinehart & Winston.

CALVINO, I. (1974). *Invisible cities* (trans. W. Weaver). New York: Harcourt Brace Jovanovich. (Original work published 1972.)

CAMPBELL, D. (1990). *If you don't know where you're going, you'll probably end up somewhere else* (rev. ed.). Allen, TX: Tabor Publication.

CANTER, L., & CANTER, M. (1976). *Assertive discipline: A take-charge approach for today's educator.* Santa Monica, CA: Canter and Associates.

CAPUZZI, D., & GROSS, D. R. (1992). *Introduction to group counseling.* Denver, CO: Love Publishing.

CARKHUFF, R. R. (1969a). *Helping and human relations: A primer for lay and professional helpers: Vol. 2. Selection and training.* New York: Holt, Rinehart & Winston.

CARKHUFF, R. R. (1969b). *Helping and human relations: A primer for lay and professional helpers: Vol. 2. Practice and research.* New York: Holt, Rinehart & Winston.

CARKHUFF, R. R. (1987). *The art of helping* (6th ed.). Amherst, MA: Human Resource Development Press.

CARKHUFF, R. R. (1988). *The age of new capitalism.* Amherst, MA: Human Resource Development Press.

CECIL, J. H., & COMAS, R. E. (1986). Faculty perceptions of CACREP accreditation. *Counselor Education and Supervision, 25,* 237–245.

CHAIKIN, A. L., DERLEGA, V. J., & MILLER, S. J. (1976). Effects of room environment on self disclosure in a counseling analogue. *Journal of Counseling Psychology, 23,* 479–481.

CHAMBERLIN, J. G. (1981). *The educating act: A phenomenological view.* Washington, DC: University Press of America.

COMBS, A. W. (Ed.). (1962). *Perceiving, behaving, becoming.* Washington, DC: Association for Supervision and Curriculum Development.

COMBS, A. W. (1965). *The professional education of teachers: A perceptual view of teacher preparation.* Boston: Allyn & Bacon.

COMBS, A. W. (1974). Why the humanist movement needs a perceptual psychology. *Journal of the Association for the Study of Perception, 9,* 1–13.

COMBS, A. W. (1982). *A personal approach to teaching: Beliefs that make a difference.* Boston: Allyn & Bacon.

COMBS, A. W. (1989). *A theory of practice: Guidelines for counseling practice.* Newbury Park, CA: Sage Publications.

COMBS, A. W., & AVILA, D. L. (1984). *The helping relationship* (3rd ed.). Boston: Allyn & Bacon.

COMBS, A. W., AVILA, D. L., & PURKEY, W. W. (1978). *Helping rela-*

tionships: Basic concepts for the helping professions (2nd ed.). Boston: Allyn & Bacon.

COMBS, A. W., BLUME, R. A., NEWMAN, A. J., & WASS, H. L. (1974). *The professional education of teachers: A humanistic approach to teacher preparation.* Boston: Allyn & Bacon.

COMBS, A. W., & GONZALEZ, D. M. (1994). *Helping relationships: Basic concepts for the helping professions* (4th ed.). Boston: Allyn & Bacon.

COMBS, A. W., RICHARDS, A. C., & RICHARDS, F. (1976). *Perceptual psychology: A humanistic approach to the study of persons.* New York: Harper & Row.

COMBS, A. W., RICHARDS, A. C., & RICHARDS, F. (1988). *Perceptual psychology: A humanistic approach to the study of persons.* Lanham, MD: University Press of America.

COMBS, A. W., & SNYGG, D. (1959). *Individual behavior: A perceptual approach to behavior* (2nd ed.). New York: Harper & Row.

COMBS, A. W., & SOPER, D. W. (1963). The perceptual organization of effective counselors. *Journal of Counseling Psychology, 10,* 222–227.

COMBS, A. W., SOPER, D. W., GOODING, C. T., BENTON, J. A., DICKMAN, J. F., & USHER, R. H. (1969). *Florida studies in the helping professions* (Social Science Monograph No. 37). Gainesville, FL: University of Florida Press.

COOPERSMITH, S. (1981). *The antecedents of self-esteem* (2nd ed.). New York: Consulting Psychologist Press.

COPELAND, A. (1939). *What to listen for in music.* New York: McGraw-Hill. (Reprinted 1985, Mentor Books.)

COREY, G. (1991). *Theory and practice of counseling and psychotherapy* (4th ed.). Pacific Grove, CA: Brooks/Cole.

COREY, G., COREY, M., & CALLANAN, P. (1993). *Issues and ethics in the helping professions* (4th ed.). Pacific Grove, CA: Brooks/Cole.

CORMIER, W. H., & CORMIER, L. S. (1991). *Interviewing strategies for helpers: Fundamental skills and cognitive behavioral interventions* (3rd ed.). Pacific Grove, CA: Brooks/Cole.

COTTLE, W. C., & DOWNIE, N. M. (1970). *Preparation for counseling* (2nd ed.). Englewood Cliffs, NJ: Prentice-Hall.

COVEY, S. R. (1989). *The seven habits of highly effective people.* New York: Simon & Schuster.

CUMMINGS, E. E. (1935). *No thanks.* New York: Golden Eagle Press.

DEAL, T. E., & KENNEDY, A. A. (1985). *Corporate cultures: The rites and rituals of corporate life.* Reading, MA: Addison-Wesley.

DELL, D. M. (1973). Counselor power base, influence attempt, and behavior change in counseling. *Journal of Counseling Psychology, 20,* 399–405.

DEMING, W. E. (1986). *Out of the crisis.* Cambridge, MA: MIT Center for Advanced Engineering Study.

DERLEGA, V. J., & CHAIKIN, A. L. (1975). *Sharing intimacy: What we reveal to others and why.* Englewood Cliffs, NJ: Prentice-Hall.

DESCARTES, R. (1912). *Principles of philosophy: A discourse on method.* New York: E. P. Dutton & Co. (Original work published 1644.)

DEWEY, J. (1933). *How we think.* Lexington, MA: Heath.

DIGGORY, J. C. (1966). *Self-evaluation: Concepts and studies.* New York: Wiley.

DINKMEYER, D., DINKMEYER, D., JR., & SPERRY, L. (1987). *Adlerian counseling and psychotherapy* (2nd ed.). Columbus, OH: Merrill.

DOWNING, C. J. (1983). A behavior classification system for counselors: A new look at psychotherapy. *Humanistic Education and Development, 21,* 138–145.

DWORKIN, A., HANEY, C., DWORKIN, R., & TELSCHOW, R. (1990). Stress and illness behavior among urban public school teachers. *Educational Administration Quarterly, 26*(1), 60–72.

EGAN, G. (1994). *The skilled helper: A model for systematic helping and interpersonal relating* (5th ed.). Pacific Grove, CA: Brooks/Cole.

EMERY, S. (1978). *Actualizations: You don't have to rehearse to be yourself.* Garden City, NY: Doubleday.

EPSTEIN, J. L. (1991). Pathways to partnership: What we can learn from federal, state, district, and school initiatives. *Phi Delta Kappan, 72*(5), 344–349.

FAIRCHILD, T. N. (1986). Time analysis: Accountability tool for counselors. *The School Counselor, 34,* 36–43.

FELKER, S. A. (1973). Intellectual ability and counseling effectiveness: Another view. *Counselor Education and Supervision, 13,* 146–150.

FERGUSON, M. (1980). *The Aquarian Conspiracy: Personal and social transformation in the 1980's.* Los Angeles, CA: J. P. Tarcher.

FRANKL, V. (1968). *The doctor and the soul: From psychotherapy to legotherapy.* New York: Knopf. (Reprinted 1986, Random House.)

FREEMAN, A., & DEWOLF, R. (1989). *Woulda, coulda, shoulda: Overcoming regrets, mistakes, and missed opportunities.* New York: Silver Arrow Books.

FROMM, E. (1956). *The art of loving: An inquiry into the nature of love.* New York: Harper & Row. (Reprinted 1989, HarperCollins.)

FUGUA, D., NEWMAN, J., ANDERSON, M. & JOHNSON, A. (1986). Preliminary study of internal dialogue in a training setting. *Psychological Reports, 58,* 163–172.

GAZDA, G. M. (1989). *Group counseling: A developmental approach* (4th ed.). Boston: Allyn & Bacon.

GAZDA, G. M., ASBURY, F. R., BALZER, F. J., CHILDERS, W. C., & WALTERS, R. P. (1991). *Human relations development: A manual for educators* (4th ed.). Boston: Allyn & Bacon.

GEORGE, R. L., & CRISTIANI, T. S. (1990). *Counseling: Theory and practice* (3rd ed.). Englewood Cliffs, NJ: Prentice-Hall.

GILLIGAN, C. (1982). *In a different voice.* Cambridge, MA: Harvard University Press.

GITLOW, H. S., & GITLOW, S. J. (1987). *The Deming guide to quality and competitive position.* Englewood Cliffs, NJ: Prentice-Hall.

GLADDING, S. T. (1991). *Group work: A counseling specialty.* New York: Macmillan.

GLADDING, S. T. (1992). *Counseling: A comprehensive profession.* New York: Macmillan.

GLASSER, W. (1981). *Stations of the mind*. New York: Harper & Row.

GLOCK, M. D. (1972). Is there a Pygmalion in the classroom? *The Reading Teacher, 25,* 405–408.

GOFFMAN, E. (1959). *The presentation of self in everyday life*. New York: Doubleday.

GOLDBERG, C. (1977). *Therapeutic partnership: Ethical concerns in psychotherapy*. New York: Springer-Verlag.

GOLDSTEIN, K. (1939). *The organism*. New York: American Book Company.

GOLDSTEIN, K. (1963). *Human nature in the light of psychopathology*. New York: Schocken Books.

GOOD, C. V. (Ed.). (1945). *Dictionary of education*. New York: McGraw-Hill.

HAASE, R. F., & DIMATTA, D. J. (1976). Special environments and verbal conditioning in a quasi-counseling interview. *Journal of Counseling Psychology, 23,* 414–421.

HACKNEY, H., & CORMIER, L. (1994). *Counseling strategies and interventions* (4th ed.). Boston: Allyn & Bacon.

HALL, E. T. (1959). *The silent language*. New York: Doubleday (Reprinted 1980, Greenwood Press.)

HAMACHEK, D. E. (1991). *Encounters with the self* (4th ed.). New York: Holt, Rinehart & Winston.

HANSEN, J. C., HIMES, B. S., & MEIER, S. (1990). *Consultation: Concepts and practices*. Englewood Cliffs, NJ: Prentice-Hall.

HARPER, K., & PURKEY, W. W. (1993). Self-concept-as-learner of middle level students. *Research in Middle Level Education, 17,* 80–89.

HATTIE, J. (1992). *Self-concept*. Hillsdale, NJ: Erlbaum.

HEILBRUN, C. G. (1988). *Writing a woman's life*. New York: Ballantine Books.

HERBERT, M. (1987). *Behavioral treatment of problem children: A practice manual* (2nd ed.). London: Academic Press.

HOBBS, N. (Ed.). (1975). *The future of children: Categories, labels, and their consequences*. Nashville, TN: Vanderbilt University Press.

HOBBS, N. (1982). *The troubled and troubling child*. San Francisco: Jossey-Bass.

HORNEY, K. (1939). *New ways in psychoanalysis*. New York: W. W. Norton. (Reprinted 1964.)

HUBER, C. H., & BACKLUND, B. A. (1992). *The twenty minute counselor*. New York: Continuum.

HUNT, J. M. (1961). *Intelligence and experience*. New York: Ronald Press.

HUNT, J. M. (1964). The implications of changing ideas on how children develop intellectually. *Children, 11,* 83–91.

HUNT, J. M. (Ed) (1972). *Human intelligence*. New Brunswick, NJ: Transaction Press.

HUSSERL, E. (1952). *Ideas: General introduction to pure phenomenology* (trans. W. R. Boyce Gibson). New York: Macmillan.

HUSSERL, E. (1977). *Phenomenological psychology: Lectures, summer semester, 1925*. (trans. John Scanlon). The Hague: Nijhoff.

HUTCHINS, D. E. (1979). Systematic counseling: The T-F-A model for counselor intervention. *Personnel and Guidance Journal, 57,* 529–531.

IVEY, A. E. (1969). The intentional individual: A process-outcome view of behavioral psychology. *The Counseling Psychologist, 1,* 56–59.

IVEY, A. E. (1991). *Developmental strategies for helpers.* Pacific Grove, CA: Brooks/Cole.

IVEY, A. E. (1994). *Intentional interviewing and counseling: Facilitating client development in a multicultural society* (3rd ed.). Pacific Grove, CA: Brooks/Cole.

IVEY, A. E. & AUTHIER, J. (1978). *Microcounseling: Innovations in interviewing, counseling, psychotherapy, and psychoeducation* (2nd ed.). Springfield, IL: Charles C. Thomas.

IVEY, A. E., & SIMEK-DOWNING, L. (1980). *Counseling and psychotherapy: Skills, theory and practice.* Englewood Cliffs, NJ: Prentice-Hall.

JANTSCH, E. (1980). *The self-organizing universe: Scientific and human implications of the emerging paradigm of evolution.* Oxford, England: Pergamon Press.

JOHNSON, D. W. (1990). *Reaching out: Interpersonal effectiveness and self-actualization* (4th ed.). Englewood Cliffs, NJ: Prentice-Hall.

JOHNSON, S. M. (1977). *First person singular: Living the good life alone.* Philadelphia: Lippincott.

JOURARD, S. M. (1964). *The transparent self: Self-disclosure and well-being.* Princeton, NJ: Van Nostrand Reinhold.

JOURARD, S. M. (1968). *Disclosing man to himself* (2nd ed.). New York: Van Nostrand Reinhold.

JOURARD, S. M. (1971a). *Self-disclosure: An experimental analysis of the transparent self.* New York: Wiley-Interscience.

JOURARD, S. M. (1971b). *The transparent self: Self-disclosure and well-being* (2nd ed.). Princeton, NJ: Van Nostrand Reinhold.

JOURARD, S. M. (1974). *The undisclosed self.* New York: Mentor Books.

JUNG, C. G. (1974). *The undiscovered self.* New York: Mentor Books.

KEGAN, R. (1982). *The evolving self: Problem and process in human development.* Cambridge, MA: Harvard University Press.

KELLEY, H. H. (1979). *Personal relationships: Their structures and processes.* Hillsdale, NJ: Erlbaum.

KELLY, G. A. (1955). *The psychology of personal constructs.* New York: W. W. Norton.

KELLY, G. A. (1963). *Theory of personality: The psychology of personal constructs.* New York: W. W. Norton.

KING, P. T., & BENNINGTON, K. F. (1972). Psychoanalysis and counseling. In B. Stefflre & W. H. Grant (Eds.), *Theories of counseling* (2nd ed., pp. 177–244). New York: McGraw-Hill.

KNOWLES, J. H. (1977). The responsibility of the individual. In J. H. Knowles (Ed.), *Doing better and feeling worse: Health in the United States.* New York: W. W. Norton.

L'ABATE, L. (1981). Classification of counseling and therapy theorists, methods, processes, and goals: The E-R-A model. *Personnel and Guidance Journal, 59,* 263–265.

LAPPÉ, F. M., & DUBOIS, P. M. (1994). *The quickening of America: Rebuilding our nation, remaking our lives.* San Francisco: Jossey-Bass.

LAZARUS, A. (1981). *Multimodal therapy*. New York: McGraw-Hill.

LEHR, J., & MARTIN, C. (1992). *We're all at risk: Inviting learning for everyone*. Minneapolis, MN: Educational Media Corporation.

LEONARD, G. (1968). *Education and ecstasy*. New York: Delacorte Press.

LEONARD, G. (1987). *Education and ecstasy: And the great school reform hoax* (rev. ed.). Berkeley, CA: North Atlantic Books.

LEWIN, K. (1951). *Field theory in social science*. New York: Harper.

LEWING, R. J., JR., & COWGER, E. L., JR. (1982). Time spent on college counselor functions. *Journal of College Student Personnel, 23*, 41–48.

LINDBERGH, A. M. (1955). *Gift from the sea*. New York: Vintage Books. (Reprinted 1991, Random House.)

LIPPITT, R., & WHITE, R. (1960). *Autocracy and democracy*. New York: Harper & Row.

LOPEZ, F. G. (1985). Brief therapy: A model for early counselor training. *Counselor Education and Supervision, 34*, 307–316.

LOWE, C. M. (1961). The self-concept: Fact or artifact? *Psychological Bulletin, 58*, 325–336.

LUDWIG, D. J., & MAEHR, M. L. (1967). Changes in self-concept and stated behavioral preferences. *Child Development, 38*, 453–467.

MACIVER, O. (1991). The "Pass It On" Exercise. Presented at the Florida Regional Conference of the National Middle School Association. Fort Lauderdale, FL.

MAHONEY, M. (1977). Personal science: A cognitive learning therapy. In A. Ellis & R. Grieger (Eds.), *Handbook of rational-emotive therapy* (pp. 352–366). New York: Springer-Verlag.

MARTIN, R., & POLLARD, E. (1980). *Learning to change: A self-management approach to adjustment*. New York: McGraw-Hill.

MARZANO, R. J., PICKERING, D., & MCTIGHE, J. (1993). *Assessing student outcomes: Performance assessment using the dimensions of learning model*. Alexandria, VA: Association for Supervision and Curriculum Development.

MASLOW, A. H. (1962). *Toward a psychology of being*. New York: Van Nostrand Reinhold.

MASLOW, A. H. (1968). *Toward a psychology of being* (2nd ed.). New York: Van Nostrand Reinhold.

MASTERS, J. C., BURISH, T. G., HOLLON, S. V. & RIMM, D. C. (1987). *Behavior therapy: Techniques and empirical findings* (3rd ed.) San Diego, CA: Harcourt-Brace.

MAY, R. (1961). The context of psychotherapy. In M. I. Stein (Ed.), *Contemporary psychotherapies* (pp. 288–304). New York: Free Press.

MAY, R. (Ed.). (1966). *Existential psychology*. New York: Random House. (Reprinted 1990, Random House.)

MAY, R. (1969). *Love and will*. New York: W. W. Norton. (Reprinted 1989, Doubleday.)

MAYEROFF, M. (1971). *On caring*. New York: Harper & Row (Reprinted 1990, HarperCollins.)

MCGINNIS, A. L. (1979). *The friendship factor*. Minneapolis, MN: Augsburg Publishing House.

MEAD, G. H. (1934). *Mind, self, and society.* Chicago: University of Chicago Press. (Revised 1967.)

MEICHENBAUM, D. (1974). Cognitive behavior modification. *University Programs Modular Studies.* Morristown, NJ: General Learning Press.

MEICHENBAUM, D. (1977). *Cognitive behavior modification: An integrative approach.* New York: Plenum Press.

MEICHENBAUM, D. (1983). *Stress reduction and prevention.* New York: Plenum Press.

MEIER, S. T., & DAVIS, S. R. (1993). *The elements of counseling* (2nd ed.). Pacific Grove, CA: Brooks/Cole.

MORRIS, V. C. (1966). *Existentialism in education.* New York: Harper & Row. (Revised 1990, Waveland Press.).

NODDINGS, N. (1984). *Caring: A feminine approach to ethics and moral education.* Berkeley, CA: University of California Press.

NODDINGS, N. (1992). *The challenge to care in schools: An alternative approach to education.* New York: Teachers College Press.

NOVAK, J. M. (Ed.). (1992). *Advancing invitational thinking.* San Francisco, CA: Caddo Gap Press.

NOVAK, J. M. (1994). Introduction: The talk and walk of democratic teacher education. In J. M. Novak (Ed.), *Democratic teacher education: Programs, processes, problems, and prospects.* Albany, NY: State University of New York Press.

O'HANLON, W. H., & WEINER-DAVIS, M. (1989). *In search of solutions: A new direction in psychotherapy.* New York: Guilford.

ORR, D. W. (1965). *Professional counseling on human behavior: Its principles and practices.* New York: Franklin Watts.

PAJARES, M. F. (1992). Teachers' beliefs and educational research: Cleaning up a messy construct. *Review of Educational Research, 62*(3), 307–332.

PARSONS, R. D., & WICKS, R. J. (1994). *Counseling strategies and intervention techniques for the human services* (4th ed.). Boston: Allyn & Bacon.

PATTERSON, C. H. (1959). *Counseling and psychotherapy: Theory and practice.* New York: Harper & Row.

PATTERSON, C. H. (1984). Empathy, warmth and genuineness in psychotherapy: A review of reviews. *Psychotherapy, 21,* 431–438.

PATTERSON, C. H. (1985a). New light for counseling theory. *Journal of Counseling and Development, 63,* 349–350.

PATTERSON, C. H. (1985b). *The therapeutic relationship: Foundations for an eclectic psychotherapy.* Pacific Grove, CA: Brooks/Cole.

PATTERSON, L. E., & EISENBERG, S. (1983). *The counseling process* (3rd ed.). Boston: Houghton Mifflin.

PAXTON, P. (1993). Total Quality Management and invitational theory. *Journal of Invitational Theory and Practice, 2*(1), 29–34.

PECK, M. S. (1978). *The road less traveled: A new psychology of love, traditional values and spiritual growth.* New York: Simon & Schuster.

PEPINSKY, H. B., & PEPINSKY, P. (1954). *Counseling: Theory and practice.* New York: Ronald Press.

PETERS, T. J., & WATERMAN, R. H., JR. (1982). *In search of excellence: Lessons from America's best-run companies.* New York: Warner Books.

PIETROFESA, J. J., HOFFMAN, A., & SPLETE, H. H. (1984). *Counseling: An introduction* (2nd ed.). Boston: Houghton Mifflin.

PIETROFESA, J. J., LEONARD, G. E., & VAN HOOSE, W. (1978). *The authentic counselor* (2nd ed.) Chicago: Rand McNally.

PINES, A. M., & ARONSON, E. (1981). *Burnout: From tedium to personal growth.* New York: Free Press.

PIRSIG, R. M. (1974). *Zen and the art of motorcycle maintenance: An inquiry into values.* New York: William Morrow.

POSNER, G. J., STRIKE, K. A., HEWSON, P. W., & GERTZOG, W. A. (1982). Accommodation of a scientific conception: Toward a theory of conceptual change. *Science Education, 66,* 211–227.

POWERS, W. T. (1973). *Behavior: The control of perception.* Chicago: Aldine.

PURKEY, W. W. (1970). *Self-concept and school achievement.* Englewood Cliffs, NJ: Prentice-Hall.

PURKEY, W. W. (1978). *Inviting school success.* Belmont, CA: Wadsworth.

PURKEY, W. W. (1991). The 5-P relay: An exciting way to create an inviting school. *Invitational Education Forum.* University of North Carolina at Greensboro, *12*(2), 9–14.

PURKEY, W. W. (1992a). A brief history of the International Alliance for Invitational Education. *Journal of Invitational Theory and Practice, 1*(1), 17–20.

PURKEY, W. W. (1992b). Conflict resolution: An invitational approach. *Journal of Invitational Theory and Practice, 1*(2), 111–116.

PURKEY, W. W., & NOVAK, J. M. (1984). *Inviting school success: A self-concept approach to teaching and learning* (2nd ed.). Belmont, CA: Wadsworth.

PURKEY, W. W., & NOVAK, J. M. (1988). *Education: By invitation only.* Bloomington, IN: Phi Delta Kappa Educational Foundation.

PURKEY, W. W., & NOVAK, J. M. (1993). The Invitational Helix: A systematic guide for individual and organizational development. *Journal of Invitational Theory and Practice, 2*(2), 59–67.

PURKEY, W. W., & NOVAK, J. M. (1995). *Inviting school success: A self-concept approach to teaching, learning, and democratic practice* (3rd ed.). Belmont, CA: Wadsworth.

PURKEY, W. W., & SCHMIDT, J. J. (1987). *The inviting relationship: An expanded perspective for professional counseling.* Englewood Cliffs, NJ: Prentice-Hall.

PURKEY, W. W., & SCHMIDT, J. J. (1990). *Invitational learning for counseling and development.* Ann Arbor, MI: ERIC/CAPS.

PURKEY, W. W., SCHMIDT, J. J., & MCBRIEN, D. (1982). The professionally inviting school counselor. *The School Counselor, 30,* 84–88.

PURKEY, W. W., & STANLEY, P. H. (1991). *Invitational teaching, learning, and living.* Washington, DC: National Education Association.

PURKEY, W. W., & STANLEY, P. H. (1994). *The inviting school treasury: 1001 ways to invite student success.* New York: Scholastic Press.

REICH, C. A. (1970). *The greening of America.* New York: Random House.

RIPLEY, D. M. (1985). *Invitational teaching behaviors in the associate degree clinical setting.* Unpublished master's thesis, University of North Carolina at Greensboro.

ROEBER, E. C. (1963). *The school counselor.* Washington, DC: The Center for Applied Research in Education.

ROGERS, C. R. (1947). Some observations on the organization of personality. *American Psychologist, 2,* 358–368.

ROGERS, C. R. (1951). *Client-centered therapy: Its current practice, implications, and theory.* Boston: Houghton Mifflin.

ROGERS, C. R. (1952). Client-centered psychotherapy. *Scientific American, 187*(5), 66–74.

ROGERS, C. R. (1957). The necessary and sufficient conditions of therapeutic personality change. *Journal of Consulting Psychology, 21,* 95–103.

ROGERS, C. R. (1958). The characteristics of a helping relationship. *Personnel and Guidance Journal, 37,* 6–16.

ROGERS, C. R. (1959). *Counseling and psychotherapy: Theory and practice.* New York: Harper & Row.

ROGERS, C. R. (1961). *On becoming a person: A therapist's view of psychotherapy.* Boston: Houghton Mifflin.

ROGERS, C. R. (1967). *Coming into existence.* New York: World Publishing.

ROGERS, C. R. (1969). *Freedom to learn.* Columbus, OH: Merrill.

ROGERS, C. R. (1980). *A way of being.* Boston: Houghton Mifflin.

ROGERS, C. R. (1983). *Freedom to learn for the eighties.* Columbus, OH: Merrill.

ROKEACH, M. (1968). *Beliefs, attitudes and values: A theory of organization and change.* San Francisco: Jossey-Bass.

ROSENTHAL, R., ARCHER, D., KOIVUMAKI, J., DIMATTEO, M., & ROGERS, P. (1974). Assessing sensitivity to nonverbal communication: The PONS test. *Psychology Today, 8*(4), 64–68.

RYCHLAK, J. F. (1985). Eclecticism in psychological theorizing: Good and bad. *Journal of Counseling and Development, 63,* 351–353.

SAINT-EXUPÉRY, A. (1943). *The little prince.* New York: Harcourt-Brace.

SCHMIDT, J. J. (1984). Counselor intentionality: An emerging view of process and performance. *Journal of Counseling Psychology, 31,* 383–386.

SCHMIDT, J. J. (1988). *Invitation to friendship.* Minneapolis, MN: Educational Media.

SCHMIDT, J. J. (1991). *A survival guide for the elementary/middle school counselor.* West Nyack, NY: The Center for Applied Research in Education.

SCHMIDT, J. J. (1993). *Counseling in schools: Essential services and comprehensive programs.* Boston, MA: Allyn & Bacon.

SCHMIDT, J. J. (1994). *Living intentionally and making life happen* (rev. ed.). Greenville, NC: Brookcliff.

SCHOMMER, M. (1990). Effects of beliefs about the nature of knowledge on comprehension. *Journal of Educational Psychology, 82,* 498–504.

SCHUNK, D. H. (1984). The self-efficacy perspective on achievement behavior. *Educational Psychologist, 19,* 119–128.

SCHUNK, D. H. (1989). Social cognition theory and self-regulating learning. In B. J. Zimmerman & D. H. Schunk (Eds.), *Self-regulated learning and academic achievement: Theory, research, and practice.* New York: Springer-Verlag.

SCHUNK, D. H. (1990). Goal setting and self-efficacy during self-regulated learning. *Educational Psychologist, 25,* 70–86.

SELIGMAN, M. E. (1991). *Learned optimism.* New York: Knopf.

SEXTON, T. L., & WHISTON, S. C. (1991). A review of the empirical basis for counseling: Implications for practice and training. *Counselor Education and Supervision, 30*(4), 330–354.

SHAFFER, L. F. (1947). The problem of psychotherapy. *American Psychologist, 2,* 459–467.

SHAVELSON, R., HUBNER, J., & STANTON, G. (1976). Self-concept: Validation of construct interpretations. *Review of Educational Research, 46,* 407–441.

SHERTZER, B., & STONE, S. C. (1974). *Fundamentals of counseling* (2nd ed.). Boston: Houghton Mifflin.

SHERTZER, B., & STONE, S. C. (1980). *Fundamentals of counseling* (3rd ed.). Boston: Houghton Mifflin.

SHERTZER, R., & STONE, S. C. (1981). *Fundamentals of guidance* (4th ed.). Boston: Houghton Mifflin.

SMITH, G. F. (1955). *Counseling in the secondary school.* New York: Macmillan.

SMITH, T. A., JR., SALTS, C. J., & SMITH, C. W. (1989). Preparing marriage and family therapy students to become employee assistance professionals. *Journal of Marital and Family Therapy, 15,* 419–424.

SNYGG, D., & COMBS, A. W. (1949). *Individual behavior.* New York: Harper & Row.

SPEARS, W. D., & DEESE, M. E. (1973). Self-concept as cause. *Educational Theory, 23,* 144–153.

STAFFORD, W. B. (1992). Invitational theory and counseling. In J. M. Novak (Ed.), *Advancing invitational thinking* (pp. 195–220). San Francisco, CA: Caddo Gap Press.

STANLEY, P. H. (1992). A bibliography for invitational theory and practice. *Journal of Invitational Theory and Practice, 1*(1), 52–69.

STEFFLRE, B., & GRANT, W. H. (1972). *Theories of counseling* (2nd ed.). New York: McGraw-Hill.

STEINEM, G. (1992). *Revolution from within: A book of self-esteem.* Boston: Little, Brown.

STEINER, C. M. (1990). *Scripts people live: Transactional Analysis of life scripts.* New York: Grove Weidenfeld.

STILLION, J., & SIEGEL, B. (1985). The intentionally inviting hierarchy. *Journal of Humanistic Education, 9,* 33–39.

STUHR, J. J. (1993). Democracy as a way of life. In J. J. Stuhr (Ed.), *Philosophy and the reconstruction of culture: Pragmatic essays after Dewey.* Albany, NY: State University of New York Press.

SWEENEY, T. J. (1981). *Adlerian counseling: Proven concepts and strategies.* Muncie, IN: Accelerated Development.

VACC, N. A., & BARDON, J. (Eds.). (1982). Assessment and appraisal: Issues, practices, and programs. *Measurement and Evaluation in Guidance, 15*(1).

VACC, N. A., & LOESCH, L. C. (1994). *A professional orientation to counseling* (2nd ed.). Muncie, IN: Accelerated Development.

VAILLANT, G. E. (1977). *Adaptation to life*. Boston: Little, Brown.

VARGAS, A. M., & BORKOWSKI, J. G. (1983). Physical attractiveness: Interactive effects of counselor and client on processes. *Journal of Counseling Psychology, 30,* 146–157.

WALZ, G., & BLEUER, J. (1992). *Student self-esteem: Vol. 1. A vital element in school success*. Ann Arbor, MI: ERIC/CAPS.

WALZ, G., GAZDA, G. M., & SHERTZER, B. (Eds.). (1991). *Counseling futures*. Ann Arbor, MI: ERIC/CAPS.

WARD, D. E. (1983). The trend toward eclecticism and the development of comprehensive models to guide counseling and psychotherapy. *The Personnel and Guidance Journal, 62,* 154–157.

WILLIAMSON, E. G. (1972). Trait-factor theory and individual differences. In B. Stefflre & W. H. Grant (Eds.), *Theories of counseling* (2nd ed., pp. 136–176). New York: McGraw-Hill.

WILSON, J. H. (1986). *The Invitational Elementary Classroom*. Springfield, IL: Charles C. Thomas.

WILSON, N. H., & ROTTER, J. C. (1982). School counseling: A look into the future. *Personnel and Guidance Journal, 60,* 353–357.

WRENN, C. G. (1962). *The counselor in a changing world*. Washington, DC: American Personnel and Guidance Association.

WRENN, C. G. (1973). *The world of the contemporary counselor*. Boston: Houghton Mifflin.

WYLIE, R. C. (1979). *The self-concept: Vol. 2. Theory and research on selected topics*. Lincoln, NE: University of Nebraska Press.

YALOM, I. (1985). *The theory and practice of group psychotherapy* (3rd ed.). New York: Basic Books.

ZARSKI, J. J., SWEENEY, T. J., & BARCIKOWSKI, R. S. (1977). Counseling effectiveness as a function of counselor social interest. *Journal of Counseling Psychology, 24,* 1–5.

ZIMMERMAN, B., BANDURA, A., & MARTINEZ-PONZ, M. (1992). Self-motivation for academic attainment: The toll of self-efficacy beliefs and personal goal setting. *American Educational Research Journal, 29*(3), 663–666.

ZIMMERMAN, I. L., & ALLEBRAND, G. N. (1965). Personality characteristics and attitudes toward achievement of good and poor readers. *Journal of Educational Research, 59,* 28–30.

NAME INDEX

Abelson, R., 34
Aburdene, P., 82
Alberti, R. E., 134
Allport, G., 26, 68
Amatea, E. S., 129
Angelou, M., 82
Ansbacher, H., 4, 157
Ansbacher, R., 4, 157
Arbuckle, D., 148, 179
Arceneaux, C., 9
Archer, D., 86
Aronson, E., 99
Asbury, F. R., 84, 111, 145
Aspy, C., 170
Aspy, D., 30, 170
Aubrey, R. F., 164, 165
Authier, J., 46
Avila, D. L., 24, 28, 31, 162

Backlund, B. A., 129
Baker, S., 164
Balzer, F. J., 84, 111, 145
Bandura, A., 30, 35, 44, 157
Barcikowski, R. S., 46
Bardon, J., 127, 174
Belkin, G. S., 149
Benjamin, A., 111
Bennington, K. F., 149
Bennis, W., 10
Benton, J. A., 68
Beutler, L. E., 156
Blailiffe, B., 34
Bleuer, J., 31, 42
Bloom, B. S., 21

Bordin, E. S., 150
Borkowski, J. G., 46
Brabeck, M. M., 156
Barmmerm, L. M., 84, 86, 114
Brown, D., 134
Buber, M., 41
Bugental, J. F., 8
Burish, T. G., 157
Burnett, P., 40
Burns, G., 18
Buscaglia, L., 74

Calvino, I., 113
Campbell, D., 57, 68
Canter, L., 50
Canter, M., 50
Capuzzi, D., 122, 124
Carkhuff, R. R., 3, 46, 111, 114, 157, 170
Cecil, J. H., 70
Chaikin, A. L., 46, 145
Chamberlin, J. G., 30
Childers, W. C., 84, 111, 145
Comas, R. E., 70
Combs, A. W., 3, 24, 27, 28, 31, 32, 35, 42, 46, 68, 157, 159, 162, 163
Coopersmith, S., 41
Copeland, A., 139
Corey, G., 163
Cormier, L., 111, 113, 114
Cormier, W. H., 113, 114
Cottle, W. C., 150
Couger, E. L., Jr., 172

Covey, S., 51, 82
Cristiani, T. S., 6

Davis, S. R., 21, 76, 89
Deal, T. E., 179
Deese, M. E., 35
Dell, D. M., 46
Deming, W. E., 105
Derlega, V. J., 46, 145
Dewey, J., 21
DeWolf, R., 21
Dickman, J. F., 68
Diggory, J. C., 26, 34
DiMatta, D. J., 46
DiMatteo, M., 86
Dinkmeyer, D. C., 4, 5, 48, 157, 170
Dinkmeyer, D. C., Jr., 4, 5, 48, 157
Downie, N. M., 150
Downing, C. J., 153
Dworkin, A., 79
Dworkin, R., 79

Egan, G., 84, 86, 111, 114, 150, 155, 157
Eisenberg, S., 111
Emery, S., 82
Emmons, M. L., 134
Epstein, J. L., 105

Fairchild, T. N., 127
Felker, S. A., 46
Ferguson, M., 176, 179
Frankl, V., 7
Freeman, A., 21
Fromm, E., 33, 70

Gazda, G. M., 78, 84, 111, 122, 145, 165, 180
George, R. L., 6
Gilligan, C., 68, 83
Gitlow, H. S., 40
Gitlow, S. J., 40
Gladding, S. T., 56, 122, 148, 164, 172, 173
Glasser, W., 163
Goffman, E., 42
Goldberg, C., 88
Goldstein, K., 26, 58

Gonzalez, D. M., 3, 157, 159, 163
Good, C. V., 148
Good, E. P., 163
Gooding, C. T., 68
Grant, W. H., 148
Gross, D. R., 122, 124

Haase, R. F., 46
Hackney, H., 111, 114
Hall, E. T., 68
Hamachek, D. E., 31, 42
Haney, C., 79
Hansen, J. C., 134
Harper, K., 31, 40
Hattie, J., 31, 32, 42
Heilbrun, C. G., 82
Herbert, M., 158
Himes, B. S., 134
Hobbs, N., 97, 101
Hoffman, A., 86, 111, 127
Hollon, S. V., 157
Horney, K., 34
Huber, C. H., 129
Hubner, J., 35
Hunt, J. M., 21, 73
Husserl, E., 26
Hutchins, D. E., 156

Ivey, A. E., 46, 50, 52–55, 84, 86, 111, 113, 114, 119, 163

Jantsch, E., 179
Johnson, D. W., 69
Johnson, S. M., 82
Jourard, S. M., 2, 21, 26, 32, 51, 76, 79, 93, 181
Jung, C. G., 145

Kegan, R., 46
Kelley, H. H., 145
Kelly, G., 4, 26, 157
Kennedy, A. A., 179
King, P. T., 149
Knowles, J. H., 73
Koivumaki, J., 86

L'Abate, L., 156
Lazarus, A., 157

Lehr, J., 145
Leonard, G. E., 69, 93
Lewin, K., 4, 26
Lewing, R. J., Jr., 172
Lippitt, R., 87
Loesch, L., 56, 70, 165
Lopez, F. G., 129
Lowe, C. M., 33
Ludwig, D. J., 34

MacIver, D., 105
Maehr, M. L., 34
Mahoney, M., 157
Martin, C., 145
Martin, R., 157
Martinez-Pons, M., 30
Marzano, R. J., 127
Maslow, A., 26, 42, 56
Masters, J. C., 157
May, R., 28, 42, 52–55, 69
Mayeroff, M., 71, 146
McGinnis, A. L., 82
McTighe, J., 127
Mead, G. H., 27
Meichenbaum, D., 30, 46, 157
Meier, S. T., 21, 76, 89, 134
Miller, S. J., 46
Morris, V. C., 1

Naisbitt, J., 82
Nanus, B., 10
Noddings, N., 56, 146
Novak, J. M., 2, 4, 21, 31, 52–55,
    93, 111, 139, 140, 146, 177,
    183, 184

O'Hanlon, W. H., 129
Orr, D. W., 151

Pajares, F., 34
Parsons, R. D., 3
Patterson, C. H., 3, 46, 156, 157,
    163
Patterson, L. E., 111
Paxton, P., 105
Peck, M. S., 82
Pepinsky, H. B., 149
Pepinsky, P., 149

Peters, T. J., 22
Pickering, D., 127
Pietrofesa, J. J., 69, 86, 111, 127,
    150
Pines, A. M., 99
Pirsig, R. M., 82
Pollard, E., 157
Powers, W. T., 30
Purkey, W. W., 2, 4, 24, 28, 31, 32,
    40, 50, 52–55, 93, 105, 111,
    131, 137, 139, 140, 146, 157,
    162, 163, 177, 181–184
Pryzwansky, W. B., 134

Reich, C. A., 179
Richards, A. C., 3, 32, 163
Richards, F., 3, 32, 163
Rimm, D. C., 157
Roeber, E. C., 165
Rogers, C. R., 3, 17, 22, 26, 32, 42,
    46, 48, 69, 147, 149, 154, 157,
    164
Rogers, P., 86
Rosenthal, R., 86
Rotter, J., 78, 165
Rychlak, J. F., 156

Salts, C. J., 173
Schmidt, J. J., 2, 4, 50, 52, 69, 70,
    78, 89, 126, 127, 134, 163, 164,
    170, 177, 183
Schommer, M., 34
Schulte, A., 134
Schunk, D. H., 30
Seligman, M. E., 7, 30, 35, 42
Sexton, T. L., 113, 144
Siegel, B., 139
Shaffer, L. F., 149
Shavelson, R., 35
Shertzer, B., 78, 148, 149, 164, 165,
    180
Simek-Downing, L., 50, 52, 84
Smith, C. W., 173
Smith, G. F., 150
Smith, T. A., Jr., 173
Snygg, D., 3, 28, 157
Soper, D. W., 46, 68
Spears, W. D., 35

Sperry, L., 4, 5, 48, 157
Splete, H. H., 86, 111, 127
Stafford, W., 10, 96, 147, 157
Stanley, P. H., 2, 146, 177, 184
Stanton, G., 35
Stefflre, B., 148
Steinem, G., 42
Steiner, C. M., 48
Stillion, J., 139
Stone, S. C., 148, 149, 164
Sweeney, T., 46, 149, 157

Telschow, R., 79

Usher, R. H., 68

Vacc, N., 56, 70, 127, 165
Vaillant, G. E., 179
VanHoose, W., 69
Vargas, A. M., 46

Walters, R. P., 84, 111, 145
Walz, G., 31, 42, 78, 165, 180
Ward, D. E., 157
Waterman, R. H., 22
Weiner-Davis, M., 129
Welfel, E. R., 156
Whiston, S. C., 113, 144
White, R., 87
Wicks, R. J., 3
Williamson, E. G., 149
Wilson, J. H., 183
Wilson, N. H., 78, 165
Wrenn, C. G., 43, 56, 78, 180
Wylie, R. C., 31, 32

Yalom, I., 124

Zarski, J. J., 46

SUBJECT INDEX

Adler, Alfred, 4, 5, 170
Agency counseling, 172–173
Alliance for Invitational Education, 182–183
American Counseling Association, 166, 171
  divisions, 166–167
Attending, 115

Behaviorism, 26
Blocking, 124
Brief therapy, 129–131
Business and industry counseling, 173

Caring, 56
Chuang-tse, 67
Clarifying, 116
Collaboration, 80
College counseling, 172
Communication skills, 114–122
Comparing and contrasting, 123–124
Compromising, 120
Conflict management, 131–138
Confronting, 120–121, 135
Consulting, 134–135
Counseling, 63
  careless functioning, 62
  commitment, 59
  contemporary and future of, 167–171, 173–177
  core conditions, 3
  defined, 1

developmental, 154
focus, 149–150
future directions, 78
goals, 57
inappropriate functioning, 60, 62
preventive, 154–155
process, 151–152
professional origins, 165
remedial, 153
responsibility, 58–59
skills, 58, 113–144
settings, 150–151, 171–173
and social changes, 175–176
and technology, 174–175
theory, 148–150
Counselors
  celebrating life, 75
  characteristics, 70–81
  contribution, 80–81
  cooperation, 79–80
  emotion, 71–73
  friendships, 75
  intellectual development, 73
  physical health, 73–74
  professional development, 77–78
  proficiency, 113–114, 139–144

Existential questions, 48–49
Eclecticism, 155–160

Facilitating skill, 122–123
Five "P's", 3, 97–108, 129
  assessment of, 104
  combining, 102–103

Five "P's" (*continued*)
   people, 98–99
   places, 99–100
   policies, 100
   processes, 101–102
   programs, 100–101
   relay, 105–108

Group skills, 122–126

Instructional skills, 125–126
   evaluating, 126
   presenting, 126
   soliciting feedback, 126
Intentionally disinviting, 60–61
Intentionally inviting, 64–67
Intentionality, 10–11, 26, 50–57
   bipolarity of, 53–55
   caring, 56
   definition, 52–53
   direction, 56–57
   goals, 57
   purpose, 57
Interpreting, 119–120
Invitational counseling
   accepting, 94
   assumptions, 2, 4, 20
   balance, 158
   choices, 15–17, 92–97
   compatibility with, 160–162
   defined, 2, 6
   "doing with," 5, 159
   elements of, 7–11
   evaluation, 90–91, 127–129
   expanded perspective, 89–92,
      164
   follow-up, 89–92
   framework for, 2
   the Helix, 139–144
   holistic view, 5–6
   ingredients of, 43
   initiating and responding, 86–89
   integrated model, 3–4, 6, 147,
      160–162
   involvement, 104–105, 108–109
   levels of, 11–13, 59–67
   intentionally disinviting, 11, 60–
      61

   intentionally inviting, 13, 64–67
   unintentionally disinviting, 12
   unintentionally inviting, 12
   limitations, 109
   managing interventions, 108–109
   the Net, 96–97
   not accepting, 94
   not sending, 93–94
   preparation, 84–86
   professional stance, 9, 49–51
   rationale, 19–20
   sending, 93
   spheres, 13–15, 70–81
   stages, 84–92
   styles, 17–19
   theoretical perspectives, 23

Listening, 115

Modeling, 124–125

Optimism, 7, 85, 178

Perception, 24–30, 47–48
   assumptions, 29–30
   clients', 44
   counselors', 46
   external vs. internal view, 30
Perceptual psychology, 27–30
Preparing, 125
Probing, 117–118
Protecting, 123

Questioning, 117

Research (*see also* Invitational
      counseling,evaluating), 127–128
Respect, 8–9
Responsibility, 58–59

School counseling, 171
Self-concept theory, 24, 30–41
   attributes, 32
   categories, 32
   consistency, 36–38 dynamism, 35
   learned, 39
   lifelong process, 40–41
   modifiable, 38–39

  organized, 32–33
  qualities of self, 31–32
Self-disclosing, 76
Shared leadership, 125
Supporting, 123
Structuring, 118–119
Summarizing, 119

Trust, 9, 92
Total Quality Management, 105
Treatment, 153–154

Unintentionally disinviting, 12, 61–63
Unintentionally inviting, 12, 63–64

TO THE OWNER OF THIS BOOK:

We hope that you have enjoyed *Invitational Counseling* as much as we have enjoyed writing it. We'd like to know as much about your experiences with the book as you care to offer. Only through your comments and the comments of others can we learn how to make *Invitational Counseling* a better book for future readers.

School: _____

Instructor's name: _____

1. For what course was this book assigned? _____

_____

2. What did you like most about the book? _____

_____

_____

3. What did you like least about the book? _____

_____

_____

4. Were all of the chapters of the book assigned for you to read? _____

   If not, which ones weren't? _____

5. In the space below, or in a separate letter, please let us know what other comments about the book you'd like to make. (For example, were any chapters or concepts particularly difficult?) We'd be delighted to hear from you!

_____

_____

_____

_____

_____

Optional:

Your name: _____ Date: _____

May Brooks/Cole quote you, either in promotion for *Invitational Counseling* or
in future publishing ventures?

Yes: _____ No: _____

Sincerely,

William W. Purkey
John J. Schmidt

Brooks/Cole is dedicated to publishing quality publications for education in the human services fields. If you are interested in learning more about our publications, please fill in your name and address and request our latest catalogue, using ths prepaid mailer.

Name: _____

Street Address: _____

City, State, and Zip: _____

FOLD HERE

BUSINESS REPLY MAIL

FIRST CLASS   PERMIT NO. 358   PACIFIC GROVE, CA

POSTAGE WILL BE PAID BY ADDRESSEE

ATT: *Human Services Catalogue*

Brooks/Cole Publishing Company
511 Forest Lodge Road
Pacific Grove, California 93950-9968

FOLD HERE